THE LIPPINCOTT SERIES
IN AMERICAN GOVERNMENT
under the editorship of
WILLIAM C. HAVARD
*Virginia Polytechnic Institute
and State University*

Hanes Walton, Jr.
Savannah State College

A Theoretical and Structural Analysis

J. B. Lippincott Company
Philadelphia   New York   Toronto

Paperbound: ISBN-0-397-47205-6
Clothbound: ISBN-0-397-47206-4

Library of Congress Catalog
Card Number: 72-155878   JUL 25 '72

Printed in the United States of America

Cover design by Printing Services, Inc.

TO PROFESSOR SAMUEL DUBOIS COOK
SCHOLAR, TEACHER, HUMANIST
TO WHOM ALL STUDENTS OF BLACK
POLITICS ARE DEEPLY INDEBTED

Contents

List of Figures

List of Tables

Preface

Black politics is mysterious, colorful, continuous, and multifarious. Black politics is simple, complex, confusing, and clear. At times the politics of black people is paradoxical, redundant, and antiblack. At times it is emotional, religious, practical, salvationist, and fervently black. And at times, the politics of black people is simply politics—i.e., "the struggle for power and the values associated with and derived from the possession of power."[1] But no matter what the dimensions, the nature, or variety, black politics, in the final analysis, reflects the black experience in America.

But beyond the nature and peculiarities of black politics is the impact of its influence. Assessing this impact, William Brink and Louis Harris have remarked that although blacks comprise only 10 percent of the population with proportionately fewer members in the mainstream of the American political system, fewer black public officials, a low turnout on election day, and fewer members of the race voting, "politicians of both major parties probably talk more about the Negro . . . than about any other 10 percent of the electorate."[2]

Commenting on the same issue, Professor Samuel Cook states that "ironically black men in their powerlessness exercised tremendous power over whites, who monopolized the process and substance of power; relegated to subjects, Black men informed and inspired the basic political philosophy and practice of white citizens."[3] However, in addition to the "centrality and universality of Negro influence," regional influence has differed in its manifestations and expression. According to Alexander Heard, "southern concern over the Negro is the most deeply rooted source of political contention in American politics."[4] The late V. O. Key contended that "in the last analysis the major peculiarities of Southern politics go back to the Negro."[5] The late Clinton Rossiter, in discussing the ultimate impact of blacks in the South, asserted that "the South is a one-party area primarily because of the Negro."[6]

[1] Samuel D. Cook, ". . . The Key to Southern Liberation . . .," *Conference Proceedings: Southwide Conference of Black Elected Officials* (Atlanta: Southern Regional Council, 1968), p. 13.

[2] W. Brink and L. Harris, *The Negro Revolution in America* (New York: Simon and Schuster, 1964), pp. 78-79.

[3] Cook, *op. cit.*, p. 15.

[4] Alexander Heard, *A Two-Party South?* (Chapel Hill, N.C.: University of North Carolina Press, 1952).

[5] V. O. Key, Jr., *Southern Politics in State and Nation* (New York: Alfred A. Knopf, 1950), p. 5.

[6] Clinton Rossiter, *Parties and Politics in America* (Ithaca, N.Y.: Cornell University Press, 1960), p. 139.

In the North the impact of black political influence has been different, yet the same. While northern politics has been interpreted as machine politics, reform politics, issue politics, presidential politics, liberal politics, and personality politics, the politics of race has been omnipresent ever since the mass black migration northward.[7] In this manner, the politics of race was influential in an indirect and submerged manner. Today, northern politics, interpreted as politics of the ghetto, politics of suburbia, or the politics of urbanism, is just a new euphemism for the old politics of race. Racial politics in the North is still ever-present.

In other words, the politics of race in the South has basically an overt nature, while the politics of race in the North has a covert-subterranean nature, which is in part hypocritical in view of the recent race riots. Thus, while different in different regions, the politics of race has nevertheless had an impact on the political process. Blacks—whether northern or southern—have undeniably influenced the politics of white America. Hence, viewed in this fashion, black politics loses it mysterious and paradoxical nature, simply because the politics of black people is ultimately tied to the politics of race in this country. The dimensions, virtues, and colorfulness of black politics evolved from the nature of racism and its sundry manifestations in the American political process.

Recently, the new upsurge of black public officials on all levels of government has caused a renewed interest in blacks and the American political system. But, heretofore, due to the sectional difference in the politics of race, scholars have viewed black politics in primarily a sectional manner, i.e., black politics in the North and black politics in the South. Moreover, since voting has been a focal point of the politics of race since the Civil War and before, scholarly analyses have inevitably centered on the electoral question. Thus, one studying black politics in this manner received separate, disjointed, and incomplete analyses. And while it is important to concentrate upon the numerous differences between North and South, it is likewise significant to discuss the similarities and take into account other points of departure than the electoral system.

Therefore, this book explores black politics North and South and from the colonial period to the present day. It seeks to analyze the politics of black people in a systematic and comprehensive fashion, thereby revealing not only the differences and similarities, but the continuities and changes that have evolved. In addition to viewing the black electorate, this book seeks to deal with other political devices and entities that blacks have invoked and used not only in the black community but in the regular democratic process. And lastly, this book tries to set forth some theoretical

---

[7] See H. Gosnell, "The Chicago 'Black Belt' as a Political Battleground," *American Journal of Sociology*, 39 (November, 1933), 330-331.

insights and generalizations about black political maneuverings and manifestations in this country.

Hopefully, this comprehensive analysis will be more informative than the sectional ones, but there is no desire to adjudge the latter unworthy or useless. They are also necessary and informative. The primary aim of this book is to open new vistas left unperceived by the more limited perspective of the older studies.

In writing this volume, I was encouraged and aided at every stage in this enterprise by several people, some of whom I can, and all of whom I would like, to acknowledge. First and foremost, I would like to express my appreciation to Professors Samuel D. Cook, Emmett E. Dorsey, Robert Brisbane, Harold Gosnell, Nathaniel Tillman, and Robert Martin, who not only taught me but had great scholarly insights into black politics.

Next, thanks is given to several colleagues whose aid in sundry ways enabled the project to be completed. Among these are Professors William P. Robinson, Jr., Leslie McLemore, Mack Jones, Jewel Prestage, and Lenneal Henderson.

In terms of individuals here at the college, thanks is given to Professor E. J. Dean, E. K. Williams, Thomas Byers, and Delacy Sanford, who facilitated my research in a host of ways.

As for the librarians, much of what was accomplished came through their assistance. Thus, thanks is given to Mr. Andrew Mclemore, Mrs. M. Wallace, and Mrs. M. Dixon. Miss Luella Hawkins, the interlibrary loan librarian, made the research on this book possible at a small black college. A greater debt is owed her than I can ever hope to repay.

All tables, charts, and figures owe their clarity and explicitness to a charming and talented clinical psychologist, Miss Brenda Denyse Mobley, who took time out from her studies and clinical work at Purdue University to devise them.

To Miss Lillie Mae Key and Delores Drummond thanks are also given, for they laboriously typed and retyped this work. And finally to my parents, Mr. and Mrs. Thomas Walton, my brother Thomas Walton, my niece April, nephews Spencer and Steven, aunt, Mrs. Margaret Guest, Elinor Guest, Katie and Joe Hampton, Phil and Bonnie, Mrs. Exie and Lenora Morton, thanks are due for their patience and encouragement. As to this final outcome, I hope the results merit the work and devotion to duty that have gone into the research and writing of the book.

HANES WALTON, JR.

January, 1972

Black Politics:
A Theoretical Approach

Politics is born of societal conflict. In fact, political activities—from soapbox speeches to street riots and wars—are the means by which such conflict is perpetuated. Generally speaking, politics is concerned primarily with the "distribution of advantages and disadvantages among people."[1] It is also "concerned with the behavior of individuals and groups as they vie for a favorable distribution of these advantages."[2] Individuals and groups naturally conflict because their wants and needs differ; nevertheless, such conflict must be resolved, otherwise anarchy would result.

Governments evolved in response to this need to resolve societal conflict. They became institutions for the order and maintenance of peace and security. Government is not an impartial mediator, however. It cannot remain aloof from controversy and grant unbiased judgment on the cases that come before it. An impartial government run by a set of irreproachable decision-makers does not exist. "Government is an authority established to settle conflicts, and parties to conflict (especially those who feel intensely) are likely to try to influence the decision in their own favor."[3] In fact, one of the basic purposes of government is the management of conflict in society and the implementation of certain personal preferences into public policy.

The Founding Fathers fashioned the American political system with a view toward both the settlement of disputes and the distribution of various advantages and disadvantages. James Madison wrote: "The regulation of these various and interfering interests forms the principal task of modern legislation and involves the spirit of party and faction in the necessary and ordinary operations of Government."[4] Madison and his colleagues saw the

---

[1] Lewis A. Froman, Jr., *People and Politics: An Analysis of the American Political System* (Englewood Cliffs, N.J.: Prentice-Hall, 1965), p. 3.

[2] *Ibid.,* p. 15.

[3] *Ibid.,* p. 11. See also Dan Nimmo and Thomas Ungs, *American Political Patterns* (Boston: Little, Brown and Company, 1961), pp. 11–18.

[4] Alexander Hamilton, James Madison, and John Jay, *The Federalist,* ed. B. Wright (Cambridge, Mass.: Harvard University Press, 1961), p. 131.

source of societal conflict as rooted in human diversity; they felt that what was needed was a system of government that would prevent the few from imposing their will upon the many. A system of checks and balances was therefore established in order to frustrate any groups that might try to satisfy their special interests at the expense of society at large.

In other words, the American political system was structured at the Philadelphia convention in such a way as to keep conflict at a minimum and to prevent any one of the various groups within society from gaining dominance over the others. This would, in the Founding Fathers' view, abate continual conflict. Moreover, the Constitution and our system of courts were intended to give those who sought a redress of grievances an orderly procedure for solving their problems. Political parties, pressure groups, minor parties, and numerous other acceptable political activities supplemented the legal procedures in muting antagonism. Those who compare and contrast the American system with those of other countries devote a great amount of verbiage to explaining how well the American system is able to manage internal conflict. In fact, the American democratic system has been promoted as a model to the emerging nations of the world precisely because it has structural processes not only for the transfer of power, but also for the maintenance of peace and tranquillity.

Therefore, those who study the Americans and their political system tend to look at the unique factors in its creation, those political activities and devices that make it work so well and the balanced feedback process. In addition, these students of the American political process take pains to point out the various legal tools for the attainment of goals available to the different groups in our pluralistic society. But when these political scientists reach the black minority, they narrow their points of departure. As shall be seen later, there are many reasons why this is so.

The study of black politics—i.e., of the attempts of one group of individuals in the American political system to implement their preferences as public policy—has suffered from a narrow conceptualization. Although politics encompasses the actions of legislative assemblies, political parties, election contests, and other formal trappings of a modern government, *the beginning and end of studies on black politics have been primarily from the electoral angle.* Heretofore, those students of the American political process (black or white) have begun their scholarly analyses with the elemental assumption that if blacks could not vote, they had little chance to have any meaningful effect on the political process. In fact, the vote has come to be seen as the basis for all other political action. For though it is admitted that the vote is only one weapon among many that are available to groups, students of black politics tend to feel that the alternative devices (e.g., lobbying, pressure groups, demonstrations, etc.) derive much of their value and significance from the existence of the vote.

"Journalists, civil rights leaders, and politicians regard the vote as the ... [black man's] strongest and most accessible weapon in his struggle for full citizenship and social and economic equality."[5] They have assumed that "political rights pave the way for all others." Their view is that, given a substantial number of votes throughout the country, blacks would be able to introduce into public policy certain of their preferences.

Several presidents before the turn of the twentieth century and Presidents Eisenhower, Kennedy, Johnson, and all attorneys general since Herbert Brownell have felt that the vote was the most effective means of advancing blacks to equality.[6] In fact, whites have so emphasized the importance of the vote, that blacks themselves believe it. Henry Lee Moon, a black political analyst, held the "ballot ... as the indispensable weapon in the persistent fight for full citizenship ... a tool to be used in the ultimate demolition of the whole outmoded structure of Jim Crow."[7] Harry Bailey, Jr., likewise argues that "the vote is ... the Negro's most important weapon in his struggle for full citizenship."[8] Chuck Stone states that "the age of the ballot is upon the Black man.... It is the tool of survival."[9] W E. B. Du Bois said: "The power of the ballot we need in sheer self-defense ... else what shall save us from a second slavery?" And Martin Luther King, Jr., remarked that the biggest step that blacks can take is in the "direction of the voting booths."[10] But in addition to individual blacks and their leaders, black protest organizations and pressure groups have for the most part been committed to a struggle to secure the extension of suffrage rights to black people.[11] Recently, the Congress of Racial Equality (CORE), the Student Coordination Committee—formerly the Student Non-Violent Coordinating Committee (SNCC)—and the Southern Christian Leadership Council have waged numerous campaigns to win the ballot for black people.[12] In fact, SCLC's entire Selma drive was to secure the ballot and federal protection of it for southern blacks. And when President Johnson signed the Voting Rights Acts as a result of the Selma demonstrations, he observed that "the vote is the most powerful instrument ever devised by

[5] Donald Matthews and James Prothro, *Negroes and the New Southern Politics* (New York: Harcourt, Brace and World, 1966), p. 11.

[6] *Ibid.*

[7] Henry Lee Moon, *Balance of Power: The Negro Vote* (New York: Doubleday and Company, 1948), p. 9.

[8] Harry Bailey, Jr., ed., *Negro Politics in America* (Columbus, Ohio: Charles E. Merrill Books, 1967), p. 164.

[9] Chuck Stone, *Black Political Power in America* (Indianapolis: Bobbs-Merrill Company, 1968), p. 10.

[10] Matthews and Prothro, *op. cit.*, p. 11. See also "Civil Rights No. 1, The Right to Vote," *New York Times Magazine*, March 14, 1965, p. 26.

[11] Hanes Walton, Jr., *Black Political Parties: A Historical and Political Analysis* (New York: Free Press, 1972), chaps. 1–2.

[12] *Ibid.*

men for breaking down injustices and destroying the terrible walls that imprison men because they are different from other men."[13]

With such importance placed on the vote by the president and the attorney general, as well as by journalists, political scientists, and blacks themselves, it is hardly strange that the majority of civil rights bills (especially those since 1957) that Congress has passed or attempted to pass have dealt primarily with the right to vote. Obviously, Congress has come to feel that the ballot alone will enable blacks to solve their other problems—housing, schools, jobs, etc.

Nevertheless, those scholars who began with the assumption "that a citizen's right to vote is the sovereign remedy for all ... his grievances"[14] and who analyzed black politics solely from an electoral angle have created numerous problems, which we shall discuss presently. First, however, let us examine the analyses themselves.

PAST STUDIES OF BLACK VOTING PATTERNS

Political scientists and other academicians—black or white—who took the ballot as their point of departure could begin their analyses of black politics in areas where blacks either had the ballot or did not have it. For instance, after the Civil War and Reconstruction, blacks in the South were denied the ballot through numerous legal and extralegal devices. Since they could not vote, their problems remained and multiplied. In the North the situation was different. Blacks there had access to the ballot; in fact, their northward migration during World War I greatly increased their voting strength there, with the result that they soon reaped tangible political rewards in the form of patronage and election as aldermen, congressmen, and such.

In other words, the study of black politics has suffered from a sectional analysis based on the black man's voting strength—the electoral approach. There have been numerous case studies of black politics in the North and an equal number of studies of black politics in the South. Each group of studies, however, has been different.

Studies of black politics in the South were based upon conceptual schemes and methodologies designed to analyze the impact of the black electorate. During the 1930s, Paul Lewinson, a pioneer student of black suffrage in the South, employed the survey sampling and interviewing techniques.[15] From his data he concluded among other things that "the

---

[13] Quoted in William R. Keech, *The Impact of Negro Voting: The Role of the Vote in the Quest for Equality* (Chicago: Rand McNally and Company, 1968), p. 1.

[14] Margaret Price, *The Negro Voter in the South* (Atlanta: Southern Regional Council, 1957), p. 1.

[15] Paul Lewinson, *Race, Class, and Party* (New York: Russell and Russell, 1963), pp. 203–206.

Negro's votelessness reacted unfavorably on his general social and economic welfare."[16] V. O. Key learned from Lewinson's study that the South had only an infinitesimally small number of black voters and consequently, in his monumental study of Southern politics, he focused his attention not on black voters, but upon black concentration in the Black Belt areas of the South. His analysis of each of the Southern states examines the difference between the politics of the Black Belt region as opposed to the region where blacks were not in a majority. In each state the driving motif behind the Black Belt whites was to exclude blacks from the ballot. Key, therefore, concluded by arguing that "in its grand outlines the politics of the South revolves around the position of the Negro."[17] Alexander Heard, basing his work upon the data Key collected, found that the South was having difficulty in creating a two-party system because of the fear that blacks could become a "balance of power" in a system with two highly competitive parties.[18]

In addition to these more comprehensive analyses of black politics in the South—studies done from the electoral standpoint—there have been case studies on the same conceptual basis. H. D. Price analyzed black politics in Florida from the electoral perspective because Florida was "the only state in the South which published registration figures broken down by race for each party."[19] In addition, more blacks then voted in Florida than in any other southern state. Generally speaking, his research led him to the conclusion that the more blacks voted, the more benefits they received in their communities.[20]

After 1944, the year in which the United States Supreme Court outlawed the white primaries in the South, it became fashionable for liberal whites to aid blacks in registering to vote. By 1960, numerous liberal white organizations in the South, imbued with the belief that at the root of the black man's problems was his lack of the vote, had launched programs to increase black registration, state and federal action having not yet materialized. Black efforts were all too small to be meaningful.

Two journalists, Pat Watters and Reese Cleghorn, in a recent book, discuss the efforts of a white liberal organization—the Southern Regional Council—with some foundation support to aid blacks in obtaining the ballot during the sixties. The book details the obstacles, pressures, and

[16] *Ibid.,* p. 197.

[17] V. O. Key, Jr., *Southern Politics in State and Nation* (New York: Vintage Books, 1949).

[18] Alexander Heard, *A Two-Party South?* (Chapel Hill, N.C.: University of North Carolina Press, 1949), chaps. 13–17.

[19] Hugh D. Price, "The Negro and Florida Politics, 1944–1954," in Harry Bailey, Jr., *Negro Politics in America* (Columbus, Ohio: Charles E. Merrill Books, 1967), p. 259. See also Hugh D. Price, *The Negro and Southern Politics: A Chapter of Florida History* (New York: New York University Press, 1951).

[20] *Ibid.,* pp. 276–277.

consequences of the Voter Education Project and the immediate impact of the 1965 Voting Rights Act. However, after analyzing the weaknesses and new trends of the black community, the absence of meaningful leadership, strong socioeconomic strata, etc., the lingering racism and intransigence of the white community, and the changing economic and social bases of central southern cities, the book concludes that the sudden arrival of blacks in southern electoral politics will not produce sudden change in the things that gravely affect southern blacks—i.e., "exclusion, prejudice, slums, rural poverty."[21] In their view, it will take some time before voting will become effective for the black community in reaching its larger goals. And as one reads the work, he gets an implication that the lack of the ballot was not the answer after all. However, in the final analysis, this work, too, sees the means to black political achievement primarily by way of the ballot.

Later, William Keech, in his *The Impact of Negro Voting*, concluded that voting power has considerable limitations, and black voting even more limitations. Therefore, the achievement of blacks through the ballot will be of necessity small and minimal in nature.[22] But once again this scholar, like others, views black politics from solely an electoral standpoint.[23]

Another recent analysis of southern black politics from the same conceptual basis explores three counties, three cities, and one state.[24] This work updates the old electoral angle by grafting onto it the standard theory regarding ethnic politics without, however, noting the difference between blacks and other ethnic groups in our society. This theory argues that all ethnic groups have gone through three stages in the American political system: (1) nonparticipant, (2) semiparticipant, and (3) full participant.[25] From his analysis of the black electorate in the counties and cities selected, the author concludes that in the main blacks are between the semiparticipant stage and the full participant stage, and it is just a matter of time before blacks become full participants and reap all the benefits of the political system.[26]

Everett C. Ladd took the case study technique even further. He explored black political leadership in the South as a function of the strength of the black voter. Taking two North Carolina cities as focal points, he attempted to describe how black leaders sought to achieve racial goals through threatening white politicians with the black vote.[27] And finally, Donald Matthews

[21] Pat Watters and Reese Cleghorn, *Climbing Jacob's Ladder: The Arrival of Negroes in Southern Politics* (New York: Harcourt, Brace and World, 1967), p. 357.

[22] Keech, *op. cit.*, pp. 106-109.

[23] For remarks on this point see Gerald M. Pomper, Review of *The Impact of Negro Voting* by William Keech, *American Political Science Review*, LXIII (September, 1969), 923-924.

[24] Harry Holloway, *The Politics of the Southern Negro: From Exclusion to Big City Organization* (New York: Random House, 1969), pp. 6-8.

[25] *Ibid.*, p. 4.

[26] *Ibid.*, pp. 336-357.

[27] Everett C. Ladd, *Negro Leadership in the South* (Ithaca, N.Y.: Cornell University Press,

and James Prothro, who employed the most sophisticated behavioral techniques in political science in analyzing black political behavior in the South, began with their predecessors' electoral standpoint and concluded that the vote as a political resource for southern blacks had its limitations.[28] Although their study did go beyond the black ballot, the book in its "grand outlines" revolved around the black vote.

In the North the same conceptual frameworks were employed in one form or another. At the present time, there is no major or comprehensive study of black politics in the North. However, there have been several case studies. Harold Gosnell's pioneer study of black politics concentrated on Chicago.[29] Using the latest social science techniques, Gosnell attempted "to describe in realistic fashion the struggle of a minority group that advanced its status by political methods."[30] He detailed the impact of black northern migration on Chicago's political arena and related this to the rise of black political power, black politicians, black political machines, and to the benefits derived from this political power to the black community.

Thirty years later James Q. Wilson returned to Gosnell's Chicago and made an analysis of black leadership in the city as a function of the black electorate.[31] In it, he describes black political behavior and the numerous political influences upon it. Like Gosnell, however, Wilson also is explicitly concerned with the black voter and what he can obtain in terms of public policy.

Those analyses that have been done of black politics nationwide have also been based within an electoral framework.[32] These works either tell how significant the black voter is, or how important the black man will be when blacks acquire the right to vote; what he should do when he has the vote, or that he holds the balance of power in national elections. For instance, Bailey's work on black politics in America is devoted almost entirely to black voting and its consequences. And Stone's work does the same.

We have surveyed here only certain of the major books in the field. In addition, the professional journals, periodicals, newspapers, dissertations,

1966), pp. 17-47.

[28] Matthews and Prothro, *op. cit.,* p. 478.

[29] Harold Gosnell, *Negro Politicians: The Rise of Negro Politics in Chicago* (Chicago: University of Chicago Press, 1967), pp. 13-36.

[30] *Ibid.,* p. 12.

[31] James Q. Wilson, *Negro Politics: The Search for Leadership* (New York: Free Press, 1960), pp. 21-47.

[32] For an analysis of the black electorate on the national level, see Stone, *op. cit.;* Moon, *op. cit.;* Bailey, *op. cit.;* William R. Nowlin, *The Negro in American National Politics* (Boston: Stratford Company, 1931); and Samuel Lubell, *White and Black: The Test of a Nation* (New York: Harper and Row, 1964). One of the lone exceptions to the electoral approach is Elbert Tatum, *The Changed Political Thought of the Negro, 1915-1940* (New York: Exposition Press, 1951), which incorrectly tried to assess the black shift to the Democratic party in 1936.

and magazines are also replete with studies, analyses, and theories regarding the black electorate. Some of these deal with how the black vote has been manipulated, while others concentrate upon factors that influence the black vote. Still others deal with the legal and extralegal restrictions on the black vote. Numerous articles have described the black vote in localities throughout the nation; most of them have discussed how the granting of suffrage rights to blacks can easily solve their problems. They do not go far enough, as we shall see later on.

Of the various works on the black electorate, some have detailed how, why, when, and where blacks were disfranchised, and others have argued the point as to whether or not blacks should have been disfranchised. Some are certain that benefits have been acquired from enfranchisement; many others argue with this conclusion. In the words of V. O. Key: *"When all the exceptions are considered, when all the justifications are made and when all the insidious comparisons are drawn," the study of black politics heretofore has been the study of the black electorate.* In fact, those studies that have been done on black politics using the electoral framework have actually made it more difficult to grasp the nature, significance, and scope of black politics as a whole.

This is not to say, however, that the vote itself is insignificant or unimportant to American political life. Nor is it to argue that an approach to black politics based on the electoral methodology will reveal nothing about black political behavior. But any analysis of black political behavior that uses this conceptual framework will inevitably be incomplete. Besides the fact that the electoral framework will cause the analyst to give a micro, rather than a macro view of black politics, it will also force him to give sectional and local analyses. In fact, the analyst can never treat the entire spectrum of black political life and render it justice simply by studying blacks and their votes. One who attempts this approach is bound to leave out numerous essential items. For instance, in none of the aforementioned studies is there a comprehensive analysis of black political parties, black pressure groups, black political machines, blacks and their participation in the major and minor political parties, black public officials and their public legislation or their relationship to the black masses and community. A narrow and microscopic technique of trying to view all of black politics from the point of view of the black voter leaves out blacks in the cities, blacks in the metropolis, blacks in state and local governments, and blacks at national conventions. Most persons saw the 1964 Mississippi Freedom Democratic party's challenge as unique, but the fact of the matter is that black challenges at national conventions had begun as early as the 1880s.

THE BLACK ENVIRONMENT AND BLACK POLITICS

More than anything else the conceptual framework within which black politics has been analyzed in the past does not make clear that although blacks constituted a "largely nonvoting minority," they nevertheless wielded tremendous political power in relationship to their population percentage.[33] In other words, a failure to see black politics from any other angle than that of voter participation indicates a misunderstanding of the American political process and the numerous devices it offers to affect public policy over and beyond the vote.[34] Moreover, the practice of analyzing black politics primarily from the election angle means that one must overemphasize the significance of the vote (and it is significant) in relationship to other devices such as pressure groups, lobbying process, riots, electioneering, etc. In sum, politics can be continued by means other than the vote.

Not only does the electoral framework make for incompleteness, it is also narrow because it illuminates primarily the political behavior of the black middle class. Lewinson's questionnaire went to black graduates of black colleges, as did Matthews and Prothro's.[35] Their black interviewees were middle-class blacks, and in the main the questionnaires and interviews were concluded in black middle-class areas.[36] Gosnell and Wilson also observed for the most part the political behavior of middle-class blacks.

Generally speaking, the electoral-based analysis omits what Lerone Bennett calls "the politics of the outsiders"—the black masses.[37] Heretofore the black masses, both rural and urban, North or South, have not been significantly involved in politics. Of course, in the North there are exceptions like Harlem, Newark, Philadelphia, and Detroit. But these areas have not undergone major political studies. Thus, the major forces for involving the black masses have been the "Black Revolution" of the sixties and the political developments prior to and after the voting rights acts. The 1965 Voting Rights Act activated the black masses, especially in the South. And additional activities of the masses came with the rise of black politicians throughout the country. In other words, the atmosphere of the times has generated political enthusiasm in the black masses and brought them to the center of the political scene.

But little is known about their political behavior. For instance, Wilson

---

[33] William Brink and Louis Harris, *The Negro Revolution in America* (New York: Simon and Schuster, 1964), pp. 78–79.

[34] For insight into the sundry tools of the American political process, see V. O. Key, Jr., *Politics, Parties, and Pressure Groups* (New York: Thomas Y. Crowell, 1958); David B. Truman, *The Governmental Groups in American Society* (Englewood Cliffs, N.J.: Prentice-Hall, 1964); Lester W. Milbrath, *The Washington Lobbyists* (Chicago: Rand McNally and Company, 1963); and Jack Peltason, *Federal Courts in the Political Process* (New York: Doubleday and Company, 1955).

[35] Lewinson, *op. cit.*, p. 203.

[36] Matthews and Prothro, *op. cit.*, pp. 3–8.

[37] Lerone Bennett, Jr., "The Politics of the Outsider," *The Negro Digest*, XVII (July, 1968), p. 5

claims that middle-class blacks seek status goals, while lower-class blacks tend to seek welfare goals.[38] But is it not true that if the black masses seek welfare goals, they are in effect seeking status goals at the same time? This point, however, is not of such major concern here as is the problem of the omission of *the black masses* in past political analysis. And it can scarcely be doubted that the black masses have been left out.

The past conceptual frameworks that used electoral participation to inquire into black politics have rendered partial, incomplete, and inadequate analyses. For the most part, they have only described political behavior of middle-class blacks in certain sections and localities of America. These studies have rendered a narrow and microscopic view of black politics in American political life. And with this approach no full view or paramount picture revealing the true nature of blacks in American political life can be had. In short, a macroanalysis of black politics cannot be properly achieved by analyzing black politics from the basis of the black voter. In fact, in order to establish a meaningful conceptual framework within which to study black politics, it is necessary to go beyond the simplicity of the electoral concept to a full systematic analysis.

However, beyond the fact that an electoral approach to black politics makes a comprehensive inquiry into the field of black politics impossible because of its inherent "micro" nature,[39] it adds yet another problem. The electoral approach to black politics—or politics in general for that matter—makes for confusion and incoherence.

For instance, any black group, organization, or individual in the community can vote or can have an effect upon the black vote, the black vote turnout, the mobilization to vote, or the direction of the black vote.[40] Moreover, even the rewards from voting become significant because they may have some effect upon future voting in the black community. Concern with rewards leads to even greater concerns, however. Did these rewards accrue to the black community because of their voting strength, their protest activity, the nature of their leadership, the socioeconomic status of the black community, the white liberalism in the surrounding community, the total community's economic bases, or because of federal or state pressure?

In other words, to focus exclusively upon black electoral power is to

[38] On this point see James Q. Wilson, "The Strategy of Protest: Problems of Negro Civic Action," in Harry Bailey, ed., *Negro Politics in America* (Columbus, Ohio: Charles E. Merrill Books, 1967), pp. 57-62. See also his *Negro Politics, op. cit.,* pp. 199-213.

[39] For some insight into the narrowness and general relevance of voting studies, especially in terms of broad generalizations, see Walter Berns, "Voting Studies," in Herbert Storing, ed., *Essays on the Scientific Study of Politics* (New York: Holt, Rinehart and Winston, 1962), pp. 3-. See also G. Duncan and Steven Lukes, "The New Democracy," in Charles McCoy and John Playford, *Apolitical Politics* (New York: Thomas Y. Crowell, 1967), pp. 166-170.

[40] Watters and Cleghorn, *op. cit.,* chap. 3.

open Pandora's box, because such an approach is open-ended: the more information one obtains, the more answers he needs to verify even the first conclusion he arrives at. In short, this approach begets a spiral that sooner or later encompasses the entire white community as well as the state government and the federal government. In addition, the court system and all the pressure groups must be included. The search for specific influences upon the vote and the ramifications of these influences increase the amount of data and the difficulties of explaining it.

John H. Strange noted these difficulties in the methodology of all of the works on black politics when he reviewed the literature.[41] He felt that "the literature concerning Negroes and politics has failed to meet [the] logical requirements for delimiting a subject,"[42] although he did not attribute the lack of delimiting the studies on black politics to some inherent approach but rather to the failure to define the topic properly. It is generally obvious, however, that a specific type of methodology, like the electoral approach, can make the delimitation a hard task. And this has been the case in black politics. Strange argues that "most of those doing research concerning the Negro and politics make no explicit attempt whatever to delimit or even identify the phenomena they are investigating other than state they are studying 'Negro politicians,' 'Negro voters or registrants,' 'Negro protest,' or 'Negro politics.' "[43]

A New Approach to Analysis of Black Politics

A macroanalysis of black politics is possible, however, from a developmental approach,[44] for a developmental framework avoids the weaknesses of the electoral analysis by viewing such analysis in a much broader context. Moreover, this developmental approach is necessary because of the inherent nature of black politics.

Basically speaking, black politics springs from the particular brand of segregation practices found in different environments in which black people find themselves. In other words, the nature of segregation and the manner in which it differs not only in different localities but within a locality have caused black people to employ political activities, methods, devices, and techniques that would advance their policy preferences. In short, *black politics is a function of the particular brand of segregation found in different environments in which black people find themsleves.*

[41] John H. Strange, "The Negro in Philadelphia Politics, 1963-1965" (unpublished Ph.D. dissertation, Princeton University, 1966), p. 5.

[42] *Ibid.,* p. 6.

[43] *Ibid.,* p. 45.

[44] For an argument for the developmental approach to black politics see Jewell Prestage, "Black Politics and the Kerner Report Concerns and Directions," *Social Science Quarterly,* December, 1968, p. 463.

And the politics of blacks differs significantly from locality to locality. Although there are many striking similarities between the political activities of black Americans in different localities, there are differences far greater than geography can explain. Basically, the differences lie in the variety of forms that segregation and discrimination have taken in this country. Most observers have long noted the difference between the manner in which segregation has manifested itself in the North and in the South.[45] But they have failed to go further and state how the practice of segregation has differed even in the same region. C. Vann Woodward, describing the particularistic nature of American segregation, states that:

> The Jim Crow laws put the authority of the state or city in the voice of the street car conductor, the railway brakeman, the bus driver, the theater usher, and also into the voice of the hoodlum of the public parks and playgrounds.[46]

In essence, segregation in America became particularized, and black politics came to function in relationship to the particular brand of segregation in a particular locality. In many aspects, black politics cannot be understood outside of a particular environment.

MACROANALYSIS OF BLACK POLITICS

Because black politics is diverse, fluid, and ever changing, some general and broad categories of macroanalysis can be enumerated and characterized to provide a much more meaningful view of the political activities of black Americans. These categories or stages are mere tools for further analysis; they are not offered as final guidelines. These categories, too, need to be tested and developed. For black politics in America has moved through four basically different stages, though in some localities, regions, etc., all four stages may not have been reached because of the nature of segregation locally. The four identifiable stages or general categories are: (1) nonparticipation, (2) limited participation, (3) moderate participation, and (4) full participation.

In the initial stage of black politics, black people were excluded not only from electoral participation but also from the nonelectoral process. In short, black people in the first stage of political development were completely passive either because of local restriction or because of a lack of interest in the political process. One should not approach the initial stage of black politics from a temporal angle, however. The time element, in other

---

[45] For insight on the different manifestations of segregation in America, see Kenneth B. Clark, "The New Negro in the North," in Matthew H. Ahmann, ed., *The New Negro* (Notre Dame, Ind.: Fides Publishers, 1964), p. 36.

[46] C. Vann Woodward, *The Strange Career of Jim Crow* (New York: Oxford University Press, 1955), p. 3.

words, is insignificant because in some localities at the present time blacks are nonparticipant in the political process. In fact, in several Alabama, Georgia, and Mississippi counties black people have not cast a vote or organized a political organization since the incorporation of that county.[47] Hence, in many localities blacks are still in the initial stage of political development. And if the Voting Rights Act expires, it is possible that blacks in a more advanced stage of development will go back or be forced back into a lower stage.

As Figure 1 indicates, the move from the initial stage to another stage takes place because of some significant event or events in the political system. This event occurs because of demands made on the system by blacks themselves, by others on their behalf, or by whites because of their participation in the political arena. An excellent example of a significant event would be the denial or revision of the 1965 Voting Rights Act. Demands either to change or deny it can be significant for the black community. And these demands generated from nonelectoral and/or electoral participation can move a segment of black people to the second stage or to another stage of political development. In other words, a stage or stages may be skipped or bypassed or reversed in black political development. One stage does not necessarily have to precede another.

The second stage of black politics is characterized by extremely low participation—electoral and nonelectoral. In this stage black people generally participate in only a minimal fashion. Politics in this stage is left to a select few within the black community who can meet the particular requirements of the environment. For example, only those free blacks in New York after 1821 who could meet the freehold estate requirement could vote. And basically only this group organized and pressured for an extension of the suffrage and other political benefits. In the South, during the 1920s and 1930s and before, a few selected blacks whom the white power structure recognized were permitted to vote in the Democratic election from time to time. Thus, in a very minimal way, blacks were permitted to participate in local politics if the segregation environment decided to permit limited participation by a select few. However, it should be remembered that the time element is not important because even today in some localities throughout the country, black people are still in the second stage of political development.

The third stage of political development is characterized by more than 50 percent black political participation. In this stage, more blacks have been motivated to enter the political arena either because of outside occurrences and events in other black communities or because of the stimulants gener-

---

[47] George Slaff, "Five Seats in Congress: The Mississippi Challenge," *The Nation*, CC (May 17, 1965), 527.

Figure 1. The Black-White Political Conflict System

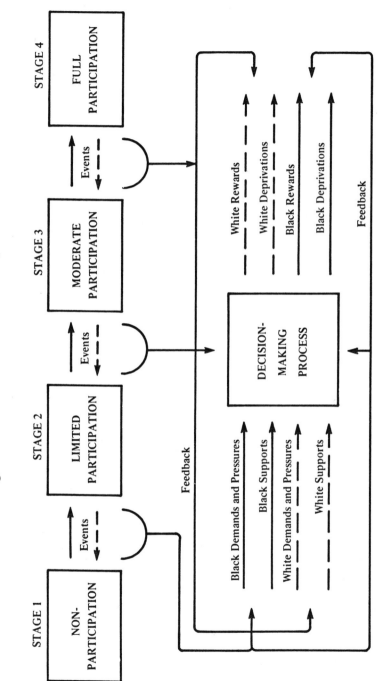

ated in their communities growing out of limited political participation by select blacks in the past. In this stage, generally speaking, blacks pressure for more participation and demand a larger voice in matters relating to their communities. In this stage, more pressure group activity and electoral activity takes place. Acquired political power is generally used to generate more power and at the same time is used to attain certain racial goals. The rewards obtained in this stage give the group additional impetus to acquire more political power and more political influence. The third stage of the ethnic political development occurs when political concession becomes frustration over inadequacies; in this stage an attempt is made to act, rather than be.

Many black people are now in the third stage of political development, others have not reached this point, and some are in the fourth stage.

The fourth stage of black political development entails full participation by blacks in the political system. In this stage, blacks are completely mobilized in acting upon the political process to translate their choices into public policy. Black political organizations, pressure groups, and electoral activities are all used to influence the governmental process. It is in this stage that blacks have acquired not only political consciousness, but also political efficiency. In this stage, blacks not only have access to the avenues of power, but tools and devices to make some impact on the power holders, and full participation represents the final stage of political development.

However, the developmental approach to black politics is not a one-way process. The era of Black Reconstruction is a perfect example of how a reversal can take place. In some southern states blacks were fully involved in the political process, but the Compromise of 1877 and the subsequent disenfranchising action of numerous southern legislatures forced most blacks back to one of the three preceding stages. Black politics came to a standstill in most southern states and remained that way up until the present time. In spite of the Fifteenth Amendment, the political status of blacks in America is a relative thing.[48] The political position of blacks is always subject to the resurgence of segregation. Even today much of the hue and cry about the renewal and extension of the 1965 Voting Rights Act is a recognition that once black people attain a certain political level they can still be forced or pushed back to a lower one.

In short, black politics in America is continually changing. The political position of the black man, like his economic, social, and intellectual position, is constantly undergoing change. James Q. Wilson states that "Any book on Negroes, particularly on their politics, ought to be published in loose-leaf bind so that it can be corrected and updated on a monthly

[48] Robert E. Martin, "The Relative Political Status of the Negro in the U. S.," in Bailey, *op. cit.*, pp. 13-16.

basis," because the political position of blacks changes just that often.[49] Hence, level attainments today may not exist next week or next month or next year. Several writers have argued that the "central theme of black [history] and thought has been the quest for freedom and equality."[50] But this is not necessarily the keystone of black politics. In fact, any analysis of black politics, within whatever frame of reference, would be hard pressed to fit black political activity into a single scheme. First of all, the constant flux of black politics itself would not necessarily permit such an interpretation because it would fail to show black politics as constantly evolving. In fact, a perspective of black politics from an evolutionary standpoint would be in opposition to the brute realities of the numerous manifestations and changes in segregation, discrimination, and racism in America. In fact, this evolutionary analysis would have to predispose that segregation is constant and the same in every American locality, which is not the case.

But not only does black politics lack a central theme because of its constant state of flux, it is also without a central element because of the very nature of politics. Politics is a quest for power, and black politics has in many cases, as we shall see later, made the acquisition of power an end in itself. The political attainment of power by black individuals and political groups has not meant that this acquisition was transmitted to the black masses and the black community.[51]

The study of black politics from an electoral framework is incomplete. A developmental approach is much more illuminating and useful. This approach gives one a means of comprehending the political involvement of blacks in each locality in American society. In fact, it gives one a macro-analysis of black political life—a panoramic view. However, it could give further insight into how much impact blacks in each stage of their political development have had upon the decision-makers and public policy. And it could render additional points of departure as to what level blacks need to attain to have sufficient impact on public policy and the decision-makers. In fact, black politics from the developmental approach not only incorporates the old electoral framework but on the whole does not deny the worth of other methodological analyses and conceptual schemes.

[49] Wilson, op. cit., p. 5.
[50] See Earl Endris Thorpe, "The Central Theme of Negro History," Carson-Newman College Faculty Studies Bulletin, II (April, 1969), 13-19. Earl Endris Thorpe, The Mind of the Negro: An Intellectual History of Afro-Americans (Baton Rouge: Ortlieb Press, 1961).
[51] See Rukudzo Murapa, "Race Pride and Black Political Thought," Negro Digest, XVIII (May, 1969), 8-9.

II

Blacks and the American Political System

Black politics flourished in colonial America. Numerous political analysts and observers have held that black political power before the Civil War was either nonexistent or basically insignificant. Nevertheless, black political activity was not only significant and ceaseless, but in many cases it was crucial in obtaining desired policy preferences for different black groups and individuals.

The arguments of Gosnell that "the direct political importance of the Negro prior to the Civil War was very slight";[1] of Gunnar Myrdal that "as a political power the Free Negroes were, of course, inconsequential, both in the South and in the North";[2] and of Henry Moon that "the vote of the Free Negro was everywhere small, and in most places insignificant,"[3] are the results of conceptualizing black politics in colonial America within an electoral framework only. Of necessity, such a conceptualization inhibits one's perspective. As Samuel Cook asserts, blacks "since early Colonial times have had a profound impact on the American political system and process."[4]

Generally speaking, the politics of blacks in colonial America can be divided into two basic categories, neither of which is exclusive of the other. The first is that of pressure or nonelectoral politics, and the second that of electoral politics. Both these categories revolve around the shifting status of blacks in the American colonies.

The pressure or nonelectoral political activities of blacks evolved from attempts to attain freedom, to maintain the status of a "free man of color,"

[1] Harold Gosnell, *Negro Politicians: The Rise of Negro Politics in Chicago* (Chicago: University of Chicago Press, 1967), p. 3.

[2] Gunnar Myrdal, *An American Dilemma*, 2nd ed. (New York: Harper and Row, 1962), p.429.

[3] Henry Lee Moon, *Balance of Power: The Negro Vote* (New York: Doubleday and Company, 1948), p. 55.

[4] Hanes Walton, Jr., *Black Political Parties: A Historical and Political Analysis* (New York: Free Press, 1972), pp. 1-2.

17

to remove discriminatory practices from different communities, and to have suffrage rights given, extended, or returned. On the other hand, black electoral politics in colonial America tended to support those who championed the idea of "suffrage for all regardless of color," those political parties (major or minor) that espoused equalitarian principles, and those political candidates who supported legislation favorable to free blacks. Irrespective of the tactics employed, however, the political activity of blacks in colonial America was an outgrowth of the particular environment involved.

The early English settlers established three kinds of colonial goverments: royal or provincial, charter or corporate, and proprietary. The charter colony was founded on land granted to a company and governed by it, the royal colony was under the rule of the English king, and the proprietary colony was owned and controlled by one or more private individuals. Most of the charter and proprietary colonies later became royal colonies. It was only in the charter colonies of Rhode Island and Connecticut, however, that the people elected their own governors and governed themselves without interference from England.

Except for Connecticut and Rhode Island, none of the early colonies allowed settlers to take much part in their government. A governor and council, chosen by king, company, or proprietor, had complete control over the government. Only later were the people able to force the crown to grant them some degree of self-government, usually by means of a bicameral legislature. The first such legislature was the House of Burgesses, which opened in Jamestown, Virginia, in 1619, the same year that blacks arrived in America from Africa.

Even in those colonies where some measure of self-government had been achieved, few colonists could vote, and then only for members of the lower house of the assembly. Universal manhood suffrage did not come early to America. The colonial era was devoid of it. Maine, for example, did not grant suffrage to all male citizens until 1820, and Rhode Island not until 1842. In 1776, universal white manhood suffrage was recognized in none of the thirteen colonies. Only after the adoption of the Constitution was the tendency toward steady extension of the franchise.

When blacks were first brought into this country, their status was closer to that of an indentured servant than to that of a slave.[5] When an attempt was made to change that status, black political activity emerged.

The status of blacks became legally fixed at different dates in colonial America. Significant black political activity began with the establishment of the slave status. Black petitions, memorials, resolutions, and proclamations were presented to local public officials, state governments, and state

---

[5] E. Franklin Frazier, *The Negro in the United States* (New York: Macmillan Company, 1957), pp. 22-26.

courts. Finally, in 1800, blacks not only petitioned Congress for a redress of their grievances, but also called upon Congress to act against the slave trade, the Fugitive Slave Act of 1793, and the institution of slavery itself.[6]

These petitions, which began around 1661, were presented to public officials not only by free blacks but by slaves as well. Not all of the earliest protest activity took the form of petitions. Some was violent, destructive, lacking coordination.[7] The slave revolts and insurrections definitely attest to this.[8] Moreover, not all of the petitions and pressure activity were focused on freedom. Numerous black protesters cried out for equal educational facilities, and some protested against being taxed without having the right to vote. In 1791, when South Carolina levied a heavy poll tax upon free blacks, two petitions were sent to the state legislature signed by 23 blacks from Camden, South Carolina, and 34 blacks from Charleston protesting these laws and the disadvantages they placed upon the free black populace. Neither petition accomplished its purpose, but the poll tax law in the state was amended in 1809 to exclude blacks who were physically incapable of earning a livelihood. Petitions like this often met with limited success; some even obtained complete success.

PRESSURE POLITICS IN COLONIAL AMERICA

Despite limited success, however, black pressure politics continued into revolutionary America. From 1773 to 1779 slaves petitioned various state legislatures to grant them their freedom. These petitions based their arguments on the revolutionary philosophy of freedom and natural law.[9] A group of blacks in New England, led by Paul Cuffee, petitioned the state legislature of Massachusetts to grant them suffrage rights since they were being taxed. A court decision in 1783 declared that blacks who were subject to taxation were entitled to vote.[10]

During the War for Independence, in which many blacks because of their gallant service gained freedom, a new form of government—a confederation—was established. Preceding the establishment of this new form of government was that eloquent document, the Declaration of Independence, that completely forgot the question of black slavery in America. Indeed,

[6] Herbert Aptheker, ed., "A Disquieting Negro Petition to Congress, 1800," Herbert Aptheker, ed., *A Documentary History of the Negro People in the United States* (New York: Citadel Press, 1959), p. 44. For an additional list of black petitions see Leslie Fishel and Benjamin Quarles, eds., *The Negro American: A Documentary* History (Glenview, Ill.: Scott, Foresman and Company, 1967), pp. 19-78.

[7] Raymond A. Bauer and Alice H. Bauer, "Day to Day Resistance to Slavery," *Journal of Negro History*, XXVII (October, 1942), 388-419.

[8] For data on the black slave revolts see Herbert Aptheker, *American Negro Slave Revolts* (New York: Columbia University Press, 1943).

[9] Fishel and Quarles, *op. cit.*, pp. 39-48.

[10] Aptheker, *op. cit.*, pp. 14-16.

the very document that proclaimed "all men are created equal" closed its eyes to the nonexistence of black equality in America.

The impact of the war pointed out the weaknesses of the Articles of Confederation and its weak central government.[11] A move, therefore, was made to create a stronger central government. This culminated in the Constitutional Convention of 1787.

No blacks attended the Constitutional Convention, but the black man's condition of servitude not only influenced the policies of the delegates and the final document, but in many respects the existence of blacks became of major concern. When the question of representation and apportionment among the states rose, slaves had to be considered. When the rendition of fugitives was discussed, fugitive slaves had to be discussed. When direct taxation was under discussion, the question of slaves as property or persons was presented for discussion also. When commerce was debated, the slave trade could not be avoided.

When the debate arose over the question of the apportionment of representation, "a compromise was reached whereby three-fifths of the slaves were to be counted in fixing representation and computing taxes."[12] In short, black slaves were to be regarded as part person and part property. On the question of rendition of fugitives, the delegates agreed that fugitives had to be returned to their masters.[13] When the question of commerce arose, the delegates reached a compromise that protected the foreign slave trade for twenty years.[14] The slave trade was not prohibited in America until 1808, and even then the prohibition was poorly enforced. Thus, even though the delegates to the Philadelphia convention managed to avoid the use of the word *slavery* in their final document, the document was colored by the very existence of the institution. Moreover, one of the first acts of the new federal government was the Northwest Ordinance of July 13, 1787, Article VI of which prohibited slavery north of the Ohio River. The same article, however, stipulated that fugitive slaves had to be returned to their masters.

Nevertheless, before the end of the Revolutionary War several northern and even some southern states had taken action against slavery and the slave trade.[15] Because of the fervor of revolutionary principles, religious beliefs, and reasons of conscience, the movement to manumit slaves, which began as a mere trickle in the North, reached major proportions.

[11] For the impact that blacks had upon the Continental Congress see Peter Bergman and Jean McCarroll, eds., *The Negro in the Continental Congress* (New York: Bergman Publications, 1970).

[12] Article 1, Section 2, U. S. Constitution.

[13] Article IV, Section 2, U. S. Constitution.

[14] Article II, Section 9, U. S. Constitution.

[15] John Hope Franklin, *From Slavery to Freedom: A History of Negro Americans* (New York: Alfred A. Knopf, 1967), pp. 138–141.

Northern blacks were gradually emancipated. In fact, it was in the struggle to achieve freedom that black pressure tactics and political activity once again reemerged. Petitions, memorials, prayers, and leaflets deluged the various state legislatures seeking, demanding, and asking for freedom. The Federalist-dominated legislature in the state of New York is a case in point.[16] Arthur Zilversmit, in his case study of black emancipation in the North, details how significant pressure tactics and activity were in the achievement of the northern abolition of slavery. Benjamin Quarles describes in detail how blacks involved themselves in the abolitionist movement from the early period until the end of slavery. In his account he discusses the impact the numerous pressures of black abolitionists had upon the early government at all levels—state, local, and national.[17]

Prior to the abolition of slavery in the North, however, a free black population had existed in both the North and the South. Even after the abolition of northern slavery, the free black population in the South continued to grow.[18] Before blacks obtained limited freedom, the tendency in both the northern and southern states was to extend the franchise generally, and no attempts had been made as yet to restrict it on the basis of color. Legally, then, blacks who obtained their freedom had the right to vote until these states withdrew that right.

ELECTORAL POLITICS IN COLONIAL AMERICA

As is shown in Figure 2, blacks had the legal right to vote in many states before the Civil War. But only in the states of Maine, New Hampshire, Vermont, Massachusetts, and Rhode Island could blacks vote without restrictions.[19] To be eligible for the franchise in New York, for example, black voters had to own at least two hundred and fifty dollars' worth of property. In several places within some states, however, such as Ohio, Wisconsin, and Michigan, there were blacks who voted and participated in numerous party conventions.[20] This was due to the nature of segregation and the attitude of the townspeople in regard to permitting blacks to vote.

Table I indicates that there was a substantial black population in the United States that would have been eligible for the right to vote in each election if the state had not restricted that right. The table further indicates that in New England the free black population tended to remain stationary

[16] Arthur Zilversmit, *The First Emancipation: The Abolition of Slavery in the North* (Chicago: University of Chicago Press, 1967), pp. 55-168.

[17] Benjamin H. Quarles, *Black Abolitionists* (New York: Oxford University Press, 1966).

[18] Frazier, *op. cit.*, pp. 62-67.

[19] Charles H. Wesley, *Neglected History: Essays in Negro American History* (Wilberforce, Ohio: Central State College Press, 1965), p. 54; Stephen B. Weeks, "The History of Negro Suffrage in the South," *Political Science Quarterly*, IX (December, 1894), 679.

[20] Weeks, *op. cit.*, pp. 673-680.

Figure 2. Black Voting before the Civil War

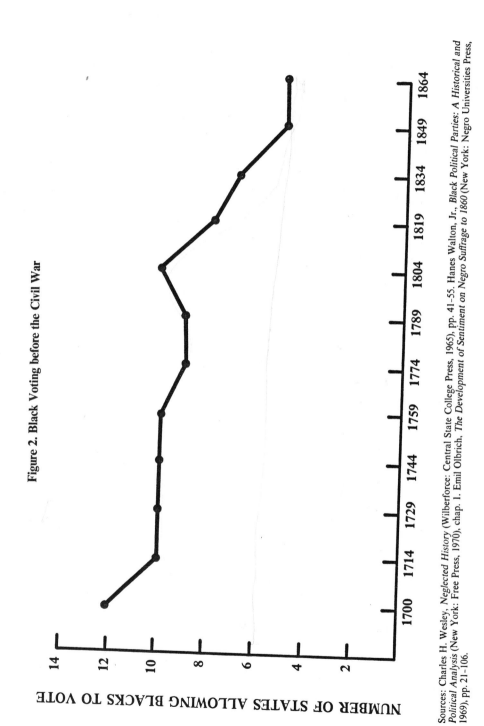

Sources: Charles H. Wesley, *Neglected History* (Wilberforce: Central State College Press, 1965), pp. 41–55. Hanes Walton, Jr., *Black Political Parties: A Historical and Political Analysis* (New York: Free Press, 1970), chap. 1. Emil Olbrich, *The Development of Sentiment on Negro Suffrage to 1860* (New York: Negro Universities Press, 1969), pp. 21–106.

Table I. Free Black Population in the United States

State	Year		
	1790	1830	1860
South Carolina	1,801	7,921	9,914
Georgia	398	2,486	3,500
Virginia	12,866	47,348	58,042
Delaware	3,899	15,855	19,829
Kentucky	114	4,917	10,684
Ohio		9,568	36,673
New Jersey	2,762	18,303	25,318
Maryland	8,043	52,938	83,942
Louisiana		16,710	18,647
Indiana		3,628	11,428
Mississippi		519	773
Illinois		1,637	7,628
Connecticut	2,771	8,047	8,627
Alabama		1,572	2,690
New York	4,682	44,870	49,005
Missouri		589	3,572
Tennessee	361	4,555	7,300
North Carolina	5,041	19,543	30,643
Arkansas		141	144
Michigan		261	6,799
Pennsylvania	6,531	37,930	56,949
Florida		844	932
Texas	0	0	355
Iowa	0	0	1,069
Wisconsin	0	0	NA
California	0	0	4,086
Minnesota	0	0	259
Oregon	0	0	128
Kansas	0	0	189
West Virginia	0	0	NA
Nevada	0	0	NA
Maine	536	1,190	1,327
New Hampshire	630	604	494
Vermont	269	881	709
Massachusetts	5,369	7,048	9,602
Rhode Island	3,484	3,561	3,952

Source: Bureau of the Census, *Negro Population, 1790-1915* (Washington, 1918), p. 57.

after 1840. In Vermont and New Hampshire there was actually a decline. After 1840 there was a gradual increase in the number of free blacks in New Jersey and Pennsylvania, but in New York the number remained generally the same. In all of the South Atlantic states except Florida, where the number remained nearly stationary, there was a steady growth in the free black population. In Alabama, Kentucky, and Tennessee the free black population increased, but that of Louisiana declined after 1840. The number of free blacks in Mississippi was always insignificant.

Figure 3, however, where a comparison of the population is juxtaposed against the voting status, shows that a significant number of blacks were concentrated in states and areas where blacks could vote before a restriction was placed upon them. Moreover, statistics give evidence that blacks participated sufficiently in the electoral politics of those regions to make themselves felt. Notable in this regard, as becomes clear from an examination of the graphic data in Table I, are the states of New York and Pennsylvania in the North and Tennessee and North Carolina in the South. In addition, there is the case of Rapides Parish, Louisiana (dubbed the ten-mile district), where until 1860 free blacks were mustered to the polls in numerous state and local elections either by the Democrats or by the local Know-Nothing party in order to swing the election in their favor.[21] In fact, free blacks in Maryland and Ohio, for example, voted even after the suffrage rights had been officially withdrawn from them. Here again, discriminatory practices were specialized rather than uniform. Even though prohibited, black voting continued in certain places because of uneven application, individual application, or even disregard of restrictive racist law.

At this point, however, it is as necessary to emphasize that blacks could and did vote in colonial America as it is important to discuss the nature of black electoral politics in early America.

The electoral politics of black people in early America took several patterns and forms. Once again the environment of the black voter must be considered. In New York, black voters strongly supported the Federalist party on a local and statewide basis because of its supposedly abolitionist stance.[22] When the Federalist party collapsed, this allegiance was transferred to the National Republicans, the successors of the old Federalists. This was because the Jeffersonian Republicans, upon gaining control of the state legislature, attempted to break up the black Federalist alliance by restricting black suffrage in 1821. When national party lines were eclipsed during the "Era of Good Feelings," black voters continued to support

[21] Roger Shugg, "Negro Voting in the Ante-Bellum South," *Journal of Negro History,* XXI (October, 1936), 360-364.

[22] Dixon Ryan Fox, "The Negro Vote in Old New York," *Political Science Quarterly,* XXXII (June, 1917), 252-275.

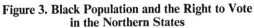

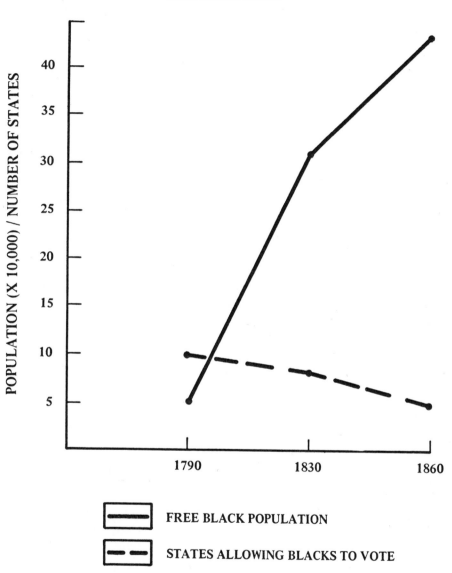

Figure 3. Black Population and the Right to Vote
in the Northern States

FREE BLACK POPULATION

STATES ALLOWING BLACKS TO VOTE

Source: Bureau of the Census, *Negro Population, 1790-1915* (Washington, D.C.: Government Printing Office, 1918), pp. 53-57.

suffrage advocates by defeating in the fifth and eighth wards politicians approved by Tammany Hall. Moreover, there was strong support from several black wards for the Workingmen's party in local elections.[23] This party, which sought to aid the workingmen by increasing technology, indirectly benefited the free blacks in their economic plight.

When party lines reformed, blacks in New York, Pennsylvania, and Rhode Island moved into the Whig camp. Black voters in New York helped elect Whig candidate William H. Seward governor because of his liberal views on retaining suffrage rights for everyone. Seward argued, "I shall not deny them any right on account of the hue they wear, or of the land in which they or their ancestors were born."[24]

In Pennsylvania black voters supported anti-Masonry, Whigs, and liberal candidates on the local and state level. But the acquisition of black voters by these political groups and individuals caused the Democrats of the state in 1838 to restrict the franchise to only white males.

In North Carolina, the political allegiance of black voters was uncertain, but in Tennessee black voters sent two white liberals, Cane Johnson and John Bell, to Congress.[25] In Ohio blacks elected a black, John M. Langston, who ran for township clerk on the Liberty party ticket.

In fact, black voters throughout the North supported the various antislavery parties and helped to elect liberals like Gerritt Smith and Charles Sumner to state and national offices respectively. These antislavery parties, altogether minor parties, gave blacks their first opportunity for political participation. The electoral politics of blacks in early America was mainly one of support for political friends and allies.

When the electoral politics of blacks in this era dwindled because of the increasing restriction and inhibition placed upon black voters, the nonelectoral black politics that had prevailed before the Revolutionary War once again became significant.

PRESSURE POLITICS IN THE ABOLITIONIST ERA

Black pressure activity prior to the war was mainly uncoordinated and limited in nature. There was no organization to funnel pressure to the appropriate decision-making agencies. As soon as blacks entered politics, however, and gained enough insight into their dilemma to question their status and see the need for improving it, a black organization was established. This was the National Negro Convention Movement,[26] which had

[23] Hanes Walton, Jr., *The Negro in Third Party Politics* (Philadelphia: Dorrance, 1969), pp. 6-7, 85.
[24] Wesley, *op. cit.*, p. 60.
[25] Weeks, *op. cit.*, p. 676. See also C. B. Patterson, *The Negro in Tennessee, 1790-1865* (New York: Negro Universities Press, 1968), pp. 167-168.
[26] Howard Bell, "The Negro Convention Movement, 1930-60: New Perspectives," *Negro*

state and local affiliates, and which employed many protest and pressure tactics in behalf of the black community. Still, a great deal of the nonelectoral politics of blacks continued on a small scale.

The first major issue on which blacks protested after the Revolutionary War was colonization—removal of free blacks outside of U. S. territorial units. Along with agitating against colonization, blacks condemned discrimination throughout the northern states. Finally, blacks joined the antislavery crusade. The numerous tactics that black abolitionists employed in seeking to destroy slavery ran from moral suasion to the support of John Brown's raid at Harper's Ferry.

On the local level the struggle for the return of the franchise became the center of much black protest activity. In 1837 blacks in New York City met in a town hall and discussed their plight and how to alleviate it. After the meeting a petition was sent to the state legislature that demanded "an alteration of the Constitution so as to give the right of voting to all the male citizens of the state on the same terms without the distinction of color."[27] In Philadelphia, where in 1838 the state legislature restricted suffrage rights to whites only, a convention of blacks met and drew up a petition entitled "An Appeal of Forty Thousand Disfranchised Citizens of Pennsylvania," which was delivered to the legislature, and which demanded a return of the suffrage rights. The petition went unheeded. In Ohio, blacks sent a protest statement to the state legislature that held that it was "unjust, anti-democratic, unpolitic, and ungenerous to withhold from us the right of suffrage." Finally, when the free blacks of Wisconsin were deprived of their suffrage rights in 1849, they demanded their return each year thereafter.

Beyond the area of suffrage, however, the nonelectoral politics of black individuals and the collective actions of the National Negro Convention Movement continued even through the Civil War. Matters such as education, equal facilities, and freedom remained the chief aims of this pressure and protest activity, which met with varying degrees of success and failure in sundry localities. Black politics in colonial and early America intensified with each passing year. Whether basically electoral or nonelectoral, the political activities of blacks continued unabated each year in varying degrees before the Civil War. There is no period in which some form of activity (electoral or nonelectoral) did not take place. And in many places the electoral politics of blacks was supplemented by their nonelectoral activities and vice versa. No matter the type of political activity, however, blacks—depending on the nature of their locality and the intensity of racial feelings and suppression—met with varying degrees of success in introducing certain of their preferences into public policy. While no major legisla-

History Bulletin, XIV (February, 1951), 103-105; Bella Gross, "The First National Negro Convention," *Journal of Negro History*, XXXI (October, 1946), 433.

[27] Aptheker, *op. cit.*, p. 165.

tion was passed as a direct result of these activities, pre-Civil War black politics was far from being insignificant. Some limited rewards were obtained. For example, the removal of a poll tax on free blacks in South Carolina and a Massachusetts court's declaration in 1783 which grew out of black protest indicated that blacks who were subject to taxation "were declared to be entitled to the suffrage." These represent only a few of the minor redresses of grievances that blacks won for themselves via politics in colonial America. Some petitions and memorials were accepted and favorably passed upon. Some blacks were elected to minor public offices. Because of black pressure tactics, some educational facilities were created for blacks, and the pressure activity of the black abolitionists did intensify the slavery controversy. On the whole, however, the dilemmas that blacks found themselves in were beyond the realm that the political power of a half-million free blacks could solve. In numerous localities blacks moved from stage one (nonparticipation) to stage two (limited participation). And as Table III indicates, there was a reversal of stages. Often blacks achieved one stage only to be thrown back at a later date to another stage. Generally speaking, however, black politics in early America never moved beyond stage two. The limited number of free blacks, the limitations placed upon black suffrage, and the limited pressure group activity—limited in terms of the number of people involved—all these kept black politics in early America in the first two stages of development. Thus, black politics was continued in nineteenth-century America by other means—the Civil War—which still left some problems of blacks unsolved. This leads to the question of how the American system of government, federalism, affected the development of black politics.

BLACKS AND FEDERALISM

As established by the Founding Fathers, the government of the United States was one of limited powers. The separate states, jealous of their sovereignty, had been reluctant to relinquish any of their prerogatives, and in order to obtain ratification of the Constitution, it had been necessary to agree to an amendment reserving to the states all powers not specifically delegated to the federal government.[28]

Furthermore, "Although the Federalists were eventually successful in establishing a strong central government, the preponderance of power still remained with the individual states."[29]

[28] Eli Ginzberg and Alfred S. Eichner, *The Troublesome Presence: American Democracy and the Negro* (Glencoe, Ill.: Free Press, 1964), p. 290.
[29] *Ibid.*

Moreover, the Founding Fathers created a federal form of government because of the advantages such a system has over either a confederation or a unitary form of government. The central weakness of a confederacy is that the central government can make regulations, but it is left up to the states to decide whether they want to accept them.[30]

In a unitary form of government all governmental power is vested in a central government, and states exercise only those powers that are given them by the federal government. In 1787, however, the American people were too "deeply attached to their state governments to permit the state to be subordinate to a central government."[31] In fact, many individuals wanted to retain the confederation, and many of the delegates to the 1787 Convention went with the understanding that the Articles of Confederation were to be revised and not that a new form of government would be established. Only a few delegates, like Madison, Hamilton, and Jay, for example, were cognizant that a move was under way to create a new form of government. That minority of delegates prevailed, however, and through numerous compromises a strong national government was created that drew its power from both the people and the states. The Supreme Court was created to decide in light of the Constitution and the Bill of Rights where the national governmental powers stopped and those of the states began. From the outset, however, the Constitution gave the national government plenary power in the area of interstate commerce.

As years passed, the nature of the American federal system changed, and its operations became more and more complex. Moreover, the relationship between the states and the national government also changed, as did the Supreme Court decisions on the nature of the national government. Federalism, from the Supreme Court's viewpoint, moved from dual federalism to what is called today cooperative federalism. Moreover, as the nature of American federalism changed, so also did the nature of the problems faced in the federal system. A perennial problem has been the establishment and protection of black civil rights. In fact, as problems have increased in this area, more and more critics have arued that federalism as a form of government has become obsolete. Harold J. Laski, the British political scientist, argued that the federal form of government enriched the rich and benefited only economic interest at the expense of other interests in society.[32] Following Laski, William Riker argues that the federal system has benefited the racist element in our southern states. He even argues that the

[30] *Ibid.*
[31] *Ibid.*
[32] Harold J. Laski, "The Obsolescence of Federalism," *New Republic,* LXLVIII (May 3, 1939), 367.

benefits accrued to southern racists are greater than those given to special economic interests.[33]

"The judgment to be passed on federalism in the United States is," he said, "therefore a judgment on the values of segregation and racial oppression."[34]

In addition to Riker's attack there are others exploring the crisis that the civil rights movement has created for our federal structure. Burke Marshall, who was assistant attorney general under President Kennedy, also has stated that it is "necessary to be realistic about the limitations on the power of the federal government to eliminate racial discrimination in this country."[35]

In Marshall's view, it is only "necessary to create again, by statutes, federal rights, and federal remedies, in a new effort to rid the nation of discriminatory practices."[36] In reality, however, the central issue of the basic protection of civil rights remains. The United States Constitution does not grant any police power to the national government. Federal marshals are only "process servants working for the courts."[37] At best they can deliver or place in custody; they do not arrest or apprehend. But without an effective police force, Marshall argues, the federal government cannot adequately protect the rights of black people.

When, for example, a black leader informs the Department of Justice that he will lead a group of blacks to register in a small town where no blacks have voted for decades, he in effect asks for federal protection. He will be told, however, that he cannot get federal protection, only federal observers, and he may feel that federal help in realizing his federal rights is being denied him. He will be told, of course, that the protection of citizens is a matter for the local police, but that if he is attacked while trying to perform a civil function, then the federal government will file a suit against the perpetrator for violating his constitutional rights.

In other words, the basic power that the national government has to protect the civil rights of blacks in our federal system of government is that of court litigations and injunctions. The question arises, however, as to the adequacy of these tools.

Generally speaking, states see these federal lawsuits to protect the rights of blacks who are exercising their civil rights as affecting their conduct only to a minimum degree. "In the view of the state it is legitimate and right not

[33] William H. Riker, *Federalism: Origin, Operation, Significance* (Boston: Little, Brown and Company, 1964), p. 153.

[34] *Ibid.*, p. 154.

[35] Burke Marshall, *Federalism and Civil Rights* (New York: Columbia University Press, 1964), p. 3.

[36] *Ibid.*, p. 83.

[37] *Ibid.*, p. 5.

to move until forced to do so—and then barely budge."[38] In addition, states consider it legitimate to use their police power to thwart any citizen's efforts to break existing and established social patterns. In effect, this ends up in endless litigation in the federal courts. It is time-consuming, costly, and it affects few individuals of either race. Nevertheless, the process continues. When the federal government feels that new action should be taken, a new legislative package is presented to Congress, which involves further delays and a weakening of the total process.

Despite these efforts, however, black protest politics has made the national government a center of its attention. In fact, the struggle of black people in America has been one of seeking to bring the federal government to their side. It is therefore not difficult to understand that when states curtailed or limited the rights of black persons, they in turn sought redress from the federal government.

In fact, the basic thrust of blacks in the American political system has been one of having their rights defined by law.[39] They have done this by pressuring the federal government into passing legislation, or by having the federal courts declare the constitutional validity of these challenged, curtailed, or limited black rights. Similarly, they expect these same political entities to protect these granted rights, since to permit a denial of them is to permit the corruption of basic democratic principles and precepts.

For the most part, the problem of federalism for blacks started through reluctance of the federal government to move in and vigorously defend the rights of blacks because of the possibility of interfering with the doctrine of states' rights. Whether the problem is simply the national government's deference to the rights of states, or whether it is the ability of states to use the least invasion of their sovereignty to embarrass the federal government by crying authoritarianism and forcing the federal government to move slowly, cautiously, or not at all, is irrelevant. Moreover, whether or not southerners have more power in Congress and more influence with presidential candidates, though significant in the final analysis, is not sufficient. The fact remains that the major problem of American federalism is neither the system itself, nor the inability of the government, nor its inbred weakness, but the unwillingness, because of entrenched racism, to effectively establish and protect black rights. The Constitution may not at the present time give the national government enough powers to protect the civil rights of blacks, but the Constitution can be amended. The states have, in fact, because of the growing technology, industrialization, and economic power, been losing more and more power to the federal government anyway.

[38] Ibid., p. 6.
[39] Emmett E. Dorsey, "The American Negro and His Government," Crisis, LXVIII (October, 1961), 472. See also Samuel Lubell, The Future of American Politics (New York: Doubleday Anchor, 1956), pp. 134-135.

Moreover, because of poor taxation policies and inefficient administration, the states have proved unable to solve their economic, social, and health problems, and it has become increasingly necessary for the federal government to take over in these areas. The states have not had their rights taken away from them; they have forfeited them, because of their antiquated legislative systems and their outmoded policies for dealing with pressing social ills.[40] The cry of states losing their rights to the federal government has become in many instances only a smoke screen to deny blacks their full civil rights.

The black conception of a relevant and valid federalism is "one which provides a relationship of the federal to the state governments that permits comprehension and effective programs of civil rights, security, and welfare."[41] Thus, the need of blacks for a government to pursue a vigorous civil rights policy is basic, basic because there are embedded in the culture of American society drastic restraints and even denials of these civil rights of blacks. In the long run, any abridgment of these rights means a denial of our constitutional and democratic principles and precepts.[42]

[40] Robert Sherrill, *Gothic Politics in the South* (New York: Grossman Publishers, 1968).
[41] Dorsey, *op. cit.*, p. 469. See also Robert S. Rankin, "The Impact of Civil Rights upon Twentieth-Century Federalism," Daniel J. Elazer et al., eds., *Cooperation and Conflict: Readings in American Federalism* (Itasca, Ill.: F. E. Peacock Publishers, 1969), pp. 581–593.
[42] Charles Hamilton, "The Political Consequences of Southern Politics," *Negro Educational Review*, XI (January, 1960), 28.

III

The Black Electorate

Black Americans have always voted. At the time of the Constitutional Convention free blacks had the legal right to suffrage in all of the states except Georgia and South Carolina. Even after the War for Independence, blacks at various times had the right to vote in almost all of the northern states and even in some southern states (see Table I). In fact, from 1838 to 1860, free blacks voted in Rapides Parish, Louisiana, even though the legislature had curtailed the right in 1812.

During the era of disfranchisement, blacks cast votes for Populists, Prohibitionists, Union Laborites, Republicans, Democrats, etc. Even after blacks had been completely disfranchised in the states of the old Confederacy, they still voted in places like San Antonio, Memphis, Atlanta, Savannah, Durham, and other cities in the South. In 1930, for example, thirty blacks voted in the municipal election in Athens, Georgia,[1] and as early as 1921 blacks in Virginia cast more than five thousand votes for John Mitchell, a black gubernatorial candidate. In short, throughout American history blacks have voted in sundry localities, even when the law forbade them to do so. This was so because the practices and application of segregation have from the start been unevenly applied.

Essentially, the black electorate has been limited by its environment. Blacks registered and voted where the political culture permitted them to do so. *The chief problems that have faced the black electorate have been the acquisition and retention of the franchise.* With permission granted, then withdrawn, then granted, the size of the black electorate has accordingly fluctuated. The quantity of the black electorate could be decreased by both legal and extralegal methods and events. State legislatures could at their whim withdraw the right to vote. North Carolina, for instance, gave blacks this freedom, the right to vote, in 1667 and withdrew it in 1715. This withdrawal was repealed in 1734, but the right to vote was again withdrawn in 1835.[2] In 1821, New York decreased its black electorate by enlarging the

---

[1] Ralph W. Wardlaw, "Negro Suffrage in Georgia, 1865-1930" (unpublished M.A. thesis, University of Georgia, 1932), p. 125.

33

amount of property that a black person had to have before he could qualify to vote.

In fact, before the ratification of the Fifteenth Amendment, numerous other states used similar methods—legal as well as illegal (i.e., violence, deception, etc.)—in order to control or manipulate the number of black voters in their boundaries.

Congress did not grant the franchise to blacks until the enactment of the Fifteenth Amendment. This grant was curtailed, however, with the Compromise of 1877, which withdrew federal protection of the black electorate. Before and since, blacks have attempted to have their right to vote firmly established by law. This chapter, then, will approach the black electorate from the standpoint of (1) the establishment of the legal right to vote, (2) the problem of registration after obtaining the right to vote, (3) the problem of the influence, manipulation, and control of the registered black voter. In other words, the story of the black electorate has been one of trying to acquire and then retain the right to vote.

Before enactment of the Fifteenth Amendment, blacks had petitioned and pressured several state legislatures as well as the state supreme courts to have their right to vote established or returned. When, in 1838, the revised constitution of Pennsylvania stripped free blacks of the right to vote, blacks contested the action in the State Supreme Court, in *Hobbs* v. *Fagg*. The court ruled that a "Negro or a mulatto was not entitled to vote." Blacks in North Carolina took to the courts to have their voting rights returned when they were withdrawn in the new constitution of 1835, but the courts ruled against them also. In New York, when the state legislature restricted the black voter, blacks petitioned the state legislature at different intervals from 1821 until the Civil War. The same situation prevailed in Connecticut when its constitution of 1818 disfranchised blacks. In fact, in all of the states that disfranchised the free blacks, and especially in those of the North and Middle West, blacks attempted to regain their suffrage rights.[3] Court action and petition alike, however, failed to aid the black electorate in its quest to acquire, regain, or retain the ballot. The free blacks who were disfranchised before the Civil War remained disfranchised.

With the coming of the Civil War, however, and the Emancipation Proclamation, efforts to have the franchise extended by the federal government to all blacks got under way. In October 1864, at Syracuse, New York, blacks established the National Equal Rights League to obtain suffrage

[2] Stephen B. Weeks, "History of Negro Suffrage," *Political Science Quarterly,* IX (December, 1894), 671–672.

[3] Leon Litwack, *North of Slavery: The Negro in the Free States* (Chicago: University of Chicago Press, 1961), chap. 1.

rights for all blacks. The president of the League, Frederick Douglass, called on President Andrew Johnson to grant blacks full enfranchisement. He refused, but a group of radical Republicans was receptive to Douglass's plea. With their backing, the Fifteenth Amendment was adopted on March 30, 1870. The federal government granted universal suffrage to blacks. With this amendment the black electorate reached its greatest heights. Although there was still some question whether blacks could vote in the North, the southern black electorate reached its greatest heights and placed black public officials in hundreds of political posts on the state and national levels. After 1877, however, the black electorate once again declined. Federal protection was withdrawn, and the southern whites devised numerous schemes designed to diminish the number of black voters; they ranged from sheer violence to the destruction of ballots.

ERA OF DISFRANCHISEMENT

In 1890, Mississippi called a state convention for the purpose of eliminating the black electorate; its plan for disfranchising the black voter became the model for the other southern states. In fact, the Mississippi precedent of not submitting the new constitution to the electorate for ratification, but simply proclaiming it the law of the land, was followed by all the southern conventions except that of Alabama.

With the arrival of the era of disfranchisement, the black electorate was reduced to insignificance in the South. Once again a struggle to regain and retain the vote ensued. That struggle has continued unabated to the present day.

Before the struggle to regain the vote commenced, however, blacks attempted to have the federal government protect their right to vote. This attempt came during President Harrison's administration when Henry Cabot Lodge introduced a bill to supervise federal elections. This bill—dubbed the "force bill" by its opponents—was buried in the Committee on Privileges and Elections on December 2, 1890. Since that time the black electorate has sought, not only to regain the ballot, but also federal protection of its usage, even though an earlier Supreme Court decision in the Slaughter House cases rendered null and void the clause in the Fourteenth Amendment which states: "No state shall make or enforce any law which shall abridge the privileges and immunities of citizens of the United States." Since this decision blacks, seeking to have the courts protect their civil rights, have not been able to avail themselves of this clause. Other amendments and other sections of the Fourteenth Amendment have had to be employed. Moreover, the Enforcement Act of May 31, 1870, and the Civil Rights Act of March 1, 1875, both of which were established for the protection of the civil rights of the black electorate, were declared unconstitutional.

DRIVE TO REGAIN THE BALLOT

The black electorate's first attempt to regain its suffrage rights came in the form of an attack on the grandfather clause of numerous southern state constitutions. This clause, which prevented blacks from voting unless they had proof that they or their ancestors voted prior to the Civil War, was declared unconstitutional in a Supreme Court decision of June 21, 1915.[4]

A sequel to the *Guinn* case was *Lane* v. *Wilson* (1939). The Oklahoma legislature passed a new suffrage law in 1916 to replace the grandfather clause provision held unconstitutional the preceding year. Since the 1914 general election had been under the disfranchising grandfather clause, the Oklahoma Act of 1916 granted voting privileges to all of those who had participated in that election. All other individuals (obviously blacks) were required to register between April 30 and May 11, 1916. An extension, until June 30, was made for those who could not make it because of poor health or because they lived too far away. "The court heeded that racial discrimination violating the Fifteenth Amendment resulted from this granting voting privileges for life to white citizens originally sheltered by the grandfather clause while subjecting colored citizens to the burden of a single twelve-day registration period as the only means of establishing voting privileges."[5]

The grandfather device having been rendered useless, the southern states next devised the "white primary," a device by which whites had the privilege of selecting those blacks who could vote in the primary elections. In about two decades after Reconstruction, the South created a one-party system, and nomination by the Democratic party became equivalent to being elected. Thus denying a person the right to vote in the primary was tantamount to disenfranchising him.

In 1923, the Texas legislature passed a law based on the doctrine of the *Newberry* v. *United States* case, which stated that a party primary is not an election within the meaning of the Constitution. This law declared that "in no event shall a Negro be eligible to participate in a Democratic primary election held in the state of Texas, and should a Negro vote in a Democratic primary election, such ballot shall be void and election officials are herein directed to throw out such ballot, and not count the same."

An El Paso black, Dr. L. A. Nixon, attempted to vote after the law had been promulgated, but election officials prevented his doing so. Nixon then

[4] See *Guinn and Beal* v. *U. S.* 347 (1914).
[5] Robert E. Cushman and Robert F. Cushman, eds., *Cases in Constitutional Law* (New York: Appleton-Century-Crofts, 1968), p. 1093.

sued the election judge, Herndon, for damages on the grounds that the legislature's exclusion act violated the Fourteenth and Fifteenth amendments. The Supreme Court declared the Texas statute unconstitutional because it denied Nixon equal protection under the law. In making this decision, the Court stated that "we find it unnecessary to consider the Fifteenth Amendment because it seems to us hard to image a more direct and obvious infringement of the Fourteenth." Thus the Court still avoided the question of federal regulation of party primaries.

The Texas legislature did not give up. In the same year the legislature enacted another stature, which authorized "every political party in this state through its state executive committee ... to prescribe the qualifications of its own members." With this grant of power, the Democratic state committee resolved that "all white Democrats who are qualified under the Constitution and laws of Texas ... and none other, [shall] be allowed to participate in the primary elections." Under this provision Dr. Nixon was again denied the ballot, and again he sued for damages. Although the white Texas Democrats argued that Nixon was excluded by party rather than by state action, the Supreme Court held that "whatever power of exclusion has been exercised by the members of the committee has come to them, therefore, not as delegates of the party but as the delegates of the state." Since the state law authorized the discrimination, this meant that blacks were denied equal protection under the laws. And once again the Supreme Court refused to say whether the party could exclude blacks. So, Texas ingenuity went to work again in order to circumvent the ruling.

This time the legislature did not take any action. Instead, the Democratic state convention adopted in 1932 a resolution that declared that "all white citizens of the state of Texas ... shall be eligible to membership in the Democratic Party and as such entitled to participate in its deliberations." When a black was denied the right to vote in the Democratic primary, the Supreme Court held that political parties "are voluntary associations for political action and are not the creature of the state." According to this decision, private persons or groups could not violate the Fourteenth Amendment; as a private association, the Democratic party, therefore, could exclude blacks from its primaries without violating the equal protection clause of the Constitution. Here again, however, the Supreme Court avoided discussion of whether or not the federal government could regulate elections.

However, in 1940, the issue of public regulation of primary elections was placed squarely before the courts in a case which turned on the question of corruption rather than on the right of blacks to vote in party primaries. But this apparently extraneous event proved to be valuable to the black electorate at a later date by setting the stage for blacks to deal a death blow to the white primary. And this was another instance in which blacks in the

political arena moved from one stage to another because of events beyond
their control rather than as a result of their own actions.

The event in question occurred in New Orleans in 1940. It grew out of an
alleged fraud committed in the primary election held for the nomination of
a United States representative. The state election officials who were
charged by federal authorities with committing this fraud defended themselves by claiming that primary elections were beyond federal regulation.
They held that the federal government could regulate only general
elections.

Thus, the issue emerged as to whether or not the federal government
could permit state officials to aid and abet the fraudulent action of congressmen. In Louisiana, the primary was the election. The Supreme Court
held that the Constitution authorizes Congress to regulate primaries when
the primary is an integral part of the procedure of choice or where the
primary effectively controls the choice. It also ruled that it was the right of
a qualified citizen of the United States to vote in a congressional primary
and to have his vote counted.

Black lawyers, seeing that the courts would protect citizens against fraud
in primaries for the nominations of congressmen, asked the Court whether
blacks could be excluded from primaries by the party or the state. The
Court decided on the basis of the *Classic* decision that the primary in Texas
was an integral part of the machine for choosing public officials and could
not be left to private individuals or groups. In declaring that "all citizens
[had] a right to participate in the choice of elected officials without restriction by any state because of race," the Court dealt a death blow to the
white primary system, and another device for restricting the black electorate was destroyed. In Virginia the white primary had died in 1929, due to a
federal district court ruling.

Like the Supreme Court decisions on the grandfather clause, however,
the Court's white primary decision did not end southern efforts to restrict
the black electorate.

Alabama, operating on a Supreme Court decision in *Williams* v. *Mississippi* (1898), which indicated that a reading and interpretation clause in
voting registration procedures did not violate the Fourteenth Amendment,
enacted the "Boswell Amendment" in 1946.[6] This amendment, which did
not by its language discriminate against blacks, did require that prospective
voters be able to "understand and explain" any part of the United States
Constitution to the satisfaction of local registration officers.[7] This sophisticated method of restricting the black electorate was declared in January

[6] Joseph M. Brittain, "Some Reflections on Negro Suffrage and Politics in Alabama: Past
and Present," *Journal of Negro History,* XLVII (April, 1962), 127-138, and Vera C. Foster,
"Boswellianism Technique in the Restriction of Negro Voting," *Phylon,* X (Fall, 1949), 26-27.
[7] *Ibid.*

1949, by a three-judge federal district court to be in violation of the Fifteenth Amendment. The court said, "We cannot ignore the impact of the Boswell Amendment upon Negro citizens because it avoids mention of race or color, to do this would be to shut our eyes to what all others can see and understand."

South Carolina tried to nullify the *Allwright* decision differently. The state legislature noted, on the basis of two clauses in the *Classic* decision, that the constitutional right to participate in primary elections existed (1) where "the state law has made the primary an integral part of the procedure of choice" and (2) "where in face the primary effectively controls the choice." It accordingly repealed some 150 statutes which mentioned, authorized, or regulated primaries. In short, the state dropped all connection with elections and left it up to private individuals to hold and regulate them, whereupon the state Democratic party leaped into the vacuum created by the state legislature and barred blacks from the polls. A federal district court, however, held that South Carolina could not wash its hands of governing elections because the democratic primary remained in actuality the only effective agency for selecting public officials. The Supreme Court upheld the lower court decision.

Texas next attempted to hold a preprimary election from which the black electorate was excluded, but the U. S. Supreme Court held such a primary to be unconstitutional.[8] Upon the defeat of these new devices, most states permitted the black electorate to register and participate in the next primary election. Some states, however, strengthened their reading and interpretation clauses.

Where state ingenuity flagged, local ingenuity flared. In Tuskegee, Alabama, where the black electorate outnumbered the white, gerrymandering was emphasized. "The city, which had been square in shape was transformed into a strangely irregular twenty-eight sided figure, with the intention and result of removing from the city all save four or five of its 400 Negro voters while not removing a single white voter or resident." As a result of the redistricting, blacks could not vote in municipal elections. In *Gomillion* v. *Lightfoot,* however, the Supreme Court held that Tuskegee's gerrymandering was an unconstitutional "essay in geometry and geography" that deprived blacks of their right to vote in city elections.[9]

Court action alone was not enough to establish the right of blacks to vote. Numerous southern communities continued to employ various discriminatory acts, ranging from intimidation to violence, to keep qualified blacks from the polls. Black pressure tactics—such as the Rev. Martin Luther King's first march on Washington in 1957—as well as the violence

---

[8] *Terry* v. *Adams,* 345 U.S. 461 (1953).
[9] 364 U.S. 339 (1961). See also Bernard Taper, *Gomillion Versus Lightfoot* (New York: McGraw-Hill Book Company, 1962).

meted out to blacks and shown to the world via the news media caused Congress to act.

CONGRESS STEPS IN

Congress in 1957 passed its first law governing black-white relations in three-quarters of a century. This law, which created the Civil Rights Commission and gave it an investigative function, also gave the attorney general power to seek court injunctions whenever an individual was either being deprived or else about to be deprived of his voting rights.[10] But "during the three years prior to the Civil Rights Act of 1960, the Justice Department filed only four suits "in behalf of the black electorate."[11] This limited action by the Justice Department has led Donald Strong to conclude that "in its first 33 months of operation the Civil Rights Act of 1957 made no significant changes in the customs of Negro disfranchisement."[12] This was in part true because the Alabama state legislature made every effort to render the federal action ineffective.

In fact, on the basis of the ineffectiveness of the 1957 act, the Commission on Civil Rights recommended to the president that new legislation was needed to enable the black electorate to register and vote. Acting largely on this recommendation, Congress passed the Civil Rights Act of 1960. Since southern congressmen had diluted the effectiveness of the 1957 act by requiring the federal government to proceed one case at a time (in essence, for 5,000 disfranchised blacks, it would have taken 5,000 cases to secure redress), the 1960 act enabled the government, whenever it found a pattern or practice of depriving blacks of their vote, to enfranchise the entire area under designation. In addition, the law decreed that registrars who destroyed or withheld incriminating evidence would have to resign. But through the efforts of southern congressmen, the new law imposed no fine or sentence for failure to comply. As a result, the 1960 act was very similar to its predecessors, for it too made little change in black disfranchisement.

In 1964 a new law was instituted that made local registration follow a pattern of consistency in regard to both the blacks and whites. It also outlawed the denial of the vote to blacks because of "inconsequential error or technicality." Still, this act was very limited in scope, and the difficulty associated with numerous voter registration campaigns in which individuals actually lost their lives clearly pointed out its deficiencies. In fact, all three laws were so weak that they provoked the Reverend Martin Luther

[10] Donald S. Strong, *Negroes, Ballots, and Judges* (University, Ala.: University of Alabama Press, 1968), p. 3.
[11] *Ibid.*, pp. 4–5.
[12] *Ibid.*, p. 5.

King to lead the march from Selma to Montgomery that forced the hand of Congress in devising new legislation.

The 1965 Voting Rights Act, which authorized the attorney general to send federal registrars into counties and provided for limited suspension of literacy tests and similar devices in certain areas, went much farther than the three previous laws in establishing black voting rights. The law had only a five-year life-span; it was renewed in 1970 for another five years. Again, this limitation was due to the influence of southern congressmen. Prior to the 1965 act, however, the Twenty-fourth Amendment outlawed poll taxes in federal elections; the 1965 act waived them in certain state elections; and the Supreme Court in 1966 held them to be in violation of the equal protection clause of the Fourteenth Amendment.

Though the Civil Rights Acts of 1957, 1960, and 1964 achieved only a qualified success, that of 1965 did more than any other act since Reconstruction to invest the federal government with the responsibility for aiding blacks whose voting rights had been denied or abridged.

Thus, having explored the problems the black electorate faced in establishing the right to vote, let us turn out attention to registration.

BLACK REGISTRATION EFFORTS

When the courts and Congress established the right of blacks to vote, the foes of black voting then "turned to the registration process as their chief weapon."[13] In other words, if blacks theoretically had the right to vote, but actually could not register, then the right to vote was made insignificant and would, in effect, be nullified.

As has been pointed out, however, the four voting rights acts were in part an attempt to help blacks to register to vote. In actuality, of course, black people had begun to register to vote in some localities and had attempted to register to vote in others—depending on the nature of the enforcement of segregation—as soon as barriers began to tumble. In fact, attempts at black registration began before the text of the grandfather clause and have continued until now. For the most part, however, these attempts either were stymied or unsuccessful.

Black registration increased after each successful attempt to establish the right to vote, particularly after the 1964 court decision and the enactment of the 1965 Voting Rights Act. Some attempts came via private efforts, others via black organizational efforts, and still others via white and black efforts.

In North Carolina, after the defeat of the grandfather clause by the Supreme Court, blacks attempted to register in several cities. In Tennessee

[13] *Ibid.*, p. 2.

black registration and attempts at registration were made continuously from 1910. In Alabama, the disfranchising convention of 1901 just about eliminated all blacks from state politics, but independent attempts by blacks to register helped to maintain the number at 3600 in 1908. "In January, 1926, Mrs. Indiana Little, school teacher of Birmingham, led 1000 Negro women and a few men before the board of registrars and demanded the right to vote as 'American citizens'...." As usual, "this militant Negro political leader was arrested and charged with vagrancy ..." and "not a single one of the thousand was registered."[14] In 1937 blacks in the same city launched another "gonna register" campaign with some 4,000 individuals, but it also failed. Thus, despite black efforts in the state, the number of blacks registered declined to 1800 in 1942.[15]

In some other southern cities black registration increased rather than decreased. In 1921 blacks in Atlanta registered in such a sufficient number under the political leadership of A. T. Walden, a black lawyer, that they defeated a municipal bond issue in 1921. The same situation prevailed in Savannah. In 1923 blacks in that city voted in a reformist city government. In 1928 black voters in Memphis, Tennessee, installed a responsive municipal administration. In each city black registration activity reached a peak before the election took place. Nevertheless, although these illustrations show that black registration and voting did occur in several states, it was both limited and for the most part in selected urban areas. On the whole, black registration prior to the *Smith* v. *Allwright* decision was at best limited. In short, in numerous places a few black individuals were permitted to vote either because of their connection with the white leadership or because of the laxity of segregation enforcement. Black political organizations because of their connection with white political machines could also register a few blacks from time to time if those blacks would support the white political machine. Finally, some blacks through determination and fortitude held to the ballot; for the black multitude the floodgates did not open until 1944.

Although blacks registered to vote in selected southern areas, the *Smith* v. *Allwright* decision did not work wonders overnight. It did, however, establish a basis for the emergence of white liberal supporters of black attempts to register to vote. Prior to 1944, whites shunned the responsibility of aiding black people in their efforts to register. Even in places like Memphis and Virginia, where white political machines continued their viability partly as a result of the black vote, the assistance from white political bosses to aid blacks to register to vote was mainly at a municipal

[14] Joseph M. Brittain, "The Return of the Negro to Alabama Politics, 1930-1954," *Negro History Bulletin*, XX (May, 1959), 196-199.
[15] R. Grann Lloyd, *White Supremacy in the United States* (Washington: Public Affairs Press, 1952), p. 16.

level.[16] Prospective black voters had to register on their own or with the assistance of black political bosses or by emulating Anglo-Saxon behavior that did not threaten the white power. If these alternatives failed, the prospective black voter remained that—a good prospect.

Soon, however, biracial organizations like the Southern Regional Council began to appear, and these worked quietly with indigenous black leaders, political bosses, and black voters leagues or associations to increase the number of black voters. The emergence of this concerned white movement, however, was at first cautious and limited because no one was sure how long blacks would have the right to vote. In short, white supporters of black registration in the South awaited the establishment of firm voting rights for blacks before they moved on a large scale.

Legal rights are not always "real" rights, however, and prospective black voters throughout the South did not achieve instant voting status. Numerous repressive and stalling tactics were employed against the prospective black registrants.[17] In Tuskegee, Alabama, the county registrar sat in a local bank vault so that blacks could not find him to register. Furthermore, he continually moved his office without notifying blacks of his new location.[18] In Fayette County, Tennessee, black tenants who attempted to register were evicted from their houses. Moreover, food and credit were denied them by local merchants. In South Carolina registrars constantly changed office hours or else limited their registration to one or two hours per day or per week or per month. In other southern localities the voter registration office closed indefinitely, or a slowing down of the registration process was instituted. Only one or two blacks were registered to vote per day. The Ku Klux Klan revised and issued threats to several black communities. Black leaders who urged registration and who participated in the process had their homes fire bombed, their lives threatened, or else they were run out of town. Finally, on their way to register or returning from the attempts to register, blacks were shot at from passing cars, even on the courthouse steps.

MANEUVERS TO PREVENT BLACK REGISTRATION

Intimidation, fraud, evasion, economic reprisals, terror, and murder combined to deny blacks the legal right granted by the *Smith* v. *Allwright*

[16] On the Byrd machine assistance to black registration, see Andrew Buni, *The Negro in Virginia Politics, 1902-1965* (Charlottesville: University Press of Virginia, 1967), pp. 124-141. On the Crump machine of Memphis see William D. Miller, *Mr. Crump of Memphis* (Baton Rouge: Louisiana State University Press, 1964), pp. 102-110, 206-207.

[17] On the nature of different attempts to save the white primary in Florida, Georgia, Louisiana, Mississippi, and Texas, see O. Douglas Weeks, "The White Primary, 1944-1948," *American Political Science Review,* XLII (June, 1948), 500-509.

[18] Charles Hamilton and Stokely Carmichael, *Black Power* (New York: Random House, 1969), p. 129.

Table II. The Number of Black Voters and the Percentage of
Voting Age Blacks Registered to Vote in the South, 1947–66

	1947	%	1952	%	1956	%	1966	%
Alabama	6,000	1.2	25,224	5	53,366	11	246,396	51.2
Arkansas	47,000	17.3	61,413	27	69,677	36	115,000	59.7
Florida	49,000	15.4	120,900	33	148,703	32	286,446	60.9
Georgia	128,000	18.8	144,835	23	163,384	27	289,545	47.2
Louisiana	10,000	2.6	120,000	25	161,410	31	242,130	47.1
Mississippi	5,000	0.9	20,000	4	20,000	5	139,099	32.9
N. Carolina	75,000	15.2	100,000	18	135,000	24	281,134	51.0
Oklahoma	50,000	29.6	NA	NA	NA	NA	NA	
S. Carolina	50,000	13.0	80,000	20	99,890	27	190,609	51.4
Tennessee	80,000	25.8	85,000	25	90,000	27	225,000	71.7
Texas	100,000	18.5	181,916	31	214,000	37	400,000	61.6
Virginia	48,000	13.2	69,326	16	82,603	19	205,000	46.9

Sources: Luther D. Jackson, "Race and Suffrage in the South Since 1940,"
New South, (June–July, 1948), p. 3. Margaret Price, *The Negro Voter in the
South* (Atlanta: Southern Regional Council, 1957), p. 5. P. Watters and R.
Cleghorn, *Climbing Jacob's Ladder* (New York: Harcourt, Brace and
World, 1960), pp. 376–377. U. S. Commission on Civil Rights, *Voting*
(Washington, D. C.: U. S. Government Printing Office, 1965), p. 243.

decision. Despite these repressions, however, black registration continued.
In the cities and southern urban areas, blacks were added to registration
lists without any trouble. But in the rural and underdeveloped areas, black
registration was fully suppressed. As Table II indicates, black registration
was uneven. Basically, blacks could register only in those counties where
segregation policies permitted such a step. For example, by 1950, six years
after the *Smith* v. *Allwright* decision, in 16 out of 97 counties in which
blacks constituted a majority of the voting-age population, not a single
black had registered to vote. Moreover, in 49 other counties where blacks
constituted a majority of the voting population, less than 5 percent of the
black population was registered. As Table III indicates, few blacks registered in the rural states where segregation was strictly enforced. In fact,
even with the backing of liberal white agencies, funds, and help, black
registration in the rural areas moved at a snail's pace, if at all. For the most
part, black registration has continued to find numerous stumbling blocks in
the rural and less developed areas of the southern states. In Mississippi, for
example, the most rural of the southern states, black politics is still in many
counties in the earliest stage of development. Attempts at black registration
still encounter numerous obstacles. During the summer of 1963, when five
black civil rights organizations coalesced into a super agency, the Council
of Federated Organization (COFO), in an effort to increase the number of

Table III. Black Registration in Rural Southern Counties—1959

	Counties with No Blacks Registered	Counties with Less Than 5% Registered	Total Number of Counties	%
Arkansas	14	1	75	20
Florida	3	3	67	8
Georgia	6	22	159	17
Louisiana	4	9	64	20
North Carolina	0	3	79	4
South Carolina	1	6	47	15
Virginia	3	1	100	4
Alabama	2	12	67	21
Mississippi	14	49	82	77
Texas	14	1	82	18

Source: Commission on Civil Rights, *Report of the United States Commission on Civil Rights, 1959* (Washington, D. C.: U. S. Government Printing Office, 1959), pp. 42-52.

black voters in Mississippi, only about 90,000 persons could finally be enrolled. This was with all the aid COFO could muster, which included more than a thousand white summer volunteers, the financial backing of the Southern Regional Council's Voter Education Project,[19] and federal help. Even this gigantic effort was stalled by the local segregationists and their numerous tactics to keep blacks off the voter rolls.

Moreover, in addition to the repressive tactics of the southern white supremacists, other factors also stymied and affected black registration. In general, religious affiliations of the white community affected black registration rates. Areas of heavy white Protestantism in the South seemed to depress or limit black registration. Areas of Roman Catholicism, on the other hand, tended to have a higher proportion of blacks registered to vote.[20] In other words, Catholics tended to be more amenable to black registration than Protestants.

Political, social, and cultural factors also affected black registration. Although urbanization and industrialization stimulated and aided black registration, rural whites and ruralism are not as inhibiting as they were. Since the Voting Rights Act of 1965, and before, blacks in the rural areas have moved toward the registration list. The Black Revolution of the sixties

[19] Pat Watters, "Encounter with the Future," *New South*, XX (May, 1965), 3-26.
[20] John H. Fenton and Kenneth W. Vines, "Negro Registration in Louisiana," *American Political Science Review*, LI (September, 1957), 713; Donald R. Matthews and James W. Prothro, *Negroes and the New Southern Politics* (New York: Harcourt, Brace and World, 1966), p. 130.

created a new political awareness among the black masses and the rural blacks, which aided in the emergence of several grassroots black political organizations and parties. Previously, the political and cultural factor of black concentration worked against increasing black registration, but lately black registration has increased without respect to this factor. In fact, concentration of blacks has actually increased black representation in public office. Even the educational level of whites has declined as a factor in black registration, for the new wave of black awareness has stimulated blacks to participate more in the public area. The private arena of black politics has not disappeared, but it now has a new partner, the public sector. In addition to the stimulation provided by the Black Revolution, there has also been the continued involvement of white liberals, white organizations and black liberals and black organizations. At the present time, therefore, the external factors—social, economic, and political—are not minimizing black registration as before. Political and psychological factors, however, are now more significant. Black registration did increase in a favorable political milieu, and the emergence of black political candidates spurred black registration.

BLACK POLITICAL LEADERSHIP

Besides external factors, however—social, economic, political, legal—that have hampered black registration, there have also been several internal ones. Black leadership, the lack of it in some cases and excesses on the part of black leaders in others, has been a perennial problem of the black electorate. Black leadership has motivated and made successful black political activity.[21] Likewise, it has defeated, stunted, and repressed black political activity. But in the final analysis, black leadership has proved an aid or a handicap, depending on its locality, circumstances, orientation, and general environment. Earlier, black political leadership operated within the confines of white control, but recently black political leaders have formed their own grassroots organizations and now work within the confines of the black community. They serve their constituents on the basis of their needs, wants, and desires.

Lately, black political leaders have addressed themselves to the community at large and have sought to advance their political fortunes neither on black nor on white platforms but basically on "issues." The issue-oriented black political leader—as opposed to the race-oriented leader—seeks a broader political base and is finding it in some communities. The election of a black politician like Senator Edward Brooke and some other blacks on

[21] Hanes Walton, Jr., and Leslie McLemore, "Portrait of Black Political Styles," *The Black Politician,* II (October, 1970), 9–13.

a city, county, or district-wide basis, are examples of these foundations. Thus, many of the inhibitions which black leadership once had have disappeared or are no longer obstacles. Because what blacks will not do in organizing their communities white politicians will, due to the vote potential.

The major internal inhibitors are fear and apathy. But basically, these were inhibitions of an age gone by. This is not to say that they are not still inhibiting the black community in entering the political arena; it is to say that their degree of inhibition is changing as well as the extent to which they are still operating. To begin with, numerous forces have combined to restrain the forces that perpetuate fear. The federal government, for example, by means of its legislative and executive support of black rights, has helped to decrease the waves of fear in the black community, as have federal and state attempts to prosecute violations of black civil rights.[22] In addition, the continued emphasis on self-defense, self-respect, and self-association of the Black Revolution has made it easier as well as necessary to ward off black fears and inaction.

Like fear, apathy, too, has begun to show signs of decreasing in the black community.[23] In fact, the increased number of black public officials has put an end to the idea that nothing can be achieved through politics. Moreover, the gains won as a result of protest during the 1960s have also indicated that involvement can be meaningful. As a result, apathetic notions of yesterday are fast giving way. But the changes, external and internal, are not uniform.

Generally speaking, the inhibiting and retarding factors of black registration (external or internal) depend in large measure on the nature and intensity of race prejudice or segregation in the locality. The less the intensity of these forces, the more black registration takes place. Despite, however, the variation in degree of black registration from locality to locality and the interplay of factors that inhibit it, black persons have registered to vote.

BLACK REGISTRATION IN THE NORTH

Before we discuss the effectiveness of black voters, however, we need to look at black registration in the North. In numerous northern states, blacks

[22] See Charles Sitton, "When a Southern Negro Goes to Court," in Frank Munger, *American State Politics* (New York: Thomas Y. Crowell, 1966), pp. 81–86; Harold H. Martin, "The Trial of Delay Beckwith," in Erwin Buell and William Brigman, eds., *The Grassroots: Readings in State and Local Politics* (Glenview, Ill.: Scott, Foresman and Company, 1968), pp. 381–391.

[23] Janet Wells, "43 Blacks Win Elections in Three Southern States," *Voter Education Project News,* III (May, 1969), 1–4.

who attempted to register before the Civil War met certain restrictions.[24] Only in the five New England states of Maine, New Hampshire, Vermont, Massachusetts, and Rhode Island did blacks retain the legal right to vote in the era before the war between the states. In every other northern and western state, the legal right to vote was sooner or later curtailed, withdrawn, or restricted.

The coming of the Civil War did not change this. Even after the war northern states were slow to grant full suffrage to black people. Although Massachusetts elected blacks—Edward G. Walker and Charles L. Mitchell—to its legislature in 1866, black politics remained in the dim shadows of the political system as a whole.

In establishing the black man's right to vote in the northern states, the radical Republicans and their allies, prodded by Frederick Douglass's Equal Rights League, assumed the position of front-runner.[25] They urged northern states to grant blacks the right to vote. The first state in which the radical Republicans conducted their campaign in behalf of black suffrage was Connecticut. A special election in October, 1865, placed the issue squarely before the state electorate. The radicals had strong support, but a substantial majority of voters decided against giving the black man the ballot.[26]

In Ohio, the Union party avoided the issue of whether blacks should have the right to vote and won the election in 1865 over a radical Republican candidate who took a square stand on the topic. In fact, each northern state continually avoided or sidestepped the issue that year. In 1866, Iowa and Michigan granted blacks the right to vote, though there was no cause for general rejoicing because all of the other northern states—New York, Pennsylvania, Ohio, and Illinois, for example—rejected the measure. Although Iowa granted blacks the right to vote in 1866, the radical Republicans finally assumed that federal action would be necessary in order to establish the right of blacks to vote in the North. In 1868, debate took shape in Congress on a new amendment that would coerce loyal northern Republican states to grant blacks the right to vote. Although the radical Republicans had not mentioned the equal suffrage issue in the 1868 campaign, it was through their effort that it was originated and ratified in 1870.

[24] See Chapter 1; see also G. James Fleming, "The Negro in American Politics: The Past," in J. David, ed., *American Negro Reference Book* (Englewood Cliffs, N.J.: Prentice-Hall, 1966), p. 414; and Emil Olbrich, *The Development of Sentiment on Negro Suffrage to 1860* (Madison: University of Wisconsin Press, 1912), pp. 71-106.

[25] Leslie H. Fishel, Jr., "Northern Prejudice and Negro Suffrage," *Journal of Negro History,* XXXIX (January, 1954), 10-11.

[26] LaWanda and John Cox, "Negro Suffrage and Republican Politics: The Problem of Motivation in Reconstruction Historiography," in Frank Gatell and Allen Weinstein, eds., *American Themes: Essays in Historiography* (New York: Oxford University Press, 1968), p. 112.

Moreover, it was this federal action that established the right of blacks in the northern states. Previously, prejudice had prevented this. In the North, too, federal action was needed in order to secure for blacks the right to vote.

Although the Fifteenth Amendment granted northern blacks the right to vote, it still did not make their entrance into the northern political arena an easy task. Black registration in the North took place without much difficulty. Nevertheless, if the problem of the black electorate in the South was one of establishing the right to vote, then registering to vote, and finally voting, the problem of the black electorate in the North was one of repression, control, and manipulation.

Racial prejudice in the North worked in a number of ways to make the impact of black voting insignificant. Repression came in the form of ostracism from party councils and convention meetings and exclusion from political offices and candidacies.[27] Northern whites who strongly opposed black suffrage used every method possible to negate black political potential from emerging in an independent fashion.

Before northern blacks could overcome the various forms of repression, control of the black vote appeared. The Republican party, through exploitation of its past record, dispersion of low-level patronage, judicious use of minor black politicians and prominent black leaders, showcase appointments, purchase of the black vote and introduction of new congressional legislation to protect black voters in the South, reduced the northern black electorate to a position of subordination. The Republicans squelched every effort by the blacks to establish political independence and run for office without party endorsement. Moreover, the Democrats, prior to the Civil War, had been antiblack; in every northern state they were the major force that defeated every attempt in the different state legislatures to grant blacks the franchise.[28] Meanwhile "during the years of Civil War and Reconstruction race prejudice was institutionalized in the Democratic Party."[29] The problem of the northern black electorate grew out of its attachment to party. The black voter could not become an independent, and the Democrats, at least at first, opposed his joining their ranks. Thus, the black

[27] Leslie H. Fishel, Jr., "The Negro in Northern Politics, 1870-1900," *Mississippi Valley Historical Review,* XLII (December, 1955), 466-469.

[28] See Olbrich, *op. cit.,* chap. 8. For some state studies see Leslie H. Fishel, Jr., "Wisconsin and Negro Suffrage," *Wisconsin Magazine of History,* XLVI (Spring, 1963), 180-196; Ira V. Brown, "Pennsylvania and the Rights of the Negro, 1865-1887," *Pennsylvania History,* XXVIII (January, 1961), 45-57; Edgar A. Toppin, "Negro Emancipation in Historic Retrospect: Ohio: The Negro Suffrage Issue in Post-Bellum Ohio Politics," *Journal of Human Relations,* XI (Winter, 1963), 232-246.

[29] La Wanda and John Cox, "Negro Suffrage and Republican Politics: The Problem of Motivation in Reconstruction Historiography," *Journal of Southern History,* XXXIII (August, 1967), 330.

electorate, having acquired the vote, was controlled by the Republican party.

Northern Republicans pointed to Lincoln's emancipation of the slaves, and also to their support of the Civil War and the prewar abolitionists' crusade in the North. They misled the black electorate by claiming that they sponsored the Thirteenth, Fourteenth, and Fifteenth amendments, and made the black electorate seem duty-bound to return the party's favors with unswerving allegiance.

Beginning in 1880, northern Republicans appointed blacks as mail carriers, firemen, policemen, county auditors, prison commissioners, and ward constables. In 1884, even a national party chairmanship was granted. These positions were played up as rewards for continued support and as promises of things to come. Then, to strengthen further their control over the northern black electorate, the Republicans fostered new legislation in several sessions of Congress to protect the rights of the black electorate in the South. Finally, the Republicans used one last tactic to secure control over the black electorate, that of economics. The black voter, black newspapers, and the black leaders were bought outright to insure their support of the Republican party.

Nor did the black electorate achieve freedom when GOP control declined and dissipated. In a furtive attempt to get meaningful rewards, the northern black electorate became prisoners of political machines. On the local level in several northern areas newly emerging political machines acquired the control over the black electorate that the Republicans were losing. Where machine control was not operative or when it declined, the control of the Democratic party on the local level took over. Northern black voters remained under the control of machines, either Republican or Democratic.

In the final analysis, the black electorate in the North was controlled and conditioned into subordination. Whether it wanted to or not, it was made to rely on one party. Although a break came later, the problem that faced the black electorate in the North remained largely how best to gain control of their own vote and to put that vote to effective use in their own behalf. For the circumstances that faced them once they had won the right to vote made that vote useless. Hence, if establishment and registration plagued the southern black electorate, control over their vote plagued the northern black electorate.

BLACK VOTING IN THE SOUTH

In the South, prior to *Smith* v. *Allwright*, the major factor influencing the black voter was race prejudice. This, even more than socioeconomic status, determined the nature, extent, size, and direction of the black vote. Of course, black leadership, organization, and status did play a part, but it was a part largely dependent upon practices of segregation in each locality. Moreover, since the South before 1944 was primarily a one-party region, the nature of the party, as well as the appeals of candidates, sought to preserve the caste system with only minor modification therein.[30]

The best that the black voter could choose was the least of the several evils that were offered him. How much this factor motivated or retarded the southern black electorate has not been studied, but the black vote in the South was very low at first; it increased gradually during the late forties, the fifties, and the sixties.

In fact, it was only after a large number of blacks had begun voting that one could discern the influence of social, economic, and political forces upon them. Recent studies indicate that during the late forties, the fifties, and the mid-sixties, the southern black electorate was typically American. It was basically middle class; its members were educated, were often professionals, usually belonged to some social organization, and had a Protestant religious affiliation. Even the early studies of the black electorate point out that between 1900 and 1914 the black voter tended to be middle class, educated, and Protestant in his religious orientation.

In regard to ideology, most southern black voters were liberals who believed strongly in a workable democratic form of government. There were, however, some black conservatives who, for numerous reasons, supported segregationist or reactionary candidates, parties, and viewpoints. There were likewise some left-wingers who ardently espoused communist and socialist ideas and proposals. These were never as numerous in the South, however, as in the North.

However, with the emergence of the Black Revolution of the sixties, the southern black electorate began to change. More and more efforts were made by the black civil rights organizations to bring all blacks, including those of the lower class, into the political arena, and after the passage of the Voting Rights Act of 1965, more and more lower-class blacks did register. The influences affecting them seem primarily to have been psychological, emotional, and inspirational. Black organizations, as well as white ones, helped prod the lower class into becoming voters. In short, both coercion and exclusion finally influenced their political behavior.

INFLUENCE OF RACIAL FACTORS

Race and racial issues became major influences on the political behavior of both lower and middle classes. Both groups voted at times in a manner that aided racial advancement and achievement. In political contests where

[30] Robert Black, "Southern Governors and the Negro: Race as a Campaign Issue Since 1954" (unpublished doctoral dissertation, Harvard University), p. 25.

the race issue was not interjected or exploited, the political, economic, and social factors became significant. Whenever the race issue was involved, however, all other issues became subordinate. Whether the racial factor will continue to be an important influence upon the political behavior of southern blacks obviously depends upon whether the issue continues to have an effect upon the political future of blacks in the region.

The factor that most influenced the black electorate in the North was "party or machine" control. From the outset party control was prevalent in the northern cities.[31] Before 1900, the black electorate in almost all of the major northern cities was under Republican domination.[32] At every turn the party relegated blacks to low-level patronage positions. Indissolubly bound to the party of "liberation," the black electorate voted in the manner prescribed by the party and its "colored" bosses. For all intents and purposes the northern black electorate became a Republican electorate, because independent black voters in the North were in scarce supply.

Blacks did try to break away from northern Republican control. In Youngstown, Pittsburgh, Boston, and in Great Barrington, Massachusetts, black neophytes who decided to seek political office on their own were not permitted into party caucus. In Pennsylvania and Rhode Island black independents were completely ostracized and their political future was eclipsed. In Ohio, Connecticut, and Pennsylvania three blacks who obtained place on the ballot found their names scratched off. In fact, no matter how hard he tried, the black voter remained controlled and repressed by party whims and choices.

Gradually, however, party control shifted in many northern cities to machine control. In other northern cities control remained, but the controlling party changed from the Republicans to the Democrats. This shift was also gradual, but it came. The Republicans' heavy-handed tactics forced blacks into the Democratic party. At the polls, though, the pulling effect of the Democrats was as strong as the pushing effect of Republican autocracy, because of the meaning of the social welfare policies of Democrats and their political machines. A later analysis will further illuminate these forces.

Machine control and party control did not, to be sure, subsume all the black electorate. There were, for example, some independent black voters who cast their votes in light of their socioeconomic status, ideology, and religious preferences, though most black independents turned to local minor parties or national third parties. Frank Crosswaith was a black Socialist in New York City who ran as a Socialist party candidate for

---

[31] Fishel, *op. cit.*, pp. 466-485. See George F. Robinson, Jr., "The Negro in Politics in Chicago," *Journal of Negro History*, XVII (April, 1932), 183-185, 214-215.

[32] Gilbert Osofsky, *Harlem: The Making of a Ghetto* (New York: Harper Torchbooks, 1968), pp. 159-178; Allen H. Spear, *Black Chicago: The Making of a Negro Ghetto, 1890-1920* (Chicago: Phoenix Books, 1969), pp. 111-126, 181-200.

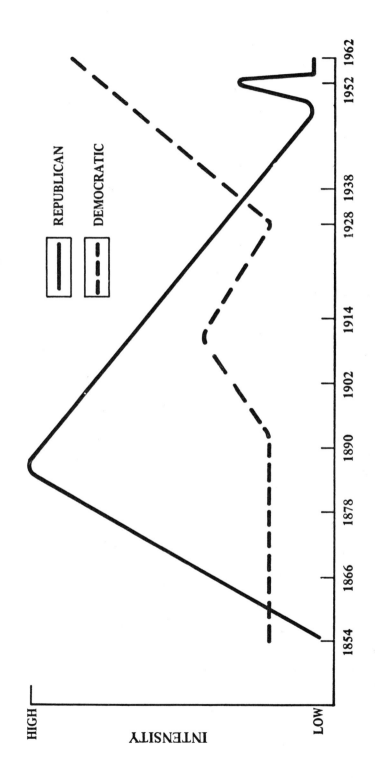

Figure 4. Black Involvement in the Republican and Democratic Parties

lieutenant governor of New York a number of times to attract more blacks
into the party's ranks. Benjamin Davis, Jr., a Harvard-trained lawyer, due
to discriminatory practices in the courtroom, joined the Communist party
in 1932, moved to New York City, and became the first black Communist
to be elected to a position on an aldermanic board. He was elected from
Harlem in 1943 and held the post until 1948. Still, the number of black
independents in the North was never significant. Most major northern
cities from the outset had political machines and bosses ingrained in their
political structure because of the influx of the large ethnic groups from
Europe. And "many immigrants turned to politics as a means to improve
their social status."[33] Therefore, the independent black voters were indeed
scared because the machine absorbed most of the black electorate through
welfare and other considerations. A politically ambitious black had little
choice except to join a political machine, for his upward mobility rested
upon his attachment to the machine and to the political structure of the
city. An exception was Adam Clayton Powell, who had a power base
outside of Tammany Hall.[34] As reformers modernized municipal governments, however, and the effects of social security, minimum wage legislation, relief programs, and collective bargaining contributed to the social
rise of underprivileged groups, machine politics began to decline.[35] Blacks
accordingly became more independent, and as they did, the influence upon
them of normal socioeconomic status increased. Since the decline of machine control over part of the northern black electorate, one of the major
influential factors has been that of race and equality. At least in presidential elections the northern black electorate has permitted the issue of civil
rights to become one of the greatest influences. In municipal and state
elections, however, there is still some lag. The northern black electorate
seemed influenced by a number of factors, such as a desire to break away
from the old party controls, the nature of the local party, and the degree of
independence of the black electorate.

SUMMARY

The socioeconomic factor is much more influential in cities where there
is no party or machine control. Even then, it is a significant influence only
when the race issue does not predominate. In other words, when a political

---

[33] Harry Bailey and Ellis Katz, *Ethnic Group Politics* (Columbus, Ohio: Charles Merrill
Book Company, 1969), p. 188.
[34] James Q. Wilson, "Two Negro Politicians: An Interpretation," in Donald G. Herzberg
and Gerald M. Pomper, eds., *American Party Politics* (New York: Holt, Rinehart and
Winston, 1967), pp. 134-136.
[35] Elmer Cornwell, Jr., "Bosses, Machines and Ethnic Politics," *ibid.*, pp. 199-200; Fred
Greenstein, "The Changing Pattern of Urban Party Politics," in Alan Shank, ed., *Political
Power and the Urban Crisis* (Boston: Holbrook Press, 1969), p. 163.

campaign is run on the basis of issues and promises, then the factors of social status, religious affiliation, economic position, and ideology become most influential. When it is played up, however, the racial issue can and often has become the overriding factor in campaigns. Moreover, this is true in both North and South.[36] Professor Everett Ladd was profoundly right when he remarked that "race advancement necessarily dominates Negro electoral participation as no issue dominates the participation of white voters." The black electorate—North or South—in state, local, and national elections is strongly influenced by the race factor.

Now that we have explored some of the influences affecting the northern black electorate, let us turn to the impact and rewards of black voting.

[36] For information on the influence of the racial issue upon the northern black electorate see James Q. Wilson, "The Strategy of Protest: Problems of Negro Civic Action," *Journal of Conflict Resolution*, IV (September, 1961), 297, and his *Negro Politics* (New York: Free Press, 1960), p. 22. For information on the influence upon the southern black electorate see Everett Ladd, Jr., *Negro Political Leadership in the South* (Ithaca, N. Y.: Cornell University Press, 1962), pp. 17-47.

IV

Blacks and
Political Machines

Any discussion of the influences on the black electorate must ultimately deal with the realities of big city bosses and machines, both of which have had a significant influence on ethnic groups and their achievements in American society. Indeed, a study of these machines will reveal black bosses and black political machines operating within the political structure. The realities and influences of black political bosses and machines must be included in any accurate discussion of the factors influencing the black electorate.

Political machines are organizations whose purpose is to elect men to office; they are held together and sustained mainly through the distribution of tangible or intangible incentives to their members. These incentives, be they tangible (largely patronage) or intangible (appeal to principles, ideology, idealism, symbolism, devotion, etc.), account for the loyalty to and enthusiasm for the machine leaders. Like any organization political machines can rely upon force to bind their followers. In other words, the persuasive influence of the machine in the political structure of the city implies force, or the dire consequences of a failure to submit. For example, ambitious members of the black electorate who seek to elevate themselves, especially black lawyers who cannot enter the large law firms, must of necessity enter the political machine in the city. Attempts to do otherwise spell certain death for possibly brilliant careers. There are exceptions, of course; some blacks who back the machine may enter the city's political life over machine opposition. More often than not, opposition to the machine proves fatal, but occasionally it proves otherwise: though a long shot, national politics sometimes places an opposing black in a high federal position. Ultimately, the sheer power of the machine hammers and suppresses its opposition into conformity.

For groups, even more than for individuals, the political forces of the machine are devastating. The early as well as the late immigrants found that the machine could perform favors and tasks that even the city welfare services were either unable or unwilling to do. Moreover, the machine also aided in tasks that city bureaucracies muddle, fumble, and half perform. Groups of newly arriving immigrants needed city services and could not afford to turn them down, and the refusal or withdrawal of these services forced blacks into a union with the urban machine. Thus, force itself became an aid to the intangible and tangible rewards which cemented the machine together.

If political machines are electoral organizations based on sundry incentives, then political bosses are the core of the machine. They are the internal cogs that give the machine its equilibrium and momentum.[1] In most cases, the political bosses were the founders of the political organization; it was they who first saw what was needed and realized that they would advance themselves by supplying it. George Washington Plunkitt, a typical political boss, described how he understood human nature and acted accordingly in order to advance himself.

> I know every man, woman, and child in the Fifteenth District, except them that's been born this summer—and I know some of them, too. I know what they like and what they don't like, what they are strong at and what they are weak in, and I reach them by approachin' at the right side.
> ... You'll find him workin' for my ticket at the polls next election day .... feller that makes a name as a waltzer on his block, the young feller that's handy with his dukes. . . .[2]

Although the political boss may be synonymous with the political machine, it does not follow that the machine's life substance is the political boss, because the machine can remain viable even after his death. In fact, the degree of its influence after the boss's death is a better indication of its stamina than anything else. Moreover, political machines often operate without bosses; a clique or a faction of a bureaucracy may run them. And they may prove just as successful without an individual boss.[3]

But despite the nature of political machines and bosses and the relationship of one to the other, they are the actualities of urban politics which are colored by the particular political culture involved. The character of the political machine derives from the character of the city. If blacks are part of the city, then they are part of the political character of the machine.

In New York blacks were involved in Tammany Hall. In Chicago they

[1] Harold Zink, *City Bosses in the United States* (Durham, N.C.: Duke University Press, 1930).

[2] Fred Greenstein, "The Coming Pattern of Urban Politics," in Alan Shank, ed., *Political Power and the Urban Crisis* (Boston: Holbrook Press, 1969), p. 163.

[3] On the nature of a bureaucratically run machine, see Theodore J. Lowi, "Gosnell's Chicago Revisited via Lindsay's New York," in Harold F. Gosnell, *Machine Politics: Chicago Model*, 2nd ed. (Chicago: University of Chicago Press, 1968), pp. 10-14.

became part of the Daley machine. In Memphis blacks were part of the Crump machine. In Richmond blacks were a part of the Byrd dynasty, and in Kansas City they were part of the Pendergast machine. Blacks, however, were *of* not *in* the white machine.

Each white machine had its black "submachine." A black boss was picked to secure black votes to support the white machine. The black electorate was in every instance subordinate to and manipulated by the white machine. Nevertheless, there were two basic types of machines: the subordinate black machine and boss, and the independent black machine and boss. Each machine differed in its nature and style; the black element in both had the same goal of race advancement.

HOW THE BLACK MACHINE EVOLVED

Either out of conviction or out of circumstance or out of both, white political bosses were usually of a segregationist persuasion.[4] They commissioned black leaders to perform a bridging function between the black electorate and the white political machine, and the black leaders derived their status and raison d'être from the white political machine.[5] They moved into the black community and established civic clubs, political leagues, voter leagues, etc., claiming to promote or advance the rights of black people. They usually picked as members of such organizations educators, prominent doctors, lawyers, etc. Although not much study has been done on black civic and political leagues, the little information that is available tends to describe them as being composed mainly of middle-class black professionals,[6] who were eager for new prestige. The black bosses tended to be individuals who could be easily manipulated and who also had some influence in the community in terms of urging other blacks to vote. Moreover, these black professionals had acquired the trappings of Anglo-Saxon political behavior and were therefore fully acceptable to the white political boss, who in turn made it easy for them to register to vote. And obtaining the vote, especially in the South during the 1920s, 1930s, and early 1940s, was a major status symbol that set its holder clearly apart from the black masses. However, the acquisition of the vote and improved status by the chosen members of the black middle class also meant that their new status depended upon the black political boss, who, in turn, depended upon the white bosses and machines. In addition, the tangible

[4] On Crump's segregationist tendencies see Harry Holloway, *The Politics of the Southern Negro* (New York: Random House, 1969), p. 297.

[5] Wendell Bell, Richard J. Hill, and Charles R. Wright, *Public Leadership* (San Francisco: Chandler Publishing Company, 1961), pp. 87–90.

[6] See Douglas S. Gatlin, "A Case Study of a Negro Voters' League Political Study Program," *Research Report*, no. 2, March, 1960 (University of North Carolina Department of Political Science).

rewards given by the machine—such as money or public recognition by whites—heightened the status of the black professional in the black community. Thus, segregationist-led political machines dominated, manipulated, and repressed the black electorate. And in this manner the same black bosses and machines were subordinate in nature.

The white political machine, moreover, did not *always* have to appoint a black boss. In many cases, especially around the turn of the century, the machine simply absorbed the black Republican leaders of the city and their defunct political clubs. With the retreat of Republicans from blacks and the evidence of antiblack attitudes in some urban Republican circles, the Democratic city political machine obviously filled part of the demand for black participation. The former black Republicans, early looking for a place to sell their wares, readily coalesced with the Democratic political bosses because the coalition meant continued viability for them. As for the bosses, it meant at least an infant black organization which only needed reviving.

In other cases, however, white political bosses could absorb the self-appointed independent leader of the black community. These black leaders, in search of power, status, meaning, and something to lead, easily coalesced with the political machine. The coalition gave them power and rewards to gather a following with which to support the machine. But the leadership abilities of these black bosses led to their rise or fall. If they could not "deliver" adequate support to the white machine and its candidates, then a new black leader was installed or absorbed to bridge the gap between the organization and the black community.

"Boss" Crump and Memphis

For example, in Memphis, Tennessee, as black bosses either failed or died, "Boss" Crump changed them. After being reelected in 1909, Crump discovered "that the Negro vote was an important element in winning elections and the successful candidates traditionally had Negro support."[7] His bid for black votes was made through black political bosses who organized and controlled and delivered the black electorate of the city to Crump.

During the earlier twenties, the Crump machine absorbed the black Republican Robert R. Church and his defunct organization. Church's connection with Crump's political machine proved fruitful for both men. According to Professor Lewinson, "Church could ... 'deliver' the Negro vote in Memphis and influence it elsewhere."[8] In fact, Church's dual con-

[7] William D. Miller, *Mr. Crump of Memphis* (Baton Rouge: Louisiana State University Press, 1964), p. 103.
[8] Paul Lewinson, *Race, Class, and Party* (New York: Russell and Russell, 1963), p. 139.

nection with Crump and the National Republicans led Senator Heflin of Alabama to read a poem into the hearing of a patronage committee investigation. In the municipal election of 1928 Church reached the peak of his influence when he delivered enough black votes to elect the Democratic mayor. However, when Church began to show some independence of the Crump machine, the coalition was dissolved.

With the destruction of Church, the Crump organization absorbed another black leader. In this case, the black selected boss was of a self-appointed nature. This man, Dr. T. E. Walker, had tried to create a black Democratic organization during the mid-1930s, although blacks were traditionally Republican in the region. The New Deal and the liberal policies of Roosevelt led him in this direction. But his individual efforts barely got him off the ground, and his absorption by the Crump machine proved beneficial to both. "But Crump's segregationist views led to a split in the 1940s on the occasion of a concert by Marian Anderson. The trouble was caused over Walker's desires for desegregated seating arrangements."[9] After the break, Walker again went independent. He supported liberals like Kefauver in 1948 and 1952. He also ran for the school board, but was defeated. But Crump died in 1954, and his death "left a political vacuum among Negroes, for it broke their main tie with the white community."[10] Thus, out of a subordinate position came one of independence. This was a unique case.

THE BYRD MACHINE IN VIRGINIA

In Virginia, the black electorate became tied to the political machine of Harry Byrd.[11] According to Robbins Gates, the "Byrd organization stands for one-partyism, economic and social status *status quo,* and white supremacy."[12] It differed, however, both in style and in form from the Crump machine. Crump's was located primarily in and around Memphis; Byrd's was statewide. Crump's was highly personal; Byrd's was mainly oligarchical. The Byrd machine was basically a pyramid in structure with numerous local leaders throughout the state. This basic difference in structure accounted for the basic difference in the relationship of the black electorate to the machine. The Byrd machine was weak in the cities, but it still obtained the black vote. In fact, the Byrd machine obtained black votes statewide.

Blacks have voted continuously in Virginia from Reconstruction until

[9] Harry Holloway, *The Politics of the Southern Negro: From Exclusion to Big City Organization* (New York: Random House, 1969), p. 279.

[10] V. O. Key, Jr., *Southern Politics in State and Nation* (New York: Vintage Books, 1949), pp. 19-24.

[11] Robbins L. Gates, *The Making of Massive Resistance: Virginia's Politics of Public School Desegregation, 1954-1956* (Chapel Hill: University of North Carolina Press, 1964), p. 24.

[12] *Ibid.*

the present. However, the number of black votes after disfranchisement in 1902 remained almost constant. After the disfranchisement law went into effect on July 10, 1902, only about 25,000 blacks voted. And in 1941, despite a panoply of black voter leagues and a nucleus of civic-minded blacks, only about 25,441 blacks voted in the entire state—a 4,500 increase over 1904.[13] These black voters had been Republican until that party purged itself of black followers. Eliminated by the Republicans, the black voters attempted an independent movement to prove to the Republicans that they needed them in their ranks, but this move failed. From the outset, however, the Democratic party had shunned their attachment, and during the early 1920s the limited black electorate found itself adrift and had "little hope of being accepted by either party."[14] It was in the midst of this limbo that a new governor, Harry Flood Byrd, attained their loyalty and allegiance for his political machine. Byrd as governor took a paternalistic attitude toward the limited black electorate. As governor, he sponsored an antilynching bill and opposed the Ku Klux Klan. Moreover, as democratic leader "he frowned upon rabble-rousing and Negro-baiting of any kind." His political machine played down violent treatment of the black community, and protected the rights of blacks to vote.

These paternalistic overtures to the black voters won their loyalty throughout the state. Black organizations such as the NAACP, the Virginia Voters League, and the Richmond Democratic Voters League helped to deliver the black vote for machine candidates and political friends. In the Byrd machine the black political boss was insignificant. There was no need for a black liaison leadership because the Byrd organization attained black allegiance via policy enactment and paternalistic overtures. It did not have to distribute tangible incentives and therefore did not need a black boss to do so. Moreover, the Byrd machine rested on a *restricted electorate* and did not need or want a large black vote. A small black vote tightly tied to the Byrd organization was sufficient. When, however, Byrd dropped his paternalism and his minimal interest in black rights and advocated poll taxes and literacy tests, when he sponsored the southern manifesto in Congress that denounced the Supreme Court decision of 1954, and when he led massive resistance to that decision in the state, the black electorate's loyalty to his machine declined.[15] However, the affiliation did not end, because the Byrd machine was still the dominant organized faction within the state. In November, 1964, black leaders met in Richmond with the

[13] Andrew Buni, *The Negro in Virginia Politics, 1902-1965* (Charlottesville. University Press of Virginia, 1967), pp. 27-28.

[14] *Ibid.*, p. 89.

[15] Paul Duke, "Southern Politics and the Negro," in Donald G. Herzberg and Gerald M. Pomper, eds., *American Party Politics: Essays and Readings* (New York: Holt, Rinehart and Winston, 1966), p. 58.

Byrd organization, and in a two-hour meeting told prominent members of the Byrd organization that blacks expected to share in the rewards of patronage and to participate in policy-making if blacks were to continue to support the machine. This move met with some success.

In the end, because of its organizational structure, the Byrd machine created only minor black political bosses and machines. This, in effect, permitted the complete subordination of the black electorate in the state.[16]

In many ways the Byrd machine paralleled the Long machine in Louisiana. Huey Long's concern for poor people and general welfare, as well as his numerous paternalistic policies toward blacks, gained tremendous black support throughout the state. Once again, black political bosses were not needed. Long's personal magnetism was the major attraction.[17]

"BOSS" COX OF CINCINNATI

"Boss" Cox's machine, which prevailed in Cincinnati before the turn of the century, was also different from the Byrd organization. Cox supported such black leaders as William "Big Bill" Copeland, "Tuscaloosa Bull," and "King of Walnut Hill" to help him run Cincinnati.[18] This was mainly because black migrants to the city lived in different clusters in the city zone with each zone clearly separated from the other.[19] Not only did the residential pattern of segregation in Cincinnati necessitate several black political bosses and political machines, the nature of race relations in the city necessitated the existence of several black leaders to bridge the gap between the numerous black enclaves or ghettos and the white community.[20] Frank Q. William "found that the tightening noose of discrimination had virtually cut off all contact between zone Negroes and the city's white community.[21] In this situation a black coalition with the Cox machine permitted the black bourgeoisie some limited mobility into other sections of the city, as well as certain material benefits. But as the coalition continued, these subordinate black bosses demanded more from the Cox machine than it was willing to give. Finally the black bosses and their machine in Cincinnati opposed Cox and defeated his machine in 1897.

THE CHICAGO MACHINE

In Chicago today a classic political machine still exists, and along with it a classic black political machine and boss. From the outset, blacks in

[16] Buni, *op. cit.*

[17] For information on blacks and the Long machine see Roy Wilkins, "Huey Long Says— An Interview with Louisiana's Kingfish," *Crisis*, XLII (February, 1935), 41–52; "The Negro in Louisiana Politics," *The Sepia Socialite*, April, 1942; and Key, *op. cit.*, p. 165.

[18] On this point see Zane Miller, *Boss Cox's Cincinnati: Urban Politics in the Progressive Era* (New York: Oxford University Press, 1968), p. 86.

[19] *Ibid.*

[20] *Ibid.*

[21] *Ibid.*, pp. 166–168.

Chicago were mainly Republicans; then because of Republican intransigence and subordination of black officers, blacks began a slow exodus to the Democratic fold. There were still some black Republicans diehards, however. During the early 1930s William Dawson was still a Republican, and served as alderman from 1935 to 1939 in the city council. Disappointed with the slow progress he was making in council, in 1939 he switched parties, and formed a coalition with the Kelly machine. Prior to his coalition with Mayor "Boss" Kelly, Dawson had personally built a machine held together by racial bonds and eventual material rewards. Once inside the Kelly-Nash machine, Dawson could at last dispense those long-promised rewards. Moreover, material benefits soon replaced the appeal to race and racial issues. His followers were now held and bound together by tangible benefits. And he could deliver the vote from the black community on the basis of these badly needed economic benefits.

Dawson's submachine, in the final analysis, was a subordinate one. He supplied the Daley organization with its needed black voters and the machine supplied him with the needed material benefits. In this manner both organizations sustained each other. And both machines are dependent on each other for a viable existence.

As a leader, Dawson was absorbed by the white machine to serve as a liaison between it and the black community. He was not, to be sure, picked because he was an established black leader before the machine included him. The white machine became his source of continued viability, and with its growing power, he was able to cement his hold over the black community. Since his absorption, Dawson has continued to secure his power, influence, and organizational strength in the black community. He has, in effect, so strengthened his submachine that he brooks no opposition, rivals, or challenges. He has separated himself from his constituency by forcing them to rely upon his political machine for racial advancement rather than upon his political accomplishments and effectiveness in Congress.[22] Whatever leadership role Dawson had in the black community is solely dependent upon his machine and organizational connection. The source of his leadership, in short, was his machine.

KANSAS CITY'S PENDERGAST

In Kansas City blacks inhabited the eastern section on the first ward of

[22] James Q. Wilson, "Two Negro Politicians: An Interpretation," in Herzberg and Pomper *op. cit.*, pp. 139-142.

the west bottom where the Pendergast machine got started.[23] Jim Pendergast, the founder of the machine, began to attract black allegiance from this area as early as 1896, when he ran for alderman. During the campaign he took time out and put up bail bonds for a black prisoner, and once in office he supported a number of projects that aided the poor and suffering blacks of his constituency.

Later, as Pendergast extended control of his machine across the entire city, he crushed black Republican organizations led by Nelson Crews and had black Republican newspapers support his son for office by 1906. Having crushed black Republicanism, however, he captured their allegiance and that of other blacks throughout the city by extending the regular party favor and consideration of welfare needs to them. In the classic sense, the Pendergast machine tied the black electorate to itself through the granting of patronage and welfare benefits to the black community.

TAMMANY HALL

Tammany Hall has always been the dominant machine in New York City, but it has not always sought black voters. From the 1820s to the 1840s, blacks voted against Tammany Hall because "it had led a determined movement to limit free Negro suffrage."[24] Moreover, from 1840 to 1870, Tammany Hall Democrats vigorously fought the Republicans in their attempts to grant blacks equal suffrage. In fact, black relations with Tammany Hall from the beginning of the nineteenth century to the end were very poor at best, and throughout the period the majority of blacks in New York remained almost totally Republican. The New York Democrats and their machine had a decidedly antiblack position and character. And although several blacks who tired of the Republican party's "take blacks for granted attitude" tried independent or mild coalition overtures to Tammany Hall Democrats, they still went unrecognized or unencouraged.

Not until the 1890s did Tammany Hall Boss Richard Croker state that political recognition and patronage would be granted to blacks "in proportion to their work and numbers." Despite that, black politicians were forced to accept the lowest political position in the city. Nevertheless, the continued display of rude tactics by white Republicans forced many blacks to support a Tammany Hall mayoralty candidate in 1892 and the formation of the first regular black Democratic club in January, 1898—the

[23] For information on blacks and the Pendergast machine, see Lyle W. Dorsett, *The Pendergast Machine* (New York: Oxford University Press, 1968), pp. 18-20, 27-28, 44, and 82.

[24] Hanes Walton, Jr., *The Negro in Third Party Politics* (Philadelphia: Dorrance and Company, 1969), p. 12.

United Colored Democracy. From the outset, however, the black "Democratic organization existed as a separate and segregated unit." "The Negro boss theoretically supervised all the Negro wards in the city." Actually, his power rose and fell at the disposition of the white Democratic county leader or mayor, not at the will of his constituency. In essence, the Democratic machine became similar to the Republican party in its techniques and methods of control.

With the turn of the century, however, things changed in the Republican party. Charlie Andrews took the presidency of the Young Men's Colored Republican Club and became a powerful black boss. He wielded so much influence that he became, with the aid of Booker T. Washington, collector of internal revenue for the second New York district. Basically, it was because of his own energy and ability that Andrews became a powerful black boss in New York City. With an active two-party system in Harlem, however, it was not long before the influence of the United Colored Democracy on the city's Democratic party elevated a Harvard-educated black to the position of the most powerful black Democrat in the city with almost dictatorial control over black patronage. According to Osofsky, "Ferdinand Q. Morton was recognized by all Democratic mayors and county chairmen as the sole spokesman of Negro Democracy." However, Morton soon moved into an alliance with Republican Fiorello H. La Guardia in 1933, and even turned to the American Labor party.

Both Morton and Andrews, who was later superseded by Abraham Grenthal, were self-styled leaders who were absorbed into the white machine on a segregated basis, and both ruled as virtual dictators. It was their dictatorial rule, in fact, that caused many independent blacks to move to minor parties such as the Socialist, Communist, and Liberal parties as outlets for selling their political wares. Frank Crosswaith was the Socialist party's candidate for lieutenant governor in 1932. He had many black supporters and party members, including Chandler Owens and A. Philip Randolph. By 1929 in Harlem such notable blacks as James Ford, Langston Hughes, and Richard Wright had joined the Communist party. And Benjamin Davis won a seat on New York City's council on the Communist ticket in 1943.[25] And James Pemberton, a young black, "rose to a dominant status" in the American Labor and Liberal party in New York.

On the other hand, when Morton, Andrews, and Grenthal passed from the rulership of the black political organization, black Republicans and Democrats became assertive and shook themselves free of Republican and Democratic machines. The situation arose in New York City in which no machine or party had dominant or significant control over the black

---

[25] Benjamin J. Davis, *Communist Councilman from Harlem* (New York: International Publishers, 1969), p. 118.

electorate. In this atmosphere of independent or weak machines, limited political bosses, and factionalized parties, a black boss and machine arose.

ADAM CLAYTON POWELL: INDEPENDENT

Not all black bosses and machines are subordinate, however. A prime case of an independent black machine was that of Adam Clayton Powell in New York City.

Powell built his machine on the foundation of his parishioners in the Abyssinian Baptist Church.[26] One of the largest Baptist churches in the city, this church provided Powell with a springboard. Although he inherited the church from his father, he had gained tremendous popularity with the people of Harlem by staging several boycotts during the late thirties in which he championed the rights of blacks and obtained for them numerous jobs and welfare benefits. Powell's organization became at once a personal machine based upon his church workers, who numbered more than ten thousand. He bound his followers to him with charismatic leadership and cries for racial equality. In short, he laid the blame for black suffrage upon the "man." And he continued to do so in vivid terms, and his parishioners continued to reward him by reelecting him to Congress.

The independence of Powell's machine stemmed from several factors. First, he represented the militant black leader who had roots in the black community. He was not appointed, selected, or chosen. He earned his position of leadership through charisma, style, and appeals to the issues which were meaningful to the black community. Furthermore, his religious connection gave him a suitable basis upon which to operate, and he was able to use that basis to move effectively into the political arena. Finally, Powell's machine bound its followers through intangible rewards which were significant to the black community.

However, history in the early sixties caught up with and passed Powell. "Out of the South came Martin Luther King, Jr., and from the North Malcolm X."[27] Powell's leadership position was challenged by new ideas and new methods. Black Americans chose new heroes. "Black people," states Julius Lester, "changed and Powell didn't. His way of life had once been an act of rebellion; it now became nothing more than self-indulgence. . . . He was not a man for all seasons, but getting through the long cold winter would have been infinitely more difficult without him."[28] With Powell's election defeat came the collapse of his personal political machine. As Powell died a political death, Dawson died a natural death, but each man's machine came to an end on his deathbed.

[26] Adam Clayton Powell, Jr., *Marching Blacks* (New York: Dial Press, 1964).
[27] Julius Lester, "Homage to Adam Clayton Powell," *The Black Politician,* July, 1971, p. 39.
[28] *Ibid.*

ATLANTA'S A. T. WALDEN

If Powell established an independent machine in New York, A. T. Walden established one in Atlanta. Georgia had disfranchised its blacks in 1908, but approximately 1,800-3,000 blacks retained the ballot. Around this small nucleus Walden became chairman of the Fifth Congressional District's Republican Committee. The lily-white movement in the South could not dislodge him from his political organization as it did from party ranks. And with the coming of Franklin Roosevelt and the New Deal, Walden moved his group of followers into the Democratic fold.[29] He also increased the black vote in Atlanta from 1,800 in 1910 to 25,000 in the late thirties. And being the only black lawyer in Atlanta, he won the admiration of the black community by his continued defense of black rights in numerous legal suits. Walden further expanded his control over the black electorate by assuming leadership of the local NAACP and directing the local YMCA; he also became president of the Atlanta Urban League. By concentrating all major black organizations under his tutelage, and also through contact with the white political leaders, Walden became the self-styled civil consultant in the black community.[30] In fact, his power and influence so grew that Walden combined his black democratic organization with the black Republican organization headed by John W. Dobbs, forming a large organization that Walden headed, and called the Atlanta Negro Voters League. Later Walden expanded even further, and consolidated all the Democratic clubs in Georgia, becoming head of the organization—the Associated Negro Democratic Clubs of Georgia.[31] In Atlanta, however, Walden's major task was to obtain some forms of racial advancement; he did this by coalescing with the white mayor William B. Hartsfield. Unfortunately, as Walden aged, he grew conservative and the coalition with Hartsfield absorbed his organization more and more without any meaningful rewards being granted to the black community. Eventually Walden's personal machine became too demanding for the aging colonel to run effectively. The more he tied himself to the white power structure for security, the weaker his machine became; by the time of his death in 1964 it had collapsed all but in name.

OTHER INDEPENDENTS

As we have seen, the blacks in Memphis still have a predominantly independent organization with no major bosses at the present time. How-

[29] Ira de Reid, "Walden the Democrat," *New Republic,* CXXIII (October 18, 1948), 13.

[30] Edward C. Banfield, *Big City Politics: A Comparative Guide to the Political Systems of Nine American Cities* (New York: Randon House, 1965), p. 34.

[31] Reid, *op. cit.,* p. 12.

ever, other black leaders have tried to establish machines and become independent. Archibald J. Carey, Jr., a black Republican in Chicago, who combined the talents of preacher and lawyer, has tried to establish a basis for independent power.[32] He has not succeeded. The black population of Chicago has continued to vote heavily Democratic. And this trend eventually spelled doom for Carey although he did win a seat on the city aldermanic board.

Another black, George Cannon, attempted to establish his political machine and independence by becoming the chairman of the Harlem Wallace-for-President committee. But in 1948 Harlem gave Wallace only 21,000 votes to Truman's 90,000. Thus, as the Wallace Progressive Movement failed, Cannon's political aspiration in black Harlem declined.

In Wayne County, Michigan, a black Republican organized and led the black community. Benjamin Pelham formed his own independent black political machine and "made and broke political figures and dominated Wayne County government as no person did before or has since his political retirement before World War I."[33] Since there was no white machine in Pelham's area, his black organization was the dominant force within the community and he wielded power without opposition. "During the period of Ben Pelham's administration curiously enough no other Negro emerged into prominence in Michigan politics.[34] With the coming of World War I and new European immigrants, Pelham's tightly knit organization lost control and his age forced him to retire from the political arena. With his retirement came the collapse of his political machine.

Within the last decade, the rise of numerous black politicians hints at some degree of independence but in many cases the emergence of these individuals has been due less to machine politics and more to reapportionment in the black community throughout the country. We shall discuss this matter in a later analysis.

In contrast, then, the subordinate black boss and his machine seem to have as many troubles, problems, and deficiencies as the independent. What the two have in common is that both exist principally for the advantage of the black boss himself. Benefits from both types of black machines enrich the bosses. To be sure, the independent machine distributed mainly intangible incentives, while the subordinate machine distributed mainly tangible benefits.

In regard to the foundations of both machines, the independent machine

[32] Horace Cayton, "Carey the Republican," *New Republic*, CXIII (October 18, 1948), 10-12.

[33] See Wade H. McCree, Jr., "The Negro Renaissance in Michigan Politics," *Negro History Bulletin*, XXVI (October, 1962), 7. See also Benjamin B. Pelham, *Forty Years in Politics* (Detroit: Wayne State University Press, 1957).

[34] *Ibid.*

seemed to arise in a milieu where weak party or machine control existed over the black electorate; the subordinate machine arose in areas where strong party or machine control existed. However, some independent machines began as Dawson's did, but became subordinate in order to remain viable; some subordinate machines, on the other hand, like the one in Memphis, became independent due to the collapse of the major white machine. Finally, the independent machine tended to be much more personalized than the subordinate, and depended more or less upon one individual than upon a well-built bureaucracy.

Whether the new type of emerging political machine that Theodore J. Lowi discussed will reach out and create a new relationship with the black electorate remains to be seen. Whether blacks will break all their ties with the old-style machine remains to be seen. Although one cannot at the present time measure the influence of machines and bosses upon the black electorate, they were without a doubt significant in shaping black voting behavior. And the nature of the political machine is closely aligned with the degree of black political development in the local community.

If blacks throughout America have won their fight for the right to vote, registered in spite of some obstacles, been manipulated and controlled to some degree by political bosses and machines, what then has been the impact of the black voter? What has he achieved? What is he likely to achieve? In the next chapter we will examine the effect of the black vote.

V

The Impact of Black Voting

To understand what blacks have achieved since their emergence into the political arena, one must look at black voting not only from a developmental, but from a vertical and also from a horizontal perspective. To be sure, the degree and sophistication of a black's political development in any area strongly determine what he can achieve there. If his level of development is low and whites head him to the polls on the basis of fish fries, money, whiskey, and barbecues, then his vote will gain him little if anything. If he is politically sagacious, however, effective bargaining will not only obtain political offices, appointments, and favorable policy decisions, it may even install a more liberal government and politicians. To understand this more fully, let us view the matter from a vertical perspective—i.e., from the local, state, and national level—and horizontally—i.e., from a policy, position, and treatment point of view. Although the vertical and horizontal approaches inevitably transverse, their different directions help establish clarity.

BLACK VOTERS AND STATE AND LOCAL ELECTIONS

Black politics comes alive at the local level. The political power of the black electorate assumes its greatest potential at the community level. Although black voters draw much interest and concern during presidential elections, their greatest potency and effectiveness seemingly come at the municipal and county levels.

Black enfranchisement has changed the face, if not the political patterns and structures, of American communities. In Clarksdale, Mississippi, black bloc voting brought a meaningful change and attitude on the part of the city administration toward the black community. In Greenville, Mississippi, the black electorate, holding a balance of power, had the mayor take steps to facilitate compliance with the 1964 Civil Rights Act, achieved appointment of a black to the planning commission, and placed blacks in new job vacancies. In addition, there was a positive correlation between the increase in black voting and the elimination of police brutality, as well as

70

one between voting and the willingness to accept desegregation of all types of public facilities. Black voting in the four communities in Mississippi alone increased public employment opportunities for the blacks in those counties. It also had a favorable effect upon an equitable distribution of public resources, such as garbage collection, pest control, the maintenance of roads, sidewalks, street lights, ditches, and taxation.

The same is true in Durham, North Carolina, and Tuskegee, Alabama. The black voting power in each city proved quite effective in changing and altering city services to get a fairer and more equitable treatment.[1] In southern cities where blacks had the vote even earlier, they had a tremendous effect upon city politics. In 1923 blacks in Savannah, Georgia, helped put a reform city government in power. In 1928, the black electorate in Memphis led by black boss Bob Church removed a reactionary mayor from office. In Jacksonville, Florida, the black votes proved effective in just about the same fashion. In Los Angeles the black voter, before 1963, added blacks to the city council.[2] Although the impact of the black electorate was somewhat significant in the pre-civil rights era it did not reach a new intensity until after the Voting Rights Act of 1965.

The same situation prevailed in the North. Before the civil rights era northern cities had black alderman, state assemblymen, and Chicago sent a black—Oscar DePriest—to Congress in 1928. Since the "revolution" of the 1960s, however, the power of the black electorate has proved to be quite significant. The major impact has been in the area of black representation. With more blacks concentrated in the urban areas of both North and South, has come increased black representation in the city or municipal government. Black control of central cities has resulted in the election of fourteen to twenty black mayors in such cities as Cleveland, Flint, Chapel Hill, and Fayette, Mississippi, plus a vice-mayor in Atlanta.[3] In fact, throughout the country more than 1,500 black public officials have been elected at the local level,[4] and the future promises more. For instance, in the states of Louisiana, Mississippi, Alabama, Georgia, South Carolina, North Carolina, and Virginia, 40 percent of the eligible black electorate is still unregistered. In the North, the rise of independent black politicians, the decline of machine politics, and the rise of black politicians elsewhere,

[1] William R. Keech, The Impact of Negro Voting: The Role of the Vote in the Quest for Equality (Chicago: Rand McNally and Company, 1968), pp. 40-79.

[2] See Breman C. Patterson, "The Politics of Recognition: Negro Politics in Los Angeles, 1960-1963" (unpublished Ph.D. dissertation, UCLA, 1967), pp. 2-44.

[3] For information on the black mayors, see Jeffrey K. Hadden, L. H. Masott, and Victor Thresen, "The Making of the Negro Mayors, 1967," Trans-Action, V (January-February, 1968), 20-21; Willadeane Clayton, "Lee, Evers, Make List of Mayors Total 14," VEP News, III (May, 1969), 1.

[4] "National Meeting of Black Officials Slated, September 11-14," VEP News, III (May, 1969), 9.

as well as the wave of black political consciousness, foster new possibilities of black representation. This "ebony" mood, coupled with the fact that Baltimore, Cincinnati, Detroit, Newark, Pittsburgh, and St. Louis have proportionately larger black populations than New York City or Los Angeles, indicates great possibilities for more black officials in these cities.

On the local level black voting has been significant in the passage and defeat of local bond issues, the cessation of police brutality, equal treatment in the courts, and an equitable distribution of public services in the black communities. On the other hand, the black electorate has had little success in changing code enforcement, getting streets paved, improving welfare payments, and obtaining policies aimed at removing the effects of past discrimination and "most critically integration of public schools."[5] For the most part, the drama of school desegregation is played out not in the political arena at either the local or national level, but in the courts.[6] Both whites and blacks have let the courts solve the desegregation problem, and the power of the ballot, for the most part, is yet to come into play. When it does, blacks will of course make some impact in certain localities. As it now stands, blacks in both North and South have been elected to the various school boards. Whether their numbers are sufficient to change school board policies on desegregation remains to be seen.

The major problem for the black electorate has become the meaningful change of public policy. At present, because of the recent emergence of so many black public officials, it is hard to determine the full impact that black voters have had in altering public policy. Since black public officials pursue numerous forms of public policy some of which are shaped by their own basic orientation, it is even more difficult to judge their impact. For instance, some black politicians seek a policy of cultural assimilation, others legal protections, others population transfer, and still others something else. And despite their approaches, they must have a political position and ideology that will be meaningful and relevant to the black community. Otherwise, the black community will not reap any major benefits from black representation at either the local, state, or national level.

If, however, because of the strength and size of the black electorate, policy determination and outcome are hard to determine, this is just part of the present problem. An additional problem facing blacks in the lower level is the shifting of local elections from single districts (usually wards) to at large. While this also holds true at the state level, it is even more crucial at the local levels. Forcing blacks to run citywide would drastically cut black representation at the local level. In fact, the entire black electorate would

[5] Gerald M. Pomper, "Review of *The Impact of Negro Voting* by William Keech," *American Political Science Review*, LXIII (September, 1969), 923.

[6] See Robert L. Crain, *The Politics of School Desegregation* (New York: Doubleday Anchor Books, 1969), pp. 349-369.

have to concentrate on one or two black candidates in the races. With limited representation there would surely be limited influence upon local regulations and public policy.

In addition to the problem of citywide elections is the problem of metropolitanism.[7] The consolidation of city and county governments or several city and county governments is another technique in which the black vote will be effectively diluted. While blacks are coming to power in central cities, when the resources needed to deal with the problems of the central cities are moving to the suburbs, then metro-government seems to some to be the answer.[8] If the impact of the black electorate upon the political affairs of local and municipal governments is to be effective, they must be included in the planning of many new metro-governments. Metro-politanism must deal with the question of black power in the cities if it is to be equitable and sincere in solving the problems of the black community.

Impact on the State Level—South

To assess the impact of black voting on the state level one could start with the governor as the most politically significant individual. One could pose questions such as the following: Have gubernatorial candidates changed their racial attitudes and positions in relation to growing black electoral power? How has the governor's office responded to the black community, its needs and problems? Or is it necessary for the governor to even respond?

A clear-cut analysis of southern gubernatorial campaigns has proved revealing in answering the first question. Race, whether external or internal attacks on segregation have made it necessary, has always been a major issue in the South, and political observers have argued that blacks with the ballot will be able to change the southern political structure. According to Matthews and Prothro, "once Negroes in the South vote in substantial numbers, white politicians will prove responsive to the desires of the Negro community."[9] Before 1944 the impact of black voting in the South was negligible in gubernatorial elections. After the *Smith* v. *Allwright* decision, however, the southern black electorate increased and its growing political power had some minimal effect.[10] Before the decision only a limited number of blacks could vote. After black voting power increased, "race was of

[7] Frances R. Piven and Richard Cloward, "Black Control of Cities," in Alan Shank, ed., *Political Power and the Urban Crisis* (Boston: Holbrook Press, 1969), pp. 320-327.

[8] Richard Hatcher, "The Black Role in Urban Politics," *Current History*, LVII (November, 1969), 287-289. See also Pat Watters and Reese Cleghorn, *Climbing Jacob's Ladder: The Arrival of Negroes in Southern Politics* (New York: Harcourt, Brace and World, 1967), pp. 75-107.

[9] Donald R. Matthews and James W. Prothro, "Social and Economic Factors and Negro Voter Registration in the South," *American Political Science Review*, LVII (March, 1963), 24.

[10] See Margaret Price, *The Negro and the Ballot* (Atlanta: Southern Regional Council, 1960), and her *The Negro Voter in the South* (Atlanta: Southern Regional Council, 1957).

relatively little importance as an *overt* campaign issue in the early 50's."[11]
With no effective external or internal attack on segregation, most gubernatorial candidates could afford to ignore or at least deemphasize racial
questions. This was true mainly for the peripheral South, however. In the
deep South the die-hard segregationists won the day.

Between 1950 and 1953 moderate segregationists won twelve (86 percent)
of the fourteen races for governor in the South. These moderate segregationists tended to have conservative economic views. They called for econ-
omy in government and "held the line with fiscal policies." In their inaugu-
ral addresses, liberal southern governors hardly mentioned race except in
the deep southern states. And these discussions were only minor and
limited in scope. Before 1954 few candidates for governor expressed liberal
views on race. Then the Brown decision, acting as an external force attacking segregation, caused a major reorientation of gubernatorial candidates
in the South toward civil rights. After the Brown decision strong segregationist candidates increased from 18 to 46 percent. Racial liberalism did
not exist during the early 1950s of course, and this increase came entirely at
the expense of the moderates. The number of moderate candidates declined
considerably, but they ran more frequently in the peripheral South than in
the deep South. In addition to the increase in strong segregationist candidates and a decrease in moderate segregation, racially moderate candidates
rose from 0 to 11 percent.

In the post-Brown decision era strong segregationists won a majority (51
percent) of the southern governorships. According to Professor Black
"ninety percent of total candidates and governors in the post-Brown period
maintained some degree of allegiance to segregation."[12]

In Georgia, Marvin Griffin won the governorship in 1954 by emphasiz-
ing his determination to preserve segregation. Governor Fielding Wright in
Mississippi "proposed to settle the integration question by issuing a gubernatorial declaration forbidding school desegregation."[13] Candidates elsewhere expressed like opinions. By the mid-1960s, however, a "sharp decline
occurred in the number of strong segregationists among major candidates,
accompanied by a modest resurgence of moderate segregationist candidates and by the gradual entry of racial liberals into gubernatorial politics."
As long as whites constituted the majority of votes in the region and as
long as they wanted politicians to resist or minimize desegregation, race
was a most exploitable issue. Most such campaigns strongly attacked black
groups like the NAACP; they described the black bloc vote as a menace to
society and their platforms contained numerous declarations for state

[11] Robert Black, "Southern Governors and the Negro: Race as a Campaign Issue since
1954" (unpublished doctoral dissertation, Harvard University), p. 77.
[12] *Ibid.*, p. 85.
[13] *Ibid.*

rights. As black voters increased, however, there was a decrease in strong segregationists. In fact, the overt racial appeal of numerous segregationists has notably declined in the region, especially in the border states of the South. Only in the deep South does the Wallace-type candidate continue.[14]

Throughout the South there has been little response to the black community by governors. Even such a segregationist governor as John Bell Williams, who received the black vote and thought it so crucial to his victory that he moderated his views, had a short memory after election day and returned to his former position. Thus, the politics of desegregation in the South remained mostly that of delay, evasion, or circumvention. In short, the influence of the black electorate upon the southern governor is limited. It may cause several candidates to modify their views in a multifactional primary race, but little more.

In the Border States, black voters had enough power to cut down on the degree of the appeal to race by white candidates. In the deep South, the power basis is emerging, but little that is meaningful can be said because the region is in such a state of transition. Southern governors like Wallace, Maddox, Barnett, and Faubus have failed to respond to the black community in any fashion. In fact, their actions have ignored the growing black electorate and have relied mainly on the white electorate because at present black electoral power is of minimal strength statewide. Moreover, this failure to respond to the black community has caused several black gubernatorial candidates to appear.

Impact on the State Level—North

In the North a different kind of situation has prevailed. Race has not been a major campaign issue,[15] and it is seldom interjected into state politics. With major control over the black electorate resting under either party or machine control, the state executive has had little to worry about. Occasional overtures were made, but before the riots of the mid-sixties, little else. Before the sixties, efforts were made in the field of civil rights commissions, FEPC organizations, and appointment of well-known black leaders to "political jobs" for window dressing. Northern state executives were not great liberal humanitarians. They were politicians first, and humanists at times.

Contrary to popular belief, "The white north [is] no more ready to accept genuine integration and real racial equality than the deep South."[16] Northerners will accept a degree of school integration, public accommodation,

[14] Hanes Walton, Jr., and Clarence Martin, "The Black Electorate and the Maddox Administration," *The Black Politician*, II (Spring, 1971), 31–34.
[15] Stewart Alsop and Oliver Q. Voyle, "What Northerners Really Think of Negroes," in Andrew M. Scott and Earle Wallace, *Politics, USA: Cases on the American Democratic Process* (New York: Macmillan Company, 1965), p. 133. See also pages 124–162.
[16] *Ibid.*, p. 137.

and equal employment opportunity, in a word, abstract justice. This sense of abstract justice is not deeply felt, however. When black advances began to infringe upon social status, the value of a house, or imminent social relationships, "the desire for abstract justice evaporates quickly and the desire to keep the colored in their place appears instead."[17] Prior to 1964, if a state executive wanted to commit political suicide, all he had to do was advocate the demands of some black organization for open occupancy, intermarriage, or equal social status. In many cases this is still true today.

In some states the governor's leadership is essentially political and the governorship is basically a halfway house or intermediate point in his career which can lead to a federal office. Thus, governors tend to avoid conflict in general in order to save their political future.[18] No governor "has had involvement thrust upon him in the way local race riots and aggressive demonstrations for school desegregation have involved mayors and three Presidents of the United States."[19] If the issue seems dangerous to a governor's political future, he will usually try to avoid a strong commitment. The actions of Governor George Romney during the Detroit riot, in which he blamed the mayor for not acting decisively and the federal government, is a clear example.

However, additional reluctance on the part of governors to act on civil rights and in relation to the needs of the black community can be seen in the creation by governors of FEPC or state commissions on human rights. Even more revealing are state civil rights laws enacted because of governors' backing. And from both items little has been accomplished. Before 1945, not a single state had either a human rights commission or fair employment practices commission. In 1945, only two northern states— New York and New Jersey—moving on the governor's pressure established FEPC.[20] After 1945, only five more northern states enacted laws creating commissions on public housing. Only seven northern states set up commissions to seek equality in the state housing situation. Before 1960, only Connecticut, New Jersey, New York, Rhode Island, and Massachusetts had commissions to enforce equal treatment in public accommodations, and in only three of them did the governor have strong powers over the budget.[21] In most cases the budget of these northern state agencies were small in comparison with the massive job assigned them. Before 1969, only two northern states had commissions that enforced civil rights in housing

[17] *Ibid.*
[18] Joseph A. Schlesinger, "The Politics of the Executive," in Herbert Jacobs and Kenneth N. Vines, eds., *Politics in the American States* (Boston: Little, Brown and Company, 1965), pp. 211–212.
[19] *Ibid.*, p. 211.
[20] Joseph Parker Witherspoon, *Administration Implementation of Civil Rights* (Austin: University of Texas Press, 1968), p. 542.
[21] Schlesinger, *op. cit.*, p. 226.

employment and public accommodation. Between 1959-1968 not more than three others increased their commission's power to encompass all three areas. In sum, northern governors have reacted only in a limited sense to the needs of the black community or electorate.

School Desegregation—North and South

Another area in which the response of the governors to the black electorate and community can be seen is in the area of school desegregation. On this matter southern governors have been most irresponsive. In 1966, in Alabama, after blacks had been somewhat enfranchised, Lurleen Wallace still won election with a covert racial appeal and a program to maintain segregated schools. In 1970 George C. Wallace was reelected governor. In Virginia the governor took an active hand in closing down public education with the "massive resistance" approach and still he won some black votes. Although public schools did not open in Prince George County, Virginia, until 1964, the governors of the state did nothing before then to aid those blacks who were denied an education while the schools were closed. The needs of the black community were ignored altogether.

In northern states, cities have experienced more controversy about school integration than they have in any other area of racial change. Governors have failed for the most part to take a hand in the crisis. The issue, in general, has been left up to the majors of the cities involved or to the local school boards. A governor's human relations commission might hear some complaints but for the most part northern governors leave the issue to the local politicians and to their administrative advisers. In fact, in regard to the entire matter of school desegregation, northern governors have shifted the responsibility, while southern governors in the deep South have made olitical "hay" out of the issue. Whether this is a trend that will continue remains to be seen. Two factors are important, however. In both North and South desegregation has proceeded legally rather than politically. Those who favor and those who oppose integration alike eventually rely on the courts to adjudicate the problem in one manner or the other. This precludes necessary political action. Recently, two political scientists have discovered that environmental factors (i.e., urbanism, income, and education) promote or aid desegregation rather than political factors (i.e., percentage of Republican votes, states' rights candidates, or race organizations).[22] This suggests that politics can also be played down if necessary. The only real political problem now posed by school desegregation is "busing" students from one neighborhood to another to insure racial

[22] See Donald Matthews and James W. Prothro, "Stateways Versus Folkways: Critical Factors in Southern Reaction to Brown v. Board of Education," in Gottfried Dietze, ed., *Essays on the American Constitution: A Commemorative Volume in Honor of Alpheus T. Mason* (Englewood Cliffs, N.J.: Prentice-Hall, 1964), pp. 139-158. See also Thomas Dye, *Politics in State and Community* (Englewood Cliffs, N. J.: Prentice-Hall, 1968), pp. 346-350.

balance, and even this has been consciously avoided or left to local school boards.

The basic response of northern governors to the black community has been to appoint blacks to key positions and organizations to handle racial problems. Generally, however, these appointments are made without consulting black party or civic leaders. Governor Nelson Rockefeller of New York, for example, has appointed men like Jackie Robinson (the first major league black baseball player) and Wyatt T. Walker (a former aid to Martin Luther King, Jr.). In the main these appointments have still left the black community without any meaningful response from the state executive. If, on the other hand, the policy is intended to acquire black voters, then at least, in the cases of Rockefeller and Mayor John V. Lindsay, it has proved to be beneficial. Whether the actions will change, or whether other governors, North and South, will adopt similar policies remains to be seen.

In sum, the impact of black voting upon the state executive's office appears to be minimal, both in the North and South. The "politicalness" of the office has caused southern governors to appeal mainly to southern whites and has caused northern governors to shift the responsibility to administrative agencies or to let the local politicians or school boards handle the crisis. Both sets of governors have reacted to insure or to improve their political futures. Even in northern states, or in those southern states where the black vote supplies the margin of victory, it is soon forgotten or token appointments with no attachment in the black community are usually made in the hope that these will please the black electorate and keep it intact.

Responding to the needs of the black community, some commissions have been established, either by statute or executive order to deal with discriminatory complaints—in housing, public accommodations, and employment. The majority of these commissions have been in northern states.[23] In the South the 1965 Civil Rights Bill had to make the states accept federal laws forbidding discriminatory practices in these areas. For the most part, the southern state executives have responded little to the black community. And if the southern states have done next to nothing, the northern state executives have done little more. At present, the black electorate is on the outside of the governor's mansion, North and South.

THE CONGRESSIONAL LEVEL

On the congressional level things are somewhat different. Black voting seems to have had a fairly significant degree of impact. Blacks may not

[23] See Duane Lockard, *Toward Equal Opportunity: A Study of State and Local Anti-Discrimination Laws* (New York: Macmillan Company, 1968).

have especially influenced public policy, but at least blacks have won election to Congress—mostly to the House of Representatives.

At present, the number of black representatives (ten in 1968) may rise to fourteen or more within the next few years. And the election of a black— Edward W. Brooke—to the U.S. Senate from Massachusetts, the first northern black to be elected to the U.S. Senate in its history as well as the first black senator to take a seat since 1881, suggests that blacks "may also win important statewide elections."[24] But the influence of the black electorate upon Congress is limited.

In the South there are only two congressional districts where black majorities exist;[25] there are more than eight in the North. Moreover, of the 96 congressional districts where blacks make up 20 percent of the constituency, only thirty-one are in the North. Three in the South are generally comprised of those blacks who will refrain from independent political action. The exception of course was Charles Evers's campaign in 1960 to capture the seat left vacant by Governor John Bell Williams. He took first place in a six-man race, but he lost in the special runoff election because the whites in the Third Mississippi Congressional District outnumbered blacks two to one.

And although it is important to elect more and more blacks to Congress, the important factor in their influence upon public policy is the influence of the black electorate upon all of the congressmen. However, since over half of all southern congressional districts have a population of one-fifth blacks and the North and West less than one-twelfth of their congressional districts black,[26] the black electorate will certainly have to rely upon a coalition of blacks and liberal white congressmen with a sizable black constituency for much of the meaningful legislation to improve the social, economic, and educational standards of blacks for the time being. Blacks are hardly 2 percent of the U. S. House of Representatives, and 1 percent of the U. S. Senate, and so far most southern congressmen have not had to react to that one-fifth of their black electorate. Only one southern congressman who voted against the Civil Rights Act changed his position as the percentage of blacks in his district rose due to new reapportionment measures in the state. But for the most part black influence in Congress remains at least for the present time in the election of black congressmen. And this can be readily seen by looking at Congress in action on black equality. Until the Civil Rights acts of 1957, 1960, and 1965 Congress had not passed any significant legislation for blacks since the Civil War and Reconstruc-

[24] Dye, op. cit., p. 354.
[25] Pat Watters, "The Negroes Enter Southern Politics," Dissent, XIII (July–August, 1966), 365.
[26] James Q. Wilson, "The Negro in Politics," in Lawrence Fuchs, ed., American Ethnic Politics (New York: Harper and Row, 1968), p. 231.

tion.[27] However, if the influence of the black electorate on Congress has been limited, what, then, has been the black electorate's influence on the presidency?

THE PRESIDENTIAL LEVEL

Before we look at the influence of the black vote upon the president and presidential politics, let us look briefly at its impact on the national political conventions. To determine this, one must being with party platforms.

Prior to the 1920s the Democrats did not want blacks and not many blacks sought membership in the Democratic party. It was not until the 1936 National Convention that blacks began to take part in the party's proceedings and deliberations. Seventy-six years after the founding of the Democratic party, blacks finally took part in the nominating proceedings. It was not until 1948, however, that the Democratic party took a strong civil rights stand in a platform that eventually led to a schism in its ranks and the creation of the Dixiecrats.

If 1948 was the beginning of the Democratic party recognition of blacks via platform enactments, the conventions of 1960, 1964, and 1968 have become so far the high point and they have shown an increasing tendency to become concerned with the black electorate as it has increased in size with each passing year. Whether this recognition will continue in the wake of the Democrats' loss of the presidency in 1968 remains to be seen.

Black involvement and participation in the national Republican Convention began when a black delegation went to the Convention of 1868. It has continued with varying degrees of intensity since then. The high-water mark of black Republicanism was during Reconstruction, but a second peak came during the Eisenhower years. Goldwater and Nixon have inaugurated policies that have caused the intensity of participation and involvement to decline measurably. Black involvement with the Republicans has gone measurably downhill since the 1880s with two small rises in 1956 and 1960. Noticeable also is the increasing absence of meaningful civil rights in the party platform. Before 1916 there were no black delegates to the Republican National Convention from the North, but there were numerous delegates from the southern states. After 1916, because of northern black migration, black delegates from the North increasingly participated in the National Convention. Despite the presence of both northern and southern black delegations, however, only marginal interest or concern was given to black rights and equality. The black delegation was used to secure nomination of party presidential candidates, and the winning candidate rewarded

---

[27] Albert P. Blaustein and Robert L. Zangrando, eds., *Civil Rights and the American Negro* (New York: Washington Square Press, 1968), p. 469.

his black supporters with a few political appointments and some patronage rather than with a strong civil rights platform and concerted action.

The Republican National conventions strongly recognized black rights in their platforms during the era of the "First" Reconstruction 1868-1876; the Democratic National Convention showed its strongest recognition from 1948-1968—the era of the "Second" Reconstruction. During each period, the black electorate had considerable power. During other periods the black voting strength was either weak or curtailed. Hence, black power has had some influence upon the national political conventions; of the two major parties it has had less on those of third parties. Black persons participated in third-party conventions long before they were able to participate in the conventions of the major parties. The antislavery parties, for example, gave blacks their first opportunity to participate in a political convention. At the national convention of the Liberty party on August 30, 1843, several black delegates were in attendance. Their influence must have been significant, since two resolutions, the 35th and 36th, referred to black citizens. The Thirty-fifth called "on all liberty-loving people to fight inequality based solely on color," and the 36th welcomed all blacks into the Liberty party. Moreover, the major idea of the party's platform was its opposition to slavery, and the party kept this platform until its collapse in 1860.

Another antislavery party, the Free Soilers, welcomed black delegates and reflected their influence and presence in the party's platform. Since the antislavery party, the Populist and the Progressive parties have strongly reflected some concern for black needs in their conventions and platforms. In addition, the socialists and the communists have also had black individuals in their conventions, party politics, and platforms. In fact, the communists have nominated and run blacks for both the presidency and vice presidency.[28]

However, despite the overture of third parties to the black electorate, the antislavery parties seemingly made the most sincere appeal and reflections in their party platforms. The other parties' overtures to blacks were born basically out of a desire to win and a need for votes. Perhaps more than any other, the Liberty party knew that the black electorate was small and its call for black equality was based on principles rather than politics.

Meaningful black influence came in the third parties' national conventions before the Civil War and in the major parties' conventions after the Civil War.

The influence of the black electorate is more readily seen in regard to the presidency and presidential politics mainly because of northern black

[28] Hanes Walton, Jr., *The Negro in Third Party Politics* (Philadelphia: Dorrance and Company, 1969), pp. 71-83.

migration at the turn of the century strategically placed blacks in New York, Illinois, Pennsylvania, Maryland, Massachusetts, and California. The president can win without the electoral votes of the South because the northern black votes located in the cities have become a balance of power factor in presidential elections. With the exception of Richard Nixon, all victorious presidents since 1936 have carried the black electorate of the northern central cities. Truman's victory in 1948 was strongly affected by the urban black populace in the North, as was Kennedy's victory in 1960 and Johnson's landslide in 1964. The concentration of the black electorate has made it tremendously powerful and useful to presidential candidates. Although Nixon achieved victory without the black vote, his victory came in the midst of the disintegration of the Democrats. Whether blacks will again prove significant in presidential elections remains to be seen. The indications are that the black electorate alone cannot defeat presidential candidates. The black vote seems to be effective only within the context of a coalition with other elements in the American electorate at large. For example, Nixon's election in 1968 proved that a presidential candidate could ignore the northern black vote by appealing to the South and by being anti-civil rights. While many political analysts have argued that the northern black vote was a balance of power factor in national elections, the Nixon strategy illuminated the loopholes in the theory.

In regard to public policy and presidential politics, the black electorate seems more significant. Beginning with Franklin D. Roosevelt, certain advances have emanated from the office of the chief executive. Roosevelt issued an executive order banning discrimination in defense industries holding federal contracts. That executive order also established a Fair Employment Practices Commission to ensure fair employment for blacks. Truman followed with an executive order banning discrimination and segregation in the armed service. Then Eisenhower employed federal troops at Little Rock to enforce the Supreme Court's 1954 integration decision. After "Ike," Kennedy issued an executive order banning segregation and discrimination in new FHA and VA financed housing. Finally, Johnson used his political acumen to get Congress to pass two civil rights bills, and a third one after the assassination of Dr. Martin Luther King, Jr. Despite numerous executive orders and political action, however, one can always argue over whether action was taken because of the power of the black electorate or because of a moral commitment; there is no clear line here between cause and effect. Even though one cannot gauge with certainty the influence of the black electorate upon the presidential policies, one can make some kind of commitment on the relationship between presidential black appointments and the black electorate.

The recent presidential policy of black political appointment seems to evolve directly out of the political power of the black electorate.[29] The spectacular appointments of blacks to the Cabinet, Supreme Court, Federal Reserve Board, District of Columbia mayorship, ambassadorial posts, and the United States Information Agency is definitely a technique for placating the black electorate. Though the appointment of blacks to high level federal positions does not improve the economic, educational or political condition of the black masses, they are nevertheless impressive to the black people.[30] Such appointments revitalize the American dream and reawaken the black community to the possibility that with significant individual achievement, the "American dream" is still workable. These positions, however, are usually more symbolic, honorific, and promotional than substantive and meaningful. Moreover, many governmental agencies can go on without blacks being appointed to them. Therefore, in the final analysis, black political appointments by presidents may be a means of improving the personal image of the president and continuing the black electorate's support for him and his party.

Thus, the impact of the black electorate upon the Presidency tends to coincide with presidential elections and can be crucial if a meaningful alliance can be formed with other elements in society.

In retrospect, some of the problems of obtaining the vote, registering, and casting the ballot are still present, and the problem of meaningfully influencing public policy and obtaining equality via the ballot has not yet been fully solved. The former problem still exists in the South and in the North, in areas of party control and machine control, while the latter problems are both temporal and legislative. Here the rise of elections at large and the rise of metropolitanism definitely act as devices to dilute the black vote. In sum, the black electorate is in the process of becoming. It is now between the past and the future. For example, whether or not the Voting Rights Act is extended again in 1975 will have a great effect upon the continuing pattern of voting behavior of black Americans.

[29] Chuck Stone, *Black Political Power in America* (Indianapolis: Bobbs-Merrill Company, 1968), p. 66. For additional information see James H. Hamilton, *Negro Suffrage and Congressional Representation* (New York: Vintage Press, 1910).

[30] Stone, *op. cit.,* p. 61.

VI

Blacks and the Republican Party

Ever since its founding, black people have been involved with the Republican party. At first, however, their attitude toward the new party was one of cautious optimism. This was because the Republican party, in the beginning, was not an antislavery political party. The party proposed not to interfere with slavery where it existed and did not try to attract black voters or to interest the American people in extending the franchise to blacks. It did, however, oppose the extension of slavery by elaborating the slogan of "no slavery outside the slave states." Moreover, in a few northern and western states the Republicans proposed legislation that would have granted suffrage to all regardless of color. In this, however, they met with little success; for the Democrats succeeded in restricting suffrage rights to white males.

BRIEF HISTORY

As early as August 26, 1856, a group of black political abolitionists meeting in Boston resolved that "the colored citizens of Boston will support with our voices and votes, John C. Frémont of California as President of the United States and William L. Dayton of New Jersey as Vice President."[1] The group added, however, that "we do not pledge ourselves to go further with the Republicans than the Republicans will go with us." By 1858, even this wariness had largely disappeared. In that year, a black suffrage convention met in Troy, New York, and advised "the eleven thousand colored voters of this state to concentrate their strength upon the Republican ticket for governor."[2] Still in 1860, the major black leader of the pre-Civil War period could advise his readers that the Republican convention and platform of 1860 were even more unsatisfactory to black people than those of 1856, and that 10,000 votes for Gerrit Smith, the

[1] *The Liberator*, September 5, 1856.
[2] *The Liberator*, October 1, 1858.

84

Liberty party candidate, "would do more for the abolition of slavery than two million for Lincoln." As the campaign developed, however, and Lincoln's thoughts on blacks in America changed, Frederick Douglass's position toward the Republicans changed also. He ended up campaigning for Lincoln and the Republican party in Wisconsin, Michigan, and Iowa. Many blacks sympathized with the Lincoln ticket, and those who could vote were reported to have voted for it. According to Benjamin Quarles, "... by election time in 1860 the Negro vote was almost solidly Republican."[3]

However, the ambivalent policy of the Republicans toward blacks continued after Lincoln's election. Even after the secession of South Carolina in December, 1860, there was hope that the seceding state would return. Even the firing on Fort Sumter did not bring an immediate emancipation policy by Republicans. Lincoln vacillated until January 1863, and even then the proclamation was limited in its applications. Moreover, Lincoln's vacillating policy had added new schisms to those he inherited with the many factions within the party itself. Some Republicans favored the abolition of slavery, others favored the nonextension of slavery and still others favored colonization. But, with the issuance of the proclamation the party seemed to have changed, and many of the factions united behind Lincoln's positions. But Lincoln's reconstruction policy once again brought to the forefront old antagonism and jealousies. Many Republicans hoped for education, the ballot, and land; others had numerous or sundry combinations of these ideas, and Lincoln's indefinite stand caused some factionalization.

These antagonisms and jealousies caused an intraparty struggle over the 1864 presidential nomination. Many free blacks felt by then that Lincoln showed a great deal of reluctance and had refused to take decisive action against slavery.[4] Furthermore, Lincoln's reconstruction policy, "which would restore the former rebels to power and leave the freedmen little more than a bean on the soil of his old mates," deeply angered black militants. Several of them met with a group of white abolitionists in Cleveland on May 3, 1864, to nominate John C. Frémont for the presidency on an equal rights platform for southern blacks. However, when Democrats nominated General George B. McClellan for president on an antiemancipation peace platform, Frémont withdrew, and blacks, North and South, endorsed Lincoln. Nevertheless, even after Lincoln's election and his assassination some

[3] For a complete analysis of the early black Republicans, see H. Walton, Jr., "Black Republicans before the Civil War, 1854-1860," paper presented at the 55th annual meeting of the Association for the Study of Negro Life and History (Philadelphia, October, 1970).

[4] James M. McPherson, The Negro's Civil War (New York: Pantheon Books, 1965), pp. 300-307.

blacks continued to express concern over his cautious policies. This attitude was destined to change, however.

In February, 1865, even before congressional Reconstruction began to change black attitudes, a Republican Supreme Court permitted the first black man to practice before it. In the following year, Charles L. Mitchell, a black Republican, was elected to the legislative assembly in Massachusetts. Although these positions were meaningful and important for black public opinion, the problem of black suffrage remained unsolved. To solve it, blacks throughout the North organized themselves into Equal Rights Leagues to agitate for the return or the extension of suffrage rights. Frederick Douglass became national president of the Equal Rights League and in this capacity approached politicians to persuade them to grant blacks national or state suffrage rights. Their first reactions, however, were mixed.

Lincoln at first was ambiguous, but he changed to a position favoring limited black suffrage based on merit, education, etc. After Lincoln's assassination, Andrew Johnson met with a black equal rights delegation led by Douglass.[5] They tried to enlist Johnson's support in their struggle for the franchise, but he spurned their attempts and argued that blacks should not be given the ballot in the South because it would simply renew antagonism between himself and his old enemies, the poor whites. After leaving the White House, however, the Douglass delegates were granted an interview with the radical Republican congressmen, who proved sympathetic.

Ten days later, Congress passed an extension of the Freedmen Bureau that Johnson in turn vetoed. This was the beginning of the end of presidential reconstruction. Increasingly, the congressional radicals took control of Reconstruction policies[6] and in so doing gained more and more support from the black masses.

If, before that, black participation and mobility in the Republican party had moved black public opinion toward a positive attitude toward the Republicans, then the activities of the radical congressional Republicans increased the positive attitude of blacks toward the party.

The passage of the Thirteenth Amendment in 1865, the passage of a bill granting blacks the right to vote in the District of Columbia in 1867, and the passage of the Fourteenth Amendment in 1869 were all pluses for Republicanism. On the national level at least, these were all firsts. Meanwhile, the Republicans worked for black enfranchisement in almost all the northern and western states. In state after state they failed. Time and again, the right to vote was denied blacks in the northern states. Still, time and

    [5] Philip S. Foner, ed., *The Life and Writings of Frederick Douglass* (New York: International Publishers, 1955), IV, 21.
    [6] Franklin L. Burdette, *The Republican Party* (Princeton, N.J.: D. Van Nostrand Company, 1968), pp. 39–42.

again, the Republicans resubmitted the question of black suffrage either for legislative or popular considerations.

After the election of 1868, however, the black suffrage issue became a national matter. And with it a major dilemma arrived. Numerous historians since Reconstruction have argued that Republicans supported the Fifteenth Amendment because it was to their advantage to do so. "To Radical leaders of the Republican Party," black enfranchisement "clearly appeared a promising means of party aggrandisement; it became essential to the perpetuation of their power."[7] It was not the southern black electorate that the Republicans desired, but the northern one.[8]

Some historians argue that the Republicans gave blacks the right to vote in order to perpetuate themselves in power. Others argue that the Republicans championed black rights out of inherent idealism, and that they had consistently promoted it in numerous northern states before the Civil War. They argue further that enfranchised blacks hurt the party more than they helped it. The opposite side, of course, claims that enfranchised blacks helped the party. The controversy over motivation continues and the problem of what caused the Republicans to support black suffrage rights still remains unsolved in modern historical literature. There is much data to support both positions and one might say that it was both expediency and idealism that motivated the Republicans to secure the passage and ratification of the Fifteenth Amendment, which granted blacks the right to vote on March 30, 1870.

With the constitutional right to suffrage secured, blacks became Republicans. The activities of Republicans in Congress endeared the party to blacks. If, moreover, the Republicans "were endeavoring to increase the political status of blacks, the Democrats were endeavoring to decrease it or, at most, to preserve the status quo." In short, congressional Republicans pushed through Reconstruction, with the beginning of which black politicians and politics came alive. Black Republicans went to the Senate and the House of Representatives, to governors' mansions, courts, state departments of education, and ambassadorial posts, to aldermen, judgeships, and to numerous positions of power throughout the South and the North. Nevertheless, though the Republican party created necessary and sufficient conditions for black Reconstruction, it also created the conditions that sounded its death knell seven years later. In the disputed election of 1876

[7] LaWanda and John H. Cox, "Negro Suffrage and Republican Politics: The Problem of Motivation in Reconstruction Historiography," in Frank Gatell and Allen Weinstein, eds., *American Themes: Essays in Historiography* (New York: Oxford University Press, 1968), p. 233.

[8] William Gillette, *The Right to Vote: Politics and the Passage of the Fifteenth Amendment* (Baltimore: Johns Hopkins Press, 1969), p. 167.

black politics, North and South, came to a sudden halt. Republican expediency this time definitely curtailed black suffrage.[9]

Rutherford B. Hayes, the Republican presidential candidate in 1876, offered a compromise to the southern states in exchange for their electoral votes in the disputed election. The compromise offered a withdrawal of the remaining federal troops from the region and a "let alone" policy in regard to blacks in the political life of the region.[10] The compromise was accepted and Hayes was inaugurated the next year. And with Hayes' inauguration the affinity between blacks and Republicans began to grow strained. The Republican attitude toward blacks, North and South, began to change.

In the South after the compromise of 1877 the Democratic party became the party of white supremacy; the Republican party was labelled the "nigger party." In order to rebuild the party in the South successive Republican presidents pursued any policy that would draw more whites into it, but the only effect of these tactics was to alienate black Republicans. By 1880, the Republican party in each of the old states of the Confederacy was involved in an intraparty conflict. White Republicans were working to oust blacks, and blacks were struggling to preserve their remaining vestige of power and patronage. During this struggle the white faction became known as the Lily White Republicans, and the black faction as the Black and Tan Republicans. Conflict between these groups continued until about 1956.

THE ROOTS OF BLACK AND TAN REPUBLICANISM

To discuss in its entirety the conflict between the Black and Taners and the Lily Whites would require a book in itself. We shall focus here on the tactics each group employed on the local, state, and national levels to suppress, quell, or eliminate the other.[11]

When the radical Republicans in Congress engineered the passage of the Fifteenth Amendment in 1870, they in effect welded southern black loyalty to the Republican party. Black Republicans in the South came alive. In addition, party loyalists—Union Leaguers, Carpetbaggers, and Scalawags—helped blacks to vote for the party, or at least saw to it that blacks supported the party of liberation. In this manner, southern whites and blacks became part of the same political organization.

Southern and northern whites became the leaders in the southern Republican party circles not only by default but because the number of

---

[9] See Paul Haworth, *The Hayes-Tilden Disputed Election of 1876* (New York: Russell and Russell, 1966).

[10] Rayford W. Logan, *The Betrayal of the Negro* (New York: Collier Books, 1965), p. 26.

[11] For a brief discussion of the Black and Tans, see Hanes Walton, Jr., *Black Political Parties: A Historical and Political Analysis* (New York: Free Press, 1972). For the first comprehensive study of the Black and Tan Republicans in each state, see my forthcoming book, *The Politics of the Black and Tan Republicans*.

educated and politically sophisticated black leaders was not sizable. More-over, these missionary whites felt it was part of their duty to lead the black electorate in the proper manner. Generally speaking, the Republican party in each southern state had a majority of whites in the top party posts and a limited number of blacks, though in most cases the newly enfranchised blacks furnished the electoral muscle. This is why southern white Demo-crats stigmatized the Republican party as the "Nigger party" and their party as the white man's party.[12]

With the Compromise of 1877 things changed in the South. A movement was begun to make the region a one-party area, where the Democratic party, or the party of white supremacy, would dominate. Any attempt to establish such a political structure would have to destroy or remove the "Nigger party." Trouble came from those whites who had attained power through the Republican party. The best they could look forward to in the Democratic party were positions as rank-and-file members; promotion to top party echelons would not be easy for these "turncoats" who had worked in the "Nigger party," and faced with the loss of power, prestige, and influence, many remained in the Republican party. Those who did sought to purge the party of its black element. In Texas, around 1880, white Republicans began to form lily-white Republican clubs in the hope that this would save the party, or at least bring some more whites into its ranks.

The problem of saving the Republican party in the South perplexed Republican presidents also. Essentially, they wanted to find some way of drawing whites back into the party, and at the same time retain the black vote.[13] A successful solution was never found, though successive Republi-can presidents, from Hayes to Hoover, did their best to find one.

The contested election of 1876 told Republican leaders that something had to be done to ingratiate the Republican party to southern whites. The compromise agreement of 1877 by Republican candidate Hayes was an early attempt to pacify southern whites and reconcile the North and the South. When the compromise only strengthened the hands of the Demo-crats, Hayes adopted a "let alone" policy toward the South, which was even more conciliatory, and which let the South solve its race problem in whatever way it deemed necessary. This, however, gave the Democrats complete control of the region and caused skepticism among black Repub-licans.

James A. Garfield succeeded Hayes, but was assassinated shortly after

[12] Forrest G. Wood, *Black Scare: The Racist Response to Emancipation and Reconstruc-tion* (Berkeley: University of California Press, 1960), pp. 18-20.

[13] Vincent DeSantis, "The Republican Party and the Southern Negro, 1877-1897," *Journal of Negro History*, XLV (April, 1960), 71-73. See also his *Republicans Face the Southern Question: The New Departure Years, 1877-1897* (Baltimore: Johns Hopkins University Press, 1959).

taking office. Garfield's successor, Chester A. Arthur, inherited the problem. Hayes had suggested that native whites should head the Republican party in the South. To make the party more acceptable to white southerners, he adopted a conciliatory policy toward them. The intent or purpose of his policy failed, however.

By the time Arthur took office an intraparty conflict was developing within the Democratic party. Numerous Democrats, mostly from rebels, bolted from the party and assumed such names as the Readjusters, the Grangers, the Funders, the Independents, the Greenbackers, Union Laborites, etc. In fact, these independents adopted every possible name except Republican. They wanted no association with the "Nigger party."

It was on these new political developments that Arthur based his hopes. He felt that this split in the Democratic ranks represented the last chance to rejuvenate the southern Republican party, and therefore he gave full recognition and support to the Independent Democratic politicians as new leaders of the southern Republican party.[14] Moreover, he unreservedly approved of cooperation between the southern Republicans and these Independent Democrats. Arthur hoped to increase the southern Republican vote so that a Republican Congress would be elected in 1882, and a southern delegation to the National Republican Convention would nominate him and help elect him in 1884.

The pursuit of his policy, however, had some reverse effects. In supporting the Independent Democrats Arthur gave considerable patronage to southern Democrats at the expense of black Republicans. Moreover, he overlooked regular black Republican leaders and consulted with the independent whites. The neglect of this common courtesy caused much concern among black Republican leaders in the North and South.

In addition, black Republican leaders such as party chairmen were pressured to vacate their positions so that whites could assume them. In Georgia, for instance, W. A. Pledger, the black state Republican chairman, was offered a permanent patronage position if he would give up his chairmanship to a white independent, Emory Spear.[15]

Arthur's southern policy failed. A Republican Congress was not elected in 1882, and a Democrat won the presidency in 1884. His policy dismayed and alienated black Republicans because it ousted them from the party leadership in their states, and gave them the same impression that Hayes's policy had given them—i.e., that their race had been abandoned by the Republican party.

[14] Vincent DeSantis, "Negro Dissatisfaction with Republican Policy in the South, 1882–1884," *Journal of Negro History*, XLVI (April, 1961), 149–150. See also Stanley P. Hirshson, *Farewell to the Bloody Shirt: Northern Republicans and the Southern Negro, 1877-1893* (Bloomington: Indiana University Press, 1962).

[15] *Ibid.* See also Oliver Hall Shadgett, *The Republican Party in Georgia: From Reconstruction through 1900* (Athens, Ga.: University of Georgia Press, 1964), pp. 74–75, 84–89.

When the Republicans returned to power with Benjamin Harrison in 1889, Lily White clubs abounded throughout the southern states. And they had intensified their efforts to save the party because southern Democrats received much help in eliminating the Democratic bolters under Cleveland's administration. Thus, the Lily White clubs were an attempt to purify the party by removing its black elements. These attempts at purification put Harrison in a difficult position. He did not know what policy to follow. He was faced with two clearly defined Republican factions and had inherited a southern policy of failure from Hayes and Arthur. Harrison finally initiated a new policy, actually a modification of the old one. In regard to southern whites, he continued the patronage policy of Arthur and the let alone policy of Hayes, but he went one step further. Harrison attempted at the same time to woo southern whites and to aid black Republicans. He gave numerous black Republicans low political appointments and fostered a bill to supervise federal elections that became known as the "force bill."

Harrison's tactics and policies supported the factionalism within the southern Republican party that Hayes and Arthur had developed. McKinley then went further; he actually played one faction off against the other for political self-interest. Prior to the Republican national convention, McKinley sent his political manager, Mark Hanna, through the South to secure or buy pledges from one faction or the other to support McKinley's nomination for the presidency at the national convention. In some states Hanna obtained the backing of the Black and Tan delegation and in others he obtained the backing of Lily Whites. After McKinley's election he rewarded with considerable patronage that faction or group in the state that had supported him prior to and at the convention.

Subsequent Republican presidential candidates learned from McKinley's tactic, and adopted a policy of playing off the two factions against each other to secure their nomination; if elected, they rewarded the supporting group with small bits of patronage.

Most Republican presidents after McKinley gave up trying to forge a viable Republican party in the South. First of all, after 1890, eight southern states through constitutional revision disfranchised the chief supporter of the southern Republican party, the black voter. Moreover, at its conventions the Democratic party thoroughly consolidated and secured itself in the region. Democratic hegemony was to prevail in the South until at least 1964. Republicanism in the South was dying.

Secondly, the infight between Taft and Roosevelt in the Republican party created a new political organization, the "Bull Moose" Progressive party of 1912, which greatly hampered the Republicans nationally. Finally—the Democrats, at least in the North—began to move toward the

black electorate. In short, Republican inertia began to give blacks reasons
to seek alternatives.

The factionalism of the southern Republicans was useful only in convention politics, since endorsement by one or the other faction might insure
the party's nomination. In 1928, Herbert Hoover finally capitulated to Lily
Whiteism after being elected, because the number of black voters in the
South and the increasing race prejudice and discrimination in America
dictated dropping the southern black Republicans as expendable. White
Republicans became the order of the day.

At national conventions, the Lily Whites and Black and Tans vied with
each other for control over state patronage, the right to be seated, the right
to be designated as the regular party in the state, and the chairmanship of
the particular state committees. In order to secure these things, each group
attempted to persuade, convince, or prove to the various presidential candidates and to credential committees that theirs was the one to support. To
prove their point and attain their goal the Black and Tans employed a
variety of tactics: legalism, electioneering, propaganda, coalescing, pressure, and even violence.

In 1920, for instance, the Texas Black and Tans nominated their own
candidate for president when they failed to get a seat at the 1920 national
convention. In the election, they cast 27,000 votes for their electors, instead
of for Harding hoping that in 1924 they could obtain recognition and seats
at the national convention.

The principal tactic of the Black and Tans in Louisiana was legalism.
The party fought over four major suits to continue its viability and to hold
numerous patronage posts, as well as the right to be the regular Republican
party in the state.

In Georgia the politics of the Black and Tans was coalition. The blacks
agreed to coalesce with the Lily White organization if black Republicans
would receive appointment to minor political positions throughout the state
as custom collectors, etc.

In Virginia the political tactics of the Black and Tans was both coalition
and electioneering. In 1921 black Republicans ran their own candidate for
governor, and he received 5,230 votes. Later a few remaining voters merged
with the Lily Whites for a few minor political offices, while some switched
parties and joined the Democratic Byrd machine.

On the national level, the Black and Tans involved themselves in preconvention and convention politics. In order to achieve recognition and
state patronage, Black and Tan groups had to pick the right candidate to
support for nomination. If that candidate won the nomination, victory was
theirs. If he lost, then their only hope lay with the credentials committee,
where elaborate briefs and persuasion were employed to secure seats. For
example, the Black and Tan faction, led by Norris Cuney, supported

William B. Allison for the presidency at the national convention; the Lily Whites supported McKinley. McKinley won, and the Black and Tan faction's quest for power and recognition suffered. If the credentials committee was sympathetic or had received great support in their behalf, the Black and Tan delegation was seated. If not, the Lily Whites achieved power.

Minor Black and Tan challenges continued until 1956, but Herbert Hoover's capitulation to Lily Whites spelled doom for the Black and Tan faction. In most southern states the organization went into decline. Moreover, by 1936 the social and economic policies of Roosevelt's New Deal had drawn most blacks into the Democratic party. In short, Hoover's lily-whiteism and the coming of the New Deal ended Black and Tan Republicanism.

BLACKS AND SOUTHERN REPUBLICANISM

Since Roosevelt's election in 1932 and the advent of the New Deal, Democratic hegemony over national politics has been almost complete. The only exceptions are the Eisenhower and Nixon administrations. Otherwise, many blacks doubt the continued viability of the Republican party.[16] Although Eisenhower had landslide victories, it was still believed that the Democratic hegemony remained intact. If southern blacks may have made a temporary shift to Republicanism during the 1956 election, they made a complete move back to the Democratic party in 1960 and 1964.[17]

Barry Goldwater's conservatism, states' rights advocacy, and anti-civil rights posture alienated blacks. There was not a single black among any of the Republican delegations from the deep South. "Nor did the Goldwaterites in the subregion display any real interest in cultivating the Negro vote."[18]

In explaining why there were no black Republicans "in the Georgia delegation," the state chairman emphasized that "the only significance this has is that . . . the leadership . . . that won . . . are people who believe in the philosophy expressed by Senator Goldwater, and there have not been many or any Negroes in the forefront of this effort." The truth of the matter is that even before Goldwater's candidacy blacks in the South did not have a

[16] See Louis Harris, *Is There a Republican Majority?* (New York: Harper and Brothers, 1954).

[17] For works on the impact of the Goldwater candidacy on the black Republican party in the South, see B. Baseman and R. T. Huckshorn, eds., *Republican Politics: The 1964 Campaign and Its Aftermath for the Party* (New York: Frederick A. Praeger, 1968); Stephen Hess and David S. Breda, *The Republican Establishment* (New York: Harper and Row, 1967); and John H. Kessel, *The Goldwater Coalition Republican Strategies in 1964* (Indianapolis: Bobbs-Merrill Company, 1968).

[18] Bernard Baseman, "Deep South Republicans: Profits and Positions," in Baseman and Huckshorn, *op. cit.*, p. 108.

favorable opinion of the Republican party.[19] Goldwaterism further destroyed any overtures toward Republicanism in general. However, the great influx of white supremacists into the party in 1964 and thereafter indicates the party's move toward a states' rights strategy rather than toward a policy of trying to rebuild a party based on both races.[20]

With Nixon's election in 1968 the Republican party basically continued its southern strategy of appeal to whites mainly. That Nixon is continuing the Goldwater formula of appeasing the South is evident from his choice of Spiro T. Agnew as his running mate, his nomination of southerners to the Supreme Court, and his easing of school desegregation guidelines. Blacks in the South are still not invited into the southern Republican councils nor are they able to participate because of the party's basic adherence to states' rights, the new guise for white supremacy. Whether the party will tamper with this winning formula of leaving blacks out remains to be seen, especially in light of the rising black electorate in the region.

BLACKS AND NORTHERN REPUBLICANISM

Black and Tan Republicans were not a meaningful factor in northern Republican politics, though, like their southern counterparts, northern Republicans did suffer from race prejudice and did engage in discriminatory practices.[21] Generally, northern Republicans supported black suffrage throughout the North,[22] but it was the black vote they cherished, not the black man. To secure this vote, northern Republicans used two means. First, they pointed to their record regarding emancipation, the three Civil War amendments, and what they were doing to help southern blacks. They felt that their national record would convince the northern black to cast his vote their way.

Secondly, the northern Republicans instituted party control over the black electorate. By granting minor offices and little bits of patronage here and there, they tied black political leaders to the party. In other instances, where black Republicans tried to break loose and establish some independence, they found Republican public officials and party members solidly against them. In some northern states they could not file for candidacy, they could not campaign, and they could not participate in party meetings.

[19] Donald R. Matthews and James W. Prothro, "Southern Images of Political Parties: An Analysis of White and Negro Attitudes," *Journal of Politics* (1964), pp. 82-111.
[20] See Gosman, *op. cit.,* p. 110-111. And his *Five States for Goldwater* (Alabama: University of Alabama Press, 1968).
[21] Leslie Fishel, Jr., "Northern Prejudice and Negro Suffrage, 1862-1870," *Journal of Negro History,* XXXIX (January, 1954), 8-26; and "The Negro in Northern Politics, 1870-1900," *Mississippi Valley Historical Review,* XLII (December, 1955), 466-489.
[22] Edgar A. Toppin, "Negro Emancipation in Historic Retrospect: The Negro Suffrage Issue in Post Bellum Ohio Politics," *Journal of Human Relations,* Winter, 1963, pp. 237-246.

In effect, they were ostracized, and ostracism meant political death, because the Democratic party also shunned blacks, and refused to permit them in any level of that party's hierarchy.

The Democratic party did not seek blacks, and before 1936 only one black (seated as a substitute in 1924) was ever permitted in the national Democratic convention. In short, there was not only an absence of blacks from Democratic ranks, "but any white man who suggested reforms in the Democratic party which would make [black] delegates possible was referred to by the opprobrious term 'Nigger lover,' and the reformer's place was likely to be occupied by another white man in subsequent conventions."

But on this score, northern Republicans were not much better. Although southern black delegates went to the national Republican convention starting in 1868, not a single black delegate was chosen from the North to attend the Republican National Convention until 1916.

Because alternatives were lacking, blacks would have voted for the northern Republicans anyway, despite their prejudice and party control. Patronage and party control merely insured the matter. Blacks became increasingly independent politically, however, and the Democrats less reluctant to accept them into their ranks. Together, these circumstances promoted the decline of black Republicanism.

Republican intransigence, race prejudice, poor political rewards to blacks, and an absolute attitude about how the black vote would be cast caused or at least laid the foundations for a black exodus from the party. At first this exodus on the part of blacks came in independent movements, candidates, and politics. Although they failed, they started a trend, for many blacks began to accept Democratic nomination for office. And as each presidential candidate passed the black issue by, and as the northern white Republicans grew more and more disinterested, black Republicanism waned.

Coupled with this push effect was the pull effect of the Democrats. In several northern localities, the Democratic party began to accept blacks, and when a Democratic candidate won the presidency in 1884, the few black Democrats that existed "found themselves suddenly in the novel position of race spokesman." This drew more blacks to the party for a short while until on the national level Republicans returned to power, when some blacks returned to the fold and others flirted with the Prohibitionist party and the national Afro-American League. By 1900 black Republicanism had reached a new low. The party's hold almost came to a halt. The effect of black migration to the northern ghetto began to change black political allegiance, but it became highly significant.

In the northern cities the basis of new political machines and clubs became almost entirely Democratic in nature. The success of these newly emerging machines depended in large part on new sources of electoral power, and the newly arriving immigrants and blacks gave the machines their sought-after viability. New blacks were enlisted in the now emerging Democratic political machine. In a word, expediency added the new blacks to the emerging Democratic organizations. Prejudice and racism were secondary to the push for power, control, and aggrandizement. Moreover, in these new political machines, blacks rose to new heights. However, the Republican party during the era of migration did not respond to the needs of the newly arriving blacks nor to the established black political allegiance. The blacks slowly began to find better opportunities via the Democratic machine rather than in the old Republican hegemony.[23] But if the Republicans failed to relate to black problems on the local level in the North, they likewise did even less on the national level. Successive Republican national presidents did little to alleviate the plight of the black Republicans. With nothing being done on the local, state, or national level, it became quite obvious that northern black Republicans, like their southern brethren, were a dying breed.

The factional quarrels of Republicans, North and South, the Progressive split of 1912, Democratic victories in national, state, and local elections, as well as the personal jealousies and conflicts in the black community aided this rapid demise. Although Oscar DePriest and other notable blacks were elected to new positions of power via the Republican label, the sway of political machines and the pull of New Deal welfarism eclipsed northern black Republicans.

Generally speaking, the Republican party, especially after the turn of the century, failed to win enough state and local elections to capture the allegiance of younger blacks. Most younger blacks in the North moved either into the Democratic party or other minor parties. With so few recruits, the old line black Republican leaders were left in unchallenged control of the party's machinery.

In New York, for instance, only one black Republican has won any elective office since the 1930s.[24] Twenty years later the black Republicans numbered little more than a dozen out of more than one hundred elected public officials in New York City.

The picture was about the same elsewhere in the North. From 1932 through 1936 thirty-seven blacks were elected to state legislatures; twenty-one were Republicans.

[23] For this trend see Oscar Glanz, "The Negro Voter in Northern Industrial Cities," *Western Political Quarterly,* XIII (December, 1960), 999-1010; Harold F. Gosnell, "The Negro Voter in Northern Cities," *National Municipal Review,* XXX (1941), 264-267, 278.

[24] Joyce Gelb, "Black Republicans in New York: A Minority Group in a Minority," paper presented at the 54th annual meeting of the Association for the Study of Negro Life and History, October 8, 1969, p. 1. For a later study see her "The Role of Negro Politicians in the Democratic, Republican, and Liberal Parties of New York City" (unpublished Ph.D. dissertation, New York University, 1969).

Furthermore, if public offices were hard for black Republicans to obtain, patronage was nonexistent. Money just to keep the party office open had to be paid by loyal party followers and leaders. Black Republicans had to provide for their own financial existence.

SUMMARY

Besides aging and lack of public offices and patronage, the relationship between local black organizations and the county, state, and national organizations is bad. Since party rewards go to areas and local organizations that are generally victorious, black Republican organizations get very few, and this in turn insures low productivity in electoral victories. Moreover, victorious Republican leaders on the state and local levels have tended to overlook the aged, morbid, and defunct black Republican organization. Once elected, these men establish a policy of building up another Republican organization in the different black communities without consulting the old line black Republican present. This means not only several competing black Republican organizations in one area, but overlapping, duplication, and incessant hostilities.

Hoover capitulated to Lily White Republicans by recognizing and condoning the movement throughout the South. He attempted to appoint a racist judge from North Carolina to the Supreme Court and even condoned the segregation of black Gold Star mothers from the whites when they planned a visit to the graves of their sons who had fallen in France during World War I. Hoover's policies served to bolster the idea that Republicans were prejudiced and biased. To blacks it seemed a withdrawal from the black community. Hence, Republican policies and the Democratic New Deal caused a major shift in black political allegiance from the 1930s to the mid-1940s.

Eisenhower's second election brought many blacks back into the Republican camp. Even Adam Clayton Powell in Harlem changed his party from Democratic to Republican and still won the election. In 1960, however, the black vote shifted back to the Democrats because of their civil rights outlook. It has stayed mainly with them since then. The racial appeal of Barry Goldwater and Nixon's law and order campaign further stifled the growth of northern and southern black Republicanism.

The Goldwater candidacy raised once again the Lily White specter of Hoover under the guise of anti-civil rights. His appeal to "in your heart you know that I am right" and the generally conservative trend of his speeches caused traditional black Republican communities in the North to go totally Democratic.[25] Goldwater's conservatism further weakened the

[25] George K. Hesslink, *Black Neighbors: Negroes in a Northern Rural Community* (Indianapolis: Bobbs-Merrill Company, 1968), pp. 98–109.

Republican image in the black community. And Nixon's policies of law and order, a lower rate of school desegregation, and an attempt to appoint southern white conservatives to the Supreme Court are not rebuilding the party's image among the black electorate.[26] Although the election of a black Republican senator, the first from a white constituency in the North, is a sign from the Republican liberals, it is still not a sign of acceptance by the northern blacks of a new Republican party allegiance.

In New York, both Governor Nelson Rockefeller and Mayor John Lindsay are guilty of this tactic. To help launch their rebuilding programs, each has appointed prominent blacks from outside the New York community, such as Jackie Robinson, James Meredith, and James Farmer. These men have no roots in the black community, however, and with no real roots in the community, these rebuilding programs do little in rebuilding the black Republican allegiance, and more in building personal coalitions.[27] And if New York is somewhat typical, then little was taking place for northern black Republicans, and they had little chance to move or progress.

In fact, North and South, the Republican party has lost the majority of its black supporters, and is doing little by way of attempting to recapture them. The party is still waiting for a policy to reconcile blacks and whites, North and South.

[26] J. I. Scott, "The President and the Supreme Court: Two-Up, Two-Down," *Negro Educational Review*, XXI (January, 1970), 2-4.

[27] See Robert S. Sigel, "Race and Religion as Factors in the Kennedy Victory in Detroit, 1960," *Journal of Negro Education*, XXXI (Fall, 1962), 436-447.

VII

Blacks and the
Democratic Party

Of the relationship between blacks and the Democratic party, political analyst Samuel Lubell states that "the economical" appeal of the New Deal ... broke the Negro's Republicanism and moved him into the Democratic party."[1] This was due, he feels, to the fact that "over the past half century, when major shifts of power have occurred from one party to another, Negroes generally have lagged one election behind the rest of the nation."[2] Blacks broke from the Republicans not in 1932, but in 1936.

Commenting on the same relationship, black historian Henry Lee Moon wrote, "by 1936, after four years of the New Deal, colored voters in the urban centers of the North and East had caught up with the procession. The mass migration out of the Republican camp was in response to the Roosevelt program which blacks were convinced ... made an effort to meet some of their urgent needs."[3]

Professor Leslie Fishel has also commented that "by midway through his first term, FDR had captured the admiration and affection of the Negro people and with that, their votes ... during the campaign of 1936 ... the second Roosevelt ... weaned the Negro away from the Republican party."[4] Gunnar Myrdal, a Swedish economist, has observed that "when the New Deal relieved the economic plight of the Negro during the depression ... Negroes began shifting to the Democratic party in large numbers."[5] A black journalist, Chuck Stone, following these leaders, argued that "by 1936, Negroes, economically benefited by the employment and welfare policies of the New Deal, began to shift their votes to the Democrats."[6]

[1] Samuel Lubell, *Black and White: Test of a Nation* (New York: Harper and Row, 1964), p. 47.
[2] *Ibid.*, p. 46.
[3] Henry Lee Moon, *Balance of Power: The Negro Vote* (New York: Doubleday and Company, 1948), p. 18.
[4] Leslie H. Fishel, Jr., "The Negro in the New Deal," in Bernard Sternsher, ed., *The Negro in Depression and War* (Chicago: Quadrangle Books, 1969), p. 9.
[5] Gunnar Myrdal, *An American Dilemma*, 2nd ed. (New York: Harper and Row, 1962), p. 494.
[6] Chuck Stone, *Black Political Power in America* (Indianapolis: Bobbs-Merrill Company,

99

Finally, Elbert Lee Tatum, a black political scientist, has argued that "the economic crisis which occurred in 1929, brought the Negro into the Democratic fold as much as any single event."[7]

These and other observers and analysts have all credited the New Deal with causing blacks overwhelmingly and instantaneously to drop their Republicanism. What these explanations and analyses overlook, however, is that a black union with the Democratic party commenced, at least on the local level, long before the New Deal. This shift began at first in the northern cities, slowly moved to the national level, and reached a climax in 1936. In short, blacks did not become Democrats because of the New Deal; they became "national" Democrats during the New Deal.

Heretofore most researchers have played down or ignored this and have made the black shift to the Democratic party seem more dramatic than it was. So far, only one scholar, a black political scientist, Professor Robert Brisbane, *has hinted that the shift of blacks from the Republican party to the Democratic party in 1936 needs reassessment.* He asserts "to deny this suggestion in its entirety would be a mistake,"[8] but in his estimation "the shift of Negro voters from the Republicans to the Democratic party became noticeable in 1920 and continued through the national election of 1936."[9] Indeed, as the foregoing analysis will reveal, in the period between 1920 and 1932 the Republicans steadily lost Negro votes, and Democratic machines continued to gain them. Part of the answer can be seen in the inbred racism of the Democratic party and its slowness in according blacks the same kind of political participation that the Republicans had given them. Black Democrats did not have the esteem and status that black Republicans had. In the eyes of the black community, the Democratic party had a negative image, especially on the national level. As we shall see, however, this image was and had been slowly changing at the grass-roots level.

BLACKS AND THE EARLY DEMOCRATS

From the inception of political parties in America, the predecessors of the present-day Democratic party emerged with or became identified with antiblack positions. This was not true in every locality, but it became the rule rather than the exception. In New York, for instance, the anti-Federalist group, a Democratic predecessor, opposed the granting of suffrage to blacks. Later, the Democratic-Republicans, a coalition of old anti-Federalists, after having captured control of the state legislature, voted to limit and

1968), p. 54.
  [7] Tatum, *op. cit.*, p. 147.
  [8] Robert H. Brisbane, *The Black Vanguard* (Valley Forge, Pa.: Judson Press, 1970), p. 119.
  [9] *Ibid.*, p. 221.

restrict black suffrage rights. Moreover, throughout the North on the issue of abolishing slavery in the different northern states, there was a general opposition by the anit-Federalist or Democratic groupings. And although New York is one example in the early colonial period, the same was true in other northern states such as Pennsylvania, New Jersey, etc.

Later, when the abolitionist issue became one of the chief issues between the North and South and of significant political importance, the predecessors of the Democratic party again took a negative stand. They appeared more conservative and cautious on the issue than did the forerunners of the Republican party. Moreover, during the 1850s while the Republicans supported the extension of suffrage to blacks, in nearly every northern state legislature, the Democrats opposed it and defeated as many bills as possible throughout the North. In fact, the Democratic party was responsible for the failure of northern states to grant even limited suffrage to the black community prior to the Civil War.

In addition to denying suffrage rights to blacks, Democratic candidates like Stephen Douglas popularized the idea of "squatter sovereignty," that culminated in the Lincoln-Douglas debates. Lincoln, the Republican, finally took a limited stand against slavery, but Douglas argued that the question should be left up to the states, not the government. The fact that some Democrats aligned with proslavery movements like the Know-Nothing and American Nationalist parties only served to enhance the parties' negative image. Finally, the image of the Democratic party in the 1860 election as fostering secession completely involved it with a proslavery stance.

Nevertheless, despite its generally proslavery or antiblack position before the Civil War, blacks for one reason or another supported the party or its predecessors in many localities. In Pennsylvania, Ohio, Tennessee, North Carolina, Louisiana, Rhode Island, Michigan, and Massachusetts, blacks cast ballots for individual Democratic candidates who were friendly or sympathetic toward suffrage rights or black emancipation. However, black support for the early predecessors of the Democratic party seemed limited and sporadic at best, and before the Civil War no major alliance existed between the two groups.

During and after the Civil War the Democratic party not only continued but also increased its antiblack stance. In fact, the party became during the war almost a race-baiting organization. To advance itself, the Democratic party, even after the Emancipation Proclamation, launched a bitter racist crusade against the Republican party and the black man. This group of extremists, known as "Copperheads," launched a relentless campaign of racist demagoguery, disseminated pamphlets, newspapers, books, sermons, and outraged oratory against the blacks and Republican party union. They based their findings on "science" as they understood it, and on the Bible.

This group partly succeeded in convincing a majority of white Americans of the supposedly innate inferiority of the blacks or the "wooly-headed Ethiopian."[10]

Horace Greeley wrote that the Copperheads "organized the hatred of the Negro and will continue to inflame the same prejudices and passions to make the government and the war unpopular by identifying both with the cause of the blacks alone."[11] Following Greeley, a prominent Republican writer, Montgomery Wilson, wrote that the first commandment of every Copperhead was "thou shalt hate the Nigger with all thy heart, and with all thy soul, and with all thy mind, and with all thy strength."[12]

In fact, the Democratic party launched the miscegenation issue in the 1864 election in order to defeat the Republican party and the advancement of blacks. In their pamphlets and speeches, the Democrats declared that the Republicans favored mixing, mingling, and intermarriage of the races. At the Democratic national convention in Chicago that year, numerous Democratic speakers attacked the "flat-nosed, wooly-headed, long-headed, cursed of God and damned of man descendants of Africa," as well as "the Negro-loving, Negro-hugging worshippers of old Abe Lincoln."[13] Despite these blatant racial appeals, the Democrats lost the election, and blacks supported the Republicans even though they were not fully satisfied with Lincoln's policies on black freedom.

Having failed in the 1864 election, the Democrats in Congress fought every attempt by the Radical Republicans to introduce and ratify the Fourteenth and Fifteenth amendments. Although the amendments were ratified and passed, Democrats, North, South, and in Congress, did whatever they could to undo the effects of the new amendments. Particularly in the South, the Democrats succeeded in passing the black codes, a new system of rules and regulations that almost forced blacks back into slavery.

Later, southern whites recaptured their state governments from the black Republicans through legal and illegal means. Once in control, they established the Democratic party in the South not only as the party of white supremacy, i.e., the white man's party, but also as the only party in the area. This Democratic hegemony has continued in the South with only four defections, i.e., 1928, 1948, 1964, and 1968 national elections.

During this period of the institutionalization of the Democratic party in the South, the party in the North became strongly segregated and did not permit black participation even when it was offered or desired. In both

---

[10] Forrest G. Wood, *Black Scare: The Racist Response to Emancipation and Reconstruction* (Berkeley: University of California Press, 1968), pp. 1-39.

[11] Quoted in *ibid.*, p. 18. See also "The Copperhead Newspapers and the Negro," *Journal of Negro History,* April, 1935, pp. 131-152.

[12] Quoted in *ibid.*, p. 18.

[13] *Ibid.*, p. 71.

North and South the Democratic party and blacks avoided and shunned each other as much as possible. However, Republican party control and poor patronage policies toward blacks as well as the desire on the part of several Democratic losers to win led to small breaches here and there, North and South.

In the South, for instance, when white Democrats were trying to regain power and undo radical Reconstruction, they called upon several trusted black voters. For their loyalty, those blacks who supported these independent Democratic movements in the South during the 1880s and the Democratic party in the 1890s against the Populists were given the right to vote.

In South Carolina blacks who supported the independent Democrat, Wade Hampton, in the "Redemption election" of 1876 retained their voting privileges through the 1930s. Upon the death of one of the Hampton Negroes "a white Columbia newspaper editor remarked that with the death Tuesday of Henry Dark, Columbia lost one of its few remaining 'old time' darkies ... that had voted the Democratic ticket since 1876."[14] "There was a quiet self-respect," the editor continued, "about Dark that somehow distinguished him from many members of his race."

In Virginia those blacks who supported the readjuster movement were also able to maintain their suffrage rights. Even in places like Birmingham, Alabama, a few blacks who viewed themselves as "leading colored citizens," and whom others saw as "uncle toms" or "safe niggers," were permitted to vote for the Democratic ticket.[15] Nor do these examples exhaust the instances of blacks supporting the Democratic party in the South in a willing manner.

In fact, in 1888, during the congressional election, blacks in many towns in Louisiana "formed Democratic clubs and cast large bloc votes" for the Democratic candidates. In 1892, blacks were elected to the Charleston City Council and to the South Carolina state legislature on the Democratic ticket. As early as 1894, black Democrats began "operating an Afro-American Democratic League in an effort to wean Negro voters away from the Republican party. Prominent Negroes gave their names and prestige to the Democratic party. The Democratic state executive committee sent Negro speakers into the field and had leading white politicians addressing Negro audiences in conciliatory times."[16] The trend continued even after the turn of the century. In 1905, J. Douglas Wetmore, a black Democrat, was elected to the Jacksonville City Council; other blacks served in the Nashville and Knoxville City Councils as late as 1912 or 1913. Moreover, as black bosses and machines arose in the South, they generally attached

[14] Paul Lewinson, *Race, Class, and Party* (New York: Russell and Russell, 1963), p. 154.
[15] *Ibid.*
[16] Sheldon Hackney, *Populism to Progressivism in Alabama* (Princeton: Princeton University Press, 1969), p. 35.

themselves to the white Democratic bosses and machines. This was primarily because only the Democratic party existed in the area.

It is possible, however, that since only one party existed in the region, the black voter had no party choice as such, but he did have a candidate choice, i.e., a choice of which Democratic candidate to support over another. Accordingly, the Democratic candidate with the best rapport with, and the most patronage to issue to the black community attained the vote. Thus, *what seems like a commitment or alignment with the Democratic party on the part of blacks in the South may have been a alignment with a particular candidate.* As Professor Brisbane has suggested in another analysis, to "those familiar with the thinking of Negroes in the years between 1932 and 1944, the black vote, in the main, was a vote for Roosevelt rather than for the Democratic party. Without the President, the diatribes and insults from some members of the Southern bloc in Congress would have long since caused the Negro to beat a retreat to the ranks of the Republican party."[17] Hence, the number of black Democrats in the South may have been minimal before policies and programs to advance the black community made membership in the party advantageous for black people.

Moreover, southern Democratic gubernatorial candidates made political capital out of the race issue. Certainly, the aforementioned white paternalists used it to advance themselves. "Nigger baiting" became the stock-in-trade of the southern demagogue, and blacks became the perennial whipping boy of southern politics, even when race was only a marginal issue in the campaign.

NORTHERN BLACKS AND THE DEMOCRATIC PARTY

Racism was a chief factor in the northern Democratic party also. Blacks began to enter the northern Democratic party as we have seen they did in the South. As early as 1868, the Democratic party in New York City secured John H. Nail, a saloon keeper and one of the leading citizens of the black community, to establish a black Democratic club in that city. Upon Nail's retirement in 1900, Ferdinand Q. Morton became the black boss of the black Democratic club, the United Color Democracy (hereafter UCD), until he quit the club in the 1930s and founded the American Labor party. Morton's successor, however, became Mrs. Bessye Bearden, who joined the club in 1920 and helped to lead it to several local electoral successes. Despite these accomplishments, the black organization was segregated within the regular Democratic party in the city. In a manner of speaking, the club became the black division of the Democratic party.

Notwithstanding the proslavery and discriminatory reputation of Demo-

[17] Brisbane, *op. cit.*, p. 225.

cratic Tammany Hall, black "Democrats represented Harlem in the State assembly and on the city board of aldermen at varying times throughout the twenties. Black movement to the Democratic party in New York has grown since its earliest beginning. In 1915, there were approximately 1,000 black Democrats. By 1920, with the black population having reached over 150,000, the majority blacks voted Democratic in local elections. In 1921, for instance, the Democratic mayoralty candidate "known as an honest leader in the black community" received 73.6 percent of black Harlem votes. In 1922 black Harlemites for the first time supported Democratic gubernatorial candidate Alfred E. Smith, who won the election. In 1928 blacks supported the Democratic mayoralty candidate, James Walker, for reelection. Any by 1930, when the black population in New York stood at 327,000, nineteen of the twenty-two political clubs were Democratic. And in 1930 New York elected two black Democrats to federal posts. As Figure 5 indicates, blacks in New York significantly supported the Democrats on the local and state level, but remained Republicans on the national level. Thus, "Harlem became the first Negro community to lend significant support to the Democratic party," at least on the local level.

In fact, the actions of the black voter in New York before the New Deal led one black observer to comment that "the Negro in Harlem has in very large degree emancipated himself from [single party domination] and become an intelligent voter."[18] Their action stimulated another observer to remark that "while there were Negro Democratic organizations in every city, they made little headway except in New York."[19]

While this last remark is somewhat illuminating, it plays down black Democratic activity elsewhere in the North. In Chicago, for instance, a few blacks broke with tradition and opened the Cook County Colored Democratic Club in 1888. Even before the organization of the club, however, the black community had given the Democratic mayoralty candidate Carter Harrison I about 50 percent of their votes. For the most part, however, the Democrats failed to consolidate their gains and support in the black community, and by 1905, the black Democratic organization had split into two rival groups, the Cook County Democratic League and the Thomas Jefferson Club.

Although dormant and particularly inefficient, the black Democratic organization continued, if only in shadow form. Moreover, Charles S. Deneen, who was the Republican governor of the state from 1905 to 1913, used every bit of patronage at his disposal to lure black voters into the Republican fold. Following Deneen on the local level in 1915 was the mayoralty winner William Hale Thompson, who likewise used patronage

[18] Osofsky, op. cit., p. 169. See also James Weldon Johnson, "The Gentleman's Agreement and the Negro Vote," Crisis, October, 1924, p. 264.
[19] Myrdal, op. cit., p. 494.

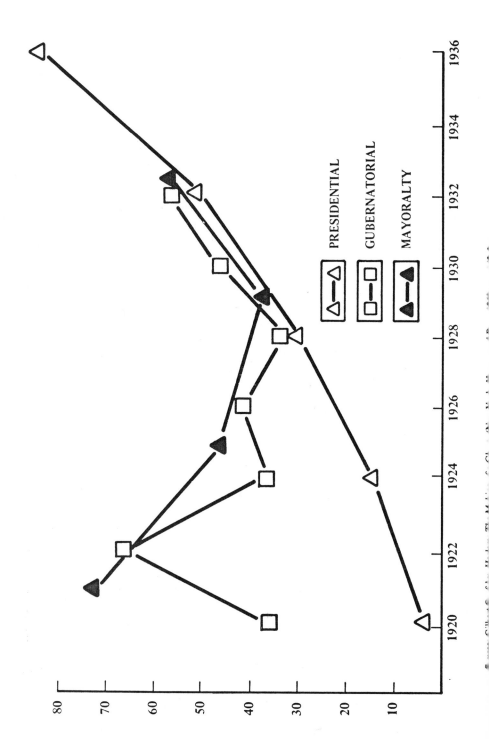

Figure 5. Percentage of Black Vote for Democratic Party in New York, 1920-1936

as freely as possible to elect himself mayor of the city three times from 1915 to 1923 and from 1927 to 1931. In fact, it would seem from the hold that these men had on the black community and the way in which the black community supported them that a Democratic tie never took shape. But to accept that thesis and the powers of suasion that these Republicans had over the black community in Chicago is to fall into the trap of numerous other analyses because despite the overt and obvious Republicanism of the black community, the Democratic party did make some gains.

In Chicago, after migration had significantly increased the black population, sentiments for the Democratic party grew. According to Professor Gosnell, as the newly arriving immigrants easily aligned themselves with the Republican political machine of Mayor Thompson, the respectable and well-to-do blacks who had been in Chicago for some time joined the Democratic party. Furthermore, they made their presence felt, at least on the national level. In 1916 nearly one-fifth of the black voters in Chicago cast Democratic ballots. In 1918, *The Broad Ax*, a black newspaper, endorsed Democratic Senator James Hamilton for reelection,[20] and the Democratic ticket in Chicago in 1918 received nearly 45 percent of the black votes. In 1920, with the *Broad Ax* still on the Democratic bandwagon, the Democratic national ticket, although it dropped in size, received about 11 percent of the black votes and 10 percent in 1924.[21] No matter how small this vote in Chicago was, it was significant because the "Republican votes cast by the Negro voters in 1920 [and 1924] was in part a protest against the Democratic Administration" of Woodrow Wilson, who almost completely segregated the federal civil service.[22]

If the black Democratic voters declined to support strongly the national Democratic ticket in 1924, they unwillingly supported it on the local level in 1923. In 1923, when Republican Bill Thompson did not run for reelection, a "clean" Democratic candidate, Judge William E. Deven, obtained the backing of two leading black Republicans, Oscar DePriest and Alderman Louis B. Anderson, plus the endorsement of *The Broad Ax*, and received 53 percent of the black votes, while the Republican candidate received less than 45 percent. Even before 1923, Big Bill Thompson had obtained all the black votes in his mayoralty campaigns. In 1919, although losing, the Democrats captured about 22 percent of the black votes and about 7 percent in 1927, 16 percent in 1931, and a grand 82 percent in 1935.

[20] John M. Allswang, "The Chicago Negro Voter and the Democratic Consensus: A Cast Study, 1918-1938," in Sternsher, *op. cit.*, p. 237.

[21] *Ibid.*, p. 238.

[22] On this point see Henry Blumenthal, "Woodrow Wilson and the Race Question," *Journal of Negro History,* April, 1963, pp. 98-114, and Kathleen Wolgemoth, "Woodrow Wilson and Federal Segregation," *Journal of Negro History,* April, 1959, pp. 158-173.

According to these calculations, if 1927 was the banner year for black Republicanism in Chicago, 1928 was the year in which the tide turned for black Democrats. Although Republicans elected the first black man—Oscar DePriest—to Congress in 1927, the black voters of Chicago, along with part of the black press, backed the Democratic nominee for the presidency, Al Smith, and gave him 28 percent of their votes. Even if this was not an overwhelming percentage, it is nonetheless significant when compared with the vote for the Democratic candidates in 1920 and 1924 of 11 percent and 10 percent respectively. It is even more significant when compared with the black vote for the Democratic mayoralty candidate one year earlier. Deven had won the black vote in 1923, and during his tenure to office had passed out patronage to the black community and had also placed a black—Julius Taylor—in his civic commission. In 1927, however, he was running against Thompson, "the second Lincoln" in black voters' eyes. Deven knew that he could not break the black voters' alliance with Thompson, so he tried to build an electoral majority through the persecution of a minority group. He distributed pictures of Thompson kissing black children and sent calliopes throughout the streets playing "Bye, Bye Blackbird." Even so, one black newspaper, the *Broad Ax*, and 7 percent of the black electorate, supported him, and a year later nearly one-third of the black voters in the city supported Smith. Commenting on this situation, Professor Allswang states that "Smith fared better among Negro voters than almost all other Democratic candidates in the national election of 1930 and 1932, including Franklin D. Roosevelt in the latter year and without benefit of the Depression."[23] In short, in Chicago during the 1928 election, there was a swing to a Democratic candidate among the black leaders and voters generally, and, "however limited an important break had been made, Chicago Negroes would never again be so overwhelmingly Republican in national politics."[24] A complete break with the Republicans on the local level in Chicago came during the 1931 mayoralty campaign. Although the Democrats in that campaign received only 16 percent of the black vote, Mayor-elect Anton Cermak smashed the old black-Thompson Republican alliance. He withdrew partonage from all of the Black Belt areas until they showed willingness to play ball with the Democrats. When Mayor Cermak was killed in 1933, his replacement, Mayor Ed Kelly, worked even more vigorously to bring black Chicagoans into the Democratic fold because the 1932 national election had indicated that only 21 percent of the black community had supported Roosevelt. "Ultimately," Kelly accomplished his task. He drafted first the black politicians and then the black masses into the Democratic party with the assistance of the national Democratic administration and its antidepression activities.

[23] Allswang, *op. cit.*, p. 246.
[24] *Ibid.*

The effects of Mayor Kelly and Cermak's activities could be seen in the 1934 election. In this election the Democrats felt so sure of themsleves that they put up a black Democrat, a novice in Chicago politics, to run against the well-known Oscar DePriest; Arthur Mitchell became the first black Democrat in Congress. In the election Mitchell received 53 percent of the black votes. The next year, Kelly ran for reelection and received 72 percent of the black vote. Kelly's black majority level had never been remotely approached by the Democrats before, and it signifies that blacks had moved to the Democratic party. By 1936 blacks in Chicago gave Roosevelt 45 percent of their total vote. Even today, blacks in Chicago seem to be the exclusive property of the Democratic party.

In sum, the trend of the black voter in Chicago toward the Democratic party is not as clear as the trend of the black voter in New York, who had already gone a long way toward the Democratic party before 1930. Nevertheless, as Figure 6 indicates, there was a steady trend on different levels by blacks toward the Democratic party even before the New Deal.

Moreover, the ineptitude of the Democrats and their failure to see the danger of raising the race issue in local elections clearly hurt them more than the overt liberalism of the local Republican candidates.[25] And this can clearly be seen in the 1927 mayoralty election when the Democrats "practically drove" the black voters into the Republican camp. But despite these weaknesses a trend in Chicago toward the Democratic party on the part of blacks did exist.

In Boston Democrats elected their first black candidate to the state legislature in 1866. Another black, Paul C. Brooks, was elected to the Common Council in 1890. A black Democratic club was not established in the city until 1895, and this, however, was confined to the eleventh ward. As the northward migration brought more and more blacks to the city, the club expanded itself to ward eighteen six years later. In 1905 about one-fourth of the black votes in Boston were cast for the Democratic mayoralty candidate. In 1910 about one-third of the black vote was cast for the Democratic gubernatorial candidate. Two years earlier the black vote was strong enough in Boston to elect a Democratic district attorney. Moreover, blacks were elected regularly to the Common Council before the city charter was reorganized during the first decade of the twentieth century. In sum, although the black population did not become great in Boston, part of that population did join the Democratic party before the New Deal.

Elsewhere the picture was about the same. In Detroit nearly one-fifth (19.5 percent) of the black vote was Democratic in 1930. And by 1932 it was more than one-third (36.7 percent) and two-thirds (63.5 percent) in

---

[25] Gosnell, *op. cit.*, p. 54. See also R. H. Bunche, "The Thompson-Negro Alliance," *Opportunity*, 7 (March, 1929), 79.

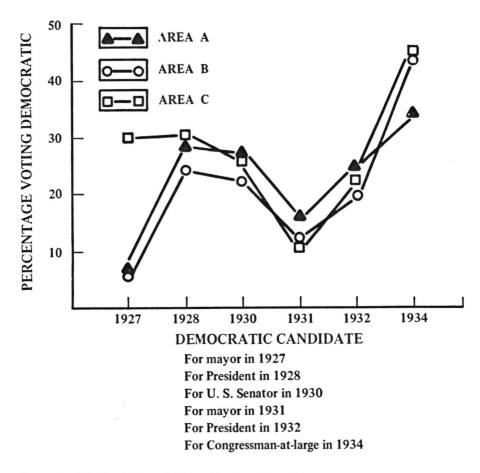

Figure 6. Percentage of the Black Vote for the Democratic Party in Three Chicago Areas, 1927–1934

DEMOCRATIC CANDIDATE

For mayor in 1927
For President in 1928
For U. S. Senator in 1930
For mayor in 1931
For President in 1932
For Congressman-at-large in 1934

Source: Harold F. Gosnell, *Negro Politicians: The Rise of Negro Politics in Chicago* (Chicago: University of Chicago Press, 1967), p. 34.

1936.[26] In Cincinnati the number of black Democrats before 1900 was very small; it was not until 1921 that the blacks in the city began to move

[26] See Edward H. Litchfield, "A Case Study of Negro Political Behavior in Detroit," *Public Opinion Quarterly*, 5 (June, 1941), 267-274, and T. R. Solomon, "Participation of Negroes in Detroit Elections" (unpublished Ph.D. thesis, University of Michigan, 1939), and Pierce F. Lewis, "Impact of Negro Migration on the Electoral Geography of Flint, Michigan, 1932-1962," *Annals of the Association of American Geographers*, 18 (March, 1965), 23-36.

toward the Democratic party. By 1932 the black population gave Roosevelt nearly one-third (28.8 percent) of their total vote.[27] In Pennsylvania the Democrats actively sought the black vote as early as 1928, and through patronage deals acquired it. By 1932 blacks cast over 35,000 votes for the Democratic presidential candidate, and since that time the blacks in Philadelphia have been staunch Democrats. Moreover, 45 percent of the black voters in Baltimore were Democrats; 25 percent in Columbus, Ohio; 41.5 percent in Kansas City, Kansas; 79.8 percent in Kansas City, Missouri; 53.3 percent in Pittsburgh; and 28.3 percent in Wilmington, Delaware, in 1932. In addition, there were a sizable number of black Democrats in several of the southern cities prior to the New Deal.

In fact, throughout the country and especially in the North, blacks, even when there seemed to be no objective reason in terms of party policies or platform, began to move into the Democratic ranks at least on the local and state levels. Even before 1936 blacks had also begun to identify themselves with the party on the national level.

BLACKS AND THE NATIONAL DEMOCRATS

The election of a Democrat, Grover Cleveland, to the White House in 1884 proved helpful. Cleveland appointed several blacks to public office and invited Frederick Douglass and his white wife to dinner. In fact, Cleveland's overtures to blacks were so different from what had been expected that Booker T. Washington was moved to write that "judging from my personal acquaintance with Mr. Cleveland ... I do not believe that he is conscious of possessing any colour prejudice. He is too great for that. ..." Cleveland's conciliatory gestures were too limited, however, to remove the stigma of the Democratic party as the party of the South from the minds of the newly emancipated freedmen. Once again, however, the Republicans faltered and continued to push blacks toward the Democratic ranks.

In fact, resentment against the "let alone" policy of the Republicans and their nonchalant attitude toward black demands caused one black leader in 1898 to endorse William Jennings Bryan, the Democratic presidential nominee. By 1900 a group of alienated black Republicans, independent blacks, and black Democrats formed the Negro National Democratic League. George E. Taylor, who became president of the league, issued a statement in 1900 that argued "that a large percentage of the ... Negro voters of the country are today arrayed with the Democratic Party."[28]

[27] James H. Brewer, "Robert Lee Van, Democrat or Republican: An Exponent of Looseleaf Politics," *Negro History Bulletin,* 21 (February, 1958), 100.

[28] Herbert Aptheker, *A Documentary History of the Negro People in the United States* (New York: Citadel Press, 1969), pp. 819-820.

Taylor went even further in his statement and held that the members of the league stood "for the principle of the Democratic party and for Bryan." When a group of black intellectuals met and organized the Niagara Movement in 1905 to protest Booker T. Washington's gradualist and conciliatory policy, they also considered some political strategies. Since Washington had close ties with Presidents Roosevelt and Taft, the members of the group, including W. E. B. Du Bois, looked favorably upon the Democratic party and endorsed Bryan in 1908.[29] About this time northern Democrats were treating blacks much better than the reactionary Republicans and southern Democrats, who combined to deprive blacks of their rights. Moreover, in 1908, whether Bryan appointed blacks to office or not, the Democratic party was anti-imperialistic, antimanagement, prolabor, and for the elimination of special privileges. Blacks would have benefited from a Democratic victory in 1908. After the election these black Democratic supporters did not give up; they formed the National Independent Political League, which replaced the National Negro American Political League that was founded earlier that year. They prepared to support northern Democrats where possible and in 1911 a national convention of black Democrats in Indianapolis "urged colored voters ... to organize together in Democratic clubs for the election of 1912." The national election of 1912 gave these fledgling black Democrats a chance to act. Upon accepting the Democratic nomination for the presidency, Woodrow Wilson had his political manager make an open bid for black support. In September the national Democratic party established a national Negro Wilson League in Richmond, Virginia, for the purpose of obtaining black orators for the party in the North.[30] After its emergence in the North, the league called for black voters to forsake the Republican party and for southern blacks to cooperate with southern whites.

Wilson personally recognized the National Independent Political League of Washington and all of its publications. To appeal further to black voters, the Democratic party spent $52,255.55 in seeking to draw them into the Democratic fold, and in a cleverly designed appeal, stated all the reasons why blacks should not vote Republican. This appeal did not mention what the Democrats would do for blacks.

These overtures from the party were not quite convincing to some black leaders. Two members of the now defunct Black Independent Political Organization, the Reverend J. M. Walden and William Monroe Trotter, along with a delegation from the United Negro Democracy of New Jersey,

[29] See also August Meier, "The Negro and the Democratic Party, 1875-1915," 2nd quarter, 1956, pp. 182-191.

[30] Arthur S. Link, "The Negro as a Factor in the Campaign of 1912," *Journal of Negro History,* 32 (January, 1947), 85.

spoke with Wilson about the race issue. When they left, Walden reconstructed from memory the details of the exchange and printed them in the September issue of *Crisis* magazine. In brief, the statement claimed that Wilson needed and sought black support and promised blacks a "fair deal." The statement concluded that Wilson would veto any legislation that was inimical to the black community.

The Walden statement upset Wilson, and he called upon his racial adviser, Oswald Garrison Villard (the grandson of William Lloyd Garrison), whose paper had supported him for the 1910 New Jersey Democratic gubernatorial contest, to help retract the message and issue a much softer one. Villard replied to the President that blacks were aware of his southern origin, his prejudiced policy at Princeton, and his generally friendly nature with southerners. With the reply, a statement by W. E. B. Du Bois was included that Villard thought would give black voters some reassurance. Wilson refused to sign it. Moreover, in October he refused to speak to the National Colored Democratic League in New York even at the request of the league's president, Bishop Alexander Walters of the African Zion Church, who had been a Democrat since 1909. Wilson politely refused, but sent a statement to the meeting expressing his desire to deal fairly with the race.

"Apparently this unequivocal promise of fair dealing, although stated in vague and general terms, had the effect of swinging Du Bois and many other leaders of militant ... [black] opinion in the North to the Wilson ranks."[31] With this limited encouragement, blacks formed additional "colored Democratic Leagues" in such places as Ramsey County, Minnesota; Kings County, New York; Providence, Rhode Island; Chicago; Denver; and other northern cities.[32] Wilson, of course, won, and, as Figure 7 indicates, the black Democratic organization had worked hard. In the selected northern cities represented in the figure, the Democrats received more black votes than the Republicans, though the Progressive party in New York outpolled Democrats in the black community. Taken as a whole, the black Democratic vote in 1912 was indeed very strong for an ethnic group that was supposedly solidly Republican. The black Democratic vote in 1912 is just one more indication that blacks had begun shifting to the Democratic party long before 1936. As Figure 5 reveals, the black presidential votes in New York showed a steady trend toward the Democratic party. By 1932 they had approximated 50 percent.

Once in office, however, Wilson quickly destroyed black optimism. He almost entirely segregated the federal civil service and introduced a new

[31] *Ibid.*, p. 93.
[32] Douglas C. Strange, "The Making of a President, 1912: The Northern Negroes' View," *Negro History Bulletin*, 31 (November, 1968), 19-20.

Figure 7. The Black Vote in the 1912 Presidential Election

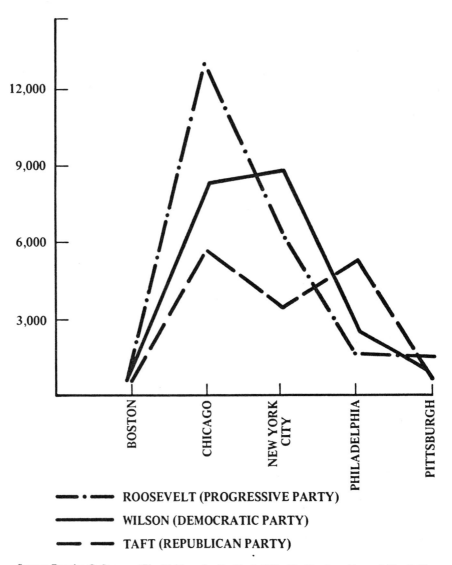

ROOSEVELT (PROGRESSIVE PARTY)

WILSON (DEMOCRATIC PARTY)

TAFT (REPUBLICAN PARTY)

Source: Douglas C. Strange, "The Making of a President, 1912: The Northern Negroes' View," *Negro History Bulletin*, 31 (November, 1968), 21. Votes include Boston's Ward 18, New York City's Assembly Districts 13 and 21, Chicago's Wards 2 and 3, Philadelphia's Wards 7 and 30, and Pittsburgh's Ward 5.

form of segregation into the nation's capital.[33] Wilson's role in segregating federal departments greatly hindered a black alliance with the Democrats. The black vote for the party in the 1920 presidential election in New York was 2.4 percent, in Chicago 10 percent, but by the 1924 presidential election it had risen in New York to 11.5 percent and in Chicago to 10 percent.

Although "there were no objective reasons for [blacks] to be attracted to the Democratic party, as a party in 1928," they nevertheless were attracted. Indeed as early as 1921 blacks had supported Smith for the governorship and found him appreciative. Five of the major black newspapers endorsed him and a black division of the national Democratic campaign committee established black Democratic Smith clubs in 22 of the 48 states. This open appeal for the black vote plus Smith's "wetness," religion, and urban background led to a vicious crusade in the South against the Democratic party and its black supporters. The campaign proved so effective that Herbert Hoover, the Republican candidate, carried forty states, including five states of the old Confederacy. Despite the Republican landslide, blacks in Chicago cast 23 percent of their votes for the Democratic nominee and the black New Yorkers cast 29.2 percent of their votes for Smith.

Although, as Professor Gosnell asserts, "the Democratic party as a national organization contained elements in 1932 which conscious Negro leaders could not very well defend," it is also equally true that blacks once again identified with the party. In fact, Robert Lee Vann, editor of the nation's largest black weekly newspaper, not only endorsed Roosevelt in 1932, but actually campaigned for him both in person and with his black paper. Prior to supporting Roosevelt, Vann in 1932 issued a bitter denunciation of the Republican party leadership and its policies toward the black community. Then, in October, after his denunciation of the Republican party had been circulated in many influential black newspapers, Vann launched an aggressive campaign for the Democrats, speaking in all the large metropolitan centers in the North and the border states. Vann's campaigning was so effective that it led the chairman of the Essex County Republican party in Newark to assert that "it was once a rare thing to find colored Democrats, now the woods are full of them ... Negro newspapers have deserted us."[34] Vann urged blacks to "Go home and turn Lincoln's picture to the wall. The debt has been paid in full." Nevertheless the black trend to the Democratic party did not come full turn. In Chicago 23 percent of the blacks voted for Roosevelt; in New York 59 percent; in Detroit, 58 percent; and in Philadelphia only 24 percent. The trend had

[33] See K. L. Walgemoth, "Woodrow Wilson's Appointment Policy and the Negro," *Journal of Southern History,* 24 (November, 1958), 457-471, and Walgemoth, "Wilson and Federal Segregation," *Journal of Negro History,* XLIV (April, 1959), 158-173.

[34] Quoted in Brewer, *op. cit.,* p. 226.

gained momentum, and with the subsequent appearance of a black Democratic congressman as well as the economic effect of the New Deal and liberal Democratic mayors and officials on the state and local level, the trend by 1936 exceeded 50 percent in most northern cities. It did not reach the 75 percent mark in some places until the 1940 election.

Nevertheless, although a trend toward the party already existed, the New Deal still had a significant influence upon black political behavior. Just as Lincoln and the Emancipation Proclamation cemented blacks to the Republican party, so Roosevelt and the New Deal became the forces that finally cemented blacks to the Democratic party.

The economic benefit from the New Deal was at first the prime motivation, but later the egalitarian policies of Roosevelt proved even more crucial. In terms of economics the agencies created to eradicate the effects of the depression—the Federal Employment Relief Administration (FERA), the Works Progress Administration (WPA), the Agricultural Adjustment Administration (AAA), the National Youth Administration (NYA), the Civilian Conservation Corps (CCC), etc.—aided blacks in a minimal fashion. But later FDR created a "Black Cabinet"—top-flight black advisers to help the president in instituting meaningful programs in the black community. In addition to the President's appointments, his wife "made it her business to reaffirm by word and deed her faith in the equality of opportunity for all." She urged party leaders to ask respected blacks like Mrs. Mary McLeod Bethune to participate among black groups, and she included black and mixed groups in her itineraries in addition to speaking up for the race at critical times and welcoming mixed groups to the White House. Later Mrs. Roosevelt secured the Lincoln Memorial as a place for Marian Anderson to sing when the DAR refused to permit her to use Constitution Hall. Roosevelt himself issued executive order 8802, which established a Fair Employment Practice Commission and also banned discrimination in industries with federal contracts. Roosevelt's death and the end of the war terminated an era in which the office of the president symbolized a concern for justice and equality, but it did not end the black alliance with the Democratic party.

The election results in 1948 showed that the black emphasis on New Deal economic benefits had given way to a primary concern for civil rights and Truman's civil rights plan in particular. Blacks remained Democrats because Truman "declared in specific terms his belief in the equality of men."

During the campaign Truman fully endorsed the sweeping recommendation of his committee on civil rights that called for strong federal action in removing state and local discriminatory practices. This endorsement led to a split in the Democratic party when the Dixiecrats walked out of the National Convention over the inclusion in the party's platform of a statement on civil rights. After the election Truman issued three significant executive orders. One abolished discrimination in the armed services, another established fair employment procedures within the federal government structure, and the third established a president's committee to insure compliance in firms with federal contracts. In short, Truman's civil rights policies complemented Roosevelt's economic and recognition policies. Both worked to increase the black vote for the Democrats.

When the Democrats left office in 1953, blacks did not abandon the party until 1956. Even then the defection was not overwhelming. Only in four southern cities did Eisenhower's vote go over 70 percent, and only eight northern cities gave him over 50 percent of their vote. But even before 1956 it must be remembered that a consistent portion of the black electorate (21 percent) had continued to support the Republican ticket, and that number significantly increased to 39 percent with the 1956 election.

By 1960, however, the black electorate, at least on the national level, was back in the Democratic column. The civil rights issue was still alive and several political observers had credited Kennedy's call to Mrs. Martin Luther King, Jr., while King was in jail as the event that caused Nixon to lose the election. The well-publicized call, many observers say, shifted the black vote to Kennedy. However, not discounting the effect of the call, it must be remembered that even when the Republicans were at the peak of their strength, in 1956, they polled less than 39 percent of the black vote. The estimates of the black vote in 1960 for the Democrats ranged from 60 percent (Gallup Poll) to 80 percent (*New York Times*), and it would seem likely that only about 7 to 15 percent of the black vote defected because of the call. In short, more than 61 percent of the black electorate remained Democratic in 1956 and this was increased not more than 20 percent during the 1960 election. This increase was enough to elect Kennedy, however. Once in office, Kennedy moved slowly through his first two years. While his brother Robert banned segregation in interstate commerce, the president vacillated and issued a mild executive order banning discrimination in federally financed housing. By 1963, however, he had sent to Congress the most comprehensive civil rights bill in the nation's history, and although he was assassinated, his Democratic successor, Lyndon B. Johnson, moved blacks toward civil rights at an even greater pace than any of his Democratic predecessors. Passing two major civil rights acts and appointing blacks to the Supreme Court, ambassadorial posts, and to the cabinet, he outstripped his Democratic forerunners and shifted even more blacks to the Democratic fold.

In 1964, although the antiblack position of the Republican party pushed blacks to the Democrats, Johnson received an overwhelming 94 percent of the black vote, and though the Democrats lost in 1968, the black voters were still in the Democratic column.

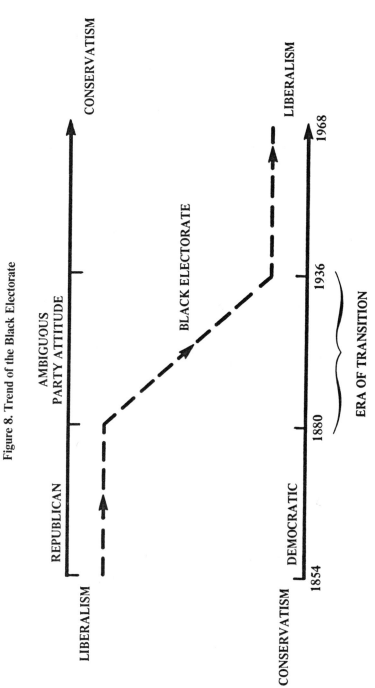

Figure 8. Trend of the Black Electorate

THE BLACK ELECTORATE: A THEORY

If the Republicans had black delegates only from the South in 1868 and none from the North until 1916, the Democrats had none from either the North or the South until 1936. The Republicans have developed a prejudicial, antiblack and ultraconservative stand since the beginning of the twentieth century; the Democratic party had such a policy during the latter part of the nineteenth and the earlier part of the twentieth century. The Republicans accorded blacks significant recognition before 1900; the Democratic party accorded blacks the same after 1932. So, if there is a black alliance with the Democratic party at the present time, there was the same kind of alliance with the Republican party in the past. Black political behavior has seemingly followed predictable patterns whether on the local, state, or national level. This, however, is not to say that when blacks have voted for Democrats on the national level they have done the same on the local and state level. Such has not always been the case. The political milieu of the city and the treatment of the black community by the political forces in power has determined which way the black vote has been cast. The benefit of a local or state political alliance is discernible much more quickly than is a national political alliance. Blacks vote basically in accordance with their interests. If to support Democrats nationally is to their interest, it is still possible that to support Republicans could be to their interest on the state level and still a third party on the local level.

The black alliance with the Democrats over the past thirty years seems no more serious than the old Republican alliance in the late nineteenth century, but one major pattern of black political behavior in regard to major political parties does become discernible, i.e., the general direction of the black electorate is toward liberalism. If our historical sketch is accurate, the Republican party seemed most liberal yesterday (during the nineteenth century) while the Democratic party holds that position today (since 1932). As seen in Figure 8, we can diagram this pattern or trend.

Blacks seemingly aligned themselves first with the Republicans until their liberal attitude toward equality and human dignity somewhat declined after the disputed 1876 election. During this period, which is labeled the period of transition, blacks were still attached to the Republican party, but a meaningful trend away from the Republicans toward third parties, independent political action, and the Democrats finally culminated in an attachment to the Democrats in 1936. Not all of the black electorate has supported or moved in a liberal fashion, however. Some blacks have always supported conservative political movements and parties, and the outlook is that as more and more blacks become economically secure more and more will vote conservatively. However, the majority has supported liberal political movements and if the past is an indication of how the future might be, then a black alliance with the most liberal party on the national or local level will continue, even if it lags at times, at least until the black community has reached a meaningful level of equality.

VIII

Black Parties, Third Parties, and Political Innovation

Since majority rule is one of the chief foundations of democracy, one of the main functions of political parties is the attainment and mobilization of a majority. Political parties must organize the electorate along party lines. Parties, however, are more concerned with winning than in the institution or propagation of a particular principle or ideology, and in their appeal to sundry groups and diverse individuals they become heterogeneous coalitions. In short, a majority in a pluralistic society is never homogeneous nor is it even in harmony with itself. To put together an unharmonious, heterogeneous, diverse coalition, political parties must modify, compromise and bargain, as well as become expedient and ambiguous. Victory is only won at a price.[1]

Nevertheless, despite the price and the nature of victory, the problems and issues of blacks have always "occupied a central place in the development of the national party organizations and in the formation of political alliances."[2] American political parties have not escaped the racist factor in American life. In many instances, as we have seen in the two previous chapters, the fortunes and misfortunes of the Democratic and Republican parties have been tied to the black problem in America. Certainly, blacks have suffered under both the Republican party of Lincoln and emancipation and the Democratic party of the common man.

The policies and activities of both major parties have drawn strong criticism from the black community and its leaders from 1856 to the present. In June, 1856, for instance, one of the major black leaders of that

[1] There are numerous books on the American party systems. For some of the most useful see Clinton Rossiter, *Parties and Politics in America* (Ithaca: Cornell University Press, 1963); Samuel J. Eldersveld, *Political Parties: A Behavioral Analysis* (Chicago: Rand McNally and Company, 1964); Frank J. Sorauf, *Party Politics in America* (Boston: Little, Brown and Company, 1968); Kay Lawson, *Political Parties and Democracy in the United States* (New York: Charles Scribner's Sons, 1968); and Judson L. James, *American Political Parties* (New York: Pegasus Press, 1969).

[2] Stephen K. Bailey, "Our National Political Parties," in Robert Goldwin, ed., *Political Parties U. S. A.* (Chicago: Rand McNally and Company, 1968), p. 17.

121

era denounced the newly emerged Republican party and characterized it as "a heterogeneous mass of political antagonism, gathered from defunct Whiggery, disaffected Democracy, and demented, defeated, and disappointed native Americanism"[3] that had at best a limited and expedient antislavery program. In the same year, a convention of Ohio blacks labelled the Democratic party as "the black-hearted apostle of American slavery." During the 1860 election, Frederick Douglass wrote in his newspaper an editorial on the Democratic party in which he said "the vital element of the party has been hatred of Negroes and love of spoils."[4] Another black newspaper, *The Anglo-African*, declared in March, 1860, that "the two great political parties separate at an angle of two roads ... [but] they meet eventually at the same goals ... the Democratic party would make the white man the master and the black man the slave ... the Republican party ... though with larger professions for humanity, is by far [our] more dangerous enemy ... their opposition to slavery means opposition to the Black man—nothing else. ...."

"We have no hope from either [of the] political parties. We must rely on ourselves. ...."[5]

Such criticism continued during and after Reconstruction and after Reconstruction there was much black involvement throughout the country with the minor or third parties. By 1916, black leaders were calling upon the black masses to create their own "Negro Political parties."[6]

In sum, "the Republican and Democratic parties have neglected to take effective steps to end disfranchisement, segregation, economic exploitation, and lynching in the South, and they have likewise been very slow in tackling such fundamental problems as trade-unions, discrimination," equitable representation at national conventions, fair housing, unemployment, poor welfare policies, police brutality, urban ghettoes, slumism, "Black poverty and general discrimination against the Black citizenry in this country."[7] In fact, because of the nature of American political parties, their preoccupation with expediency and compromise, as well as their failure to forthrightly advance freedom to the black Americans, many blacks have found it necessary to go beyond or outside the normal two-party system to express their political viewpoints. According to the Civil Rights Commission, this search for a new political alternative has led blacks "to the formation of independent [black] political organizations in many areas" of

[3] Philip Foner, ed., *The Life and Writings of Frederick Douglass* (New York: International Publishers, 1950), II, 83.

[4] *Ibid.*, p. 493.

[5] James M. McPherson, *The Negro's Civil War* (New York: Vintage Books, 1965), p. 4.

[6] R. R. Wright, Jr., "A Negro Party," *Christian Recorder*, September 28, 1919, p. 4. William Pickens, "Political Parties and the Negro," *The Messenger*, March, 1923, pp. 625-626.

[7] H. Gosnell, *Negro Politicians, op. cit.*, p. 319.

the country. They have formed political parties not only on the local, county, and state level, but on the national level as well.[8]

BLACK COUNTY AND STATE PARTIES

Blacks in Pennsylvania organized a state party, the Colored Independent party, in 1883. Although the party protest activity was much more pronounced than its political activity, it did continue in existence for several years under various names, such as the Negro Prohibition League. Agitation and protest superseded its electioneering and the party served mainly to inform the black public, as well as the public in general, about major issues facing the black community.

In Ohio, blacks organized the Negro Protective party in 1897 and cast 5,000 votes for its black gubernatorial candidate, S. J. Lewis. Lewis ran on a platform of equal rights, and promised to protect black rights that were gradually being diminished or disregarded at that time. After one election, however, the party faded into electoral oblivion.

When disfranchisement came, black voting and black organizations temporarily declined, but the rise of Black and Tan organizations in the South became rudimentary parties in some southern states. From time to time until their demise in the late 1930s, Black and Tan organizations in Louisiana, South Carolina, and other southern states supported various candidates for office. In Virginia the Black and Tan organization in 1921 protested the activities and exclusionary policy of the Lily Whites by running a black candidate, John Mitchell, for governor. The ticket drew some 5,230 votes. In Texas in 1928 the Black and Tan group nominated their own electors for president in order to protest the action of the Republican National Convention in seating the Lily White delegation. For those electors, they cast nearly 28,000 votes.

The Black and Tans were not the extent of black political parties in the South, however.

In 1944, for example, blacks in South Carolina formed the South Carolina Progressive Democratic party in a state convention in May.[9] Thirty-nine of the state's forty-six counties sent one hundred and seventy-two delegates. An outgrowth of a desire on the part of blacks to vote for Roosevelt for a fourth term and to get around the exclusiveness of the white primary rule in the state, the party decided at its state convention to send delegates to the national convention to challenge the regular state

[8] For a comprehensive analysis of the development, nature, accomplishments, and future of black political parties, see Hanes Walton, Jr., *Black Political Parties: A Historical and Political Analysis* (New York: Free Press, 1972).

[9] *Ibid.* See also W. D. Robinson, "Democracy Frontiers," *Journal of Human Relations,* 3 (Spring, 1954), 63–71, and Alexander Heard, *A Two-Party South?* (Chapel Hill: University of North Carolina Press, 1965), pp. 192–194.

party delegates. Although the challenge was quietly rejected, Osceola Mc-
Kaine, the PDP's executive secretary, ran for the United States Senate and
received about 4,000 votes. Nor did the party give up after 1944. It
mounted seating challenges at the Democratic national conventions in
1948 and 1956, also. While none of these challenges succeeded, the party
did enlarge the black electorate in South Carolina and also succeeded in
getting some of its members accepted by the white Democratic organization.

By 1969, however, the party had dissolved, and blacks within the state
began forming the United Citizens party, which in 1970 sent three blacks to
the state legislature—the first to go since Reconstruction.

On April 26, 1964, another black state party, the Mississippi Freedom
Democratic Party (MFDP) was organized in Jackson, Mississippi. This
party, which was bent on bringing blacks who were excluded from the
regular Democratic party organization in Mississippi to power in state
politics, held precinct, county, district, meetings plus a state convention. At
the last, the party decided to challenge seating of the regular state Democratic delegation at the 1964 national convention at Atlantic City. This
convention challenge was rejected. Instead, as a compromise the convention offered two seats at large, without the right to vote. The MFDP
delegates in turn rejected this compromise as too mild for all their troubles
and efforts. The party returned to Mississippi and held a "Freedom"
election—one conducted by the party itself—for the MFDP candidates
who could not obtain places on the ballot of the regular Democratic party
ticket. On this ballot Johnson and Humphrey received more votes than on
the regular ticket.

In January, 1965, the MFDP challenged the seating in Congress of five
white congressmen from Mississippi on the grounds that they were nominated and elected in a primary and general election that excluded blacks,
which was in violation of Section 2 of the Fourteenth Amendment. The
second part of the MFDP challenge argued that the black candidate who
had defeated the white candidate in the "Freedom" election be permitted
to take his seat.

In September, despite protests and pleas to the contrary, the House
voted 228 to 143 to dismiss the MFDP challenge. Nevertheless, from 1965
to 1966, the MFDP continued to participate in numerous local and state
elections, though without any success. It also continued to file many suits
against the continued legal hurdles that the state legislature placed in the
party's path. Moreover, in many sections of the state, the MFDP found
itself challenged by the NAACP. The party continued to flourish, however,
despite obstacles and limited financial resources, and in 1967 it met with
success.

In the general election of 1967 the MFDP elected five blacks to county posts and one, Robert Clark, to the state legislature (he was the first black elected to that position since Reconstruction). For this election, the MFDP and the NAACP coalesced in order to enable their respective candidate to obtain surety bonds, which almost all insurance companies in the state had denied them. The coalition was effective and each candidate obtained the necessary bonding.

After the candidates took office in January, 1968, the coalition between the MFDP and NAACP continued. Then, Charles Evers, who was the field secretary of the NAACP and is now mayor of Fayette, Mississippi, decided to run for the congressional seat recently vacated by the state's new governor. Evers won first place in a six-way race, but he withdrew from the special run-off upon the assassination of civil rights leader Martin Luther King, Jr.

At the national Democratic convention in 1968 the MFDP formed with other groups under the banner of the Loyal Democratic Party of Mississippi (the LDM) and was seated over the regular white delegation, which had only one black member. After the convention, the party returned to the state and participated in the municipal elections of 1969 and once again achieved several victories. At present, the MFDP is still participating in and changing the political scene in the state of Mississippi.

Two years after the MFDP was formed the Lowndes County freedom organization (the Black Panther party) and the Dallas County Freedom organization were formed in Alabama. Each put up black candidates for every office in its respective county. Unfortunately, if the MFDP is an example of a black organization that overcame state suppression, the LCFO is an example of a black party that was destroyed by state repression as well as by internal organizational weaknesses. All its candidates, like those in Dallas County also, lost the election on an average of 400 votes per candidate, though blacks constituted a majority in both. After the election, the party faded from the scene.

In 1968, however, the party was superseded by the National Democratic Party of Alabama, which challenged the regular state party at the national convention, but without success. It also ran more than a hundred candidates in state elections, again without success. Recently, however, twenty-one of its candidates won local office, and with this success the party hopes to continue in the future. Finally, in 1968, blacks in Georgia organized a district party (the Party of Christian Democracy). This party organized in the 76th House district of Georgia, ran a black for that office, and lost. The party seems to have declined somewhat since then, and whether it will try again in the 1970s is not known.

BLACK NATIONAL PARTIES

Radical blacks opposed supporting any one of the two major parties, because of the inconsistency of their records on the question of race. Even before 1900, these radicals had established several different national black independent leagues. Not until 1904, however, did they establish a national black political party. This, the National Liberty party, was an outgrowth of black civil and personal liberty leagues, which had thrived in black communities North and South since the Civil War. It held its first national convention at the Douglas Hotel in St. Louis, Missouri, on the fifth and sixth days of July, 1904. Thirty-six states sent delegates to the convention and George Edwin Taylor, the president of the Negro National Democratic League, was nominated as the presidential candidate. In his presidential address, Taylor deplored how the Democrats and Republicans permitted injustices to continue against their black supporters and declared that the National Liberty party would stand for "popular rights, i.e., 'a government of all the people, for all the people, and by all the people.'" Nevertheless, the party faded shortly after its formation, and several other black national political organizations claiming a nonpartisan posture emerged, such as the National Negro American Political League (1908), the National Independent Political League (1912), the National Labor Congress (1924), and the National Negro Congress (1936). Not until 1960 did another national black party appear. This, the Afro-American party, organized in Alabama and ran two blacks, the Reverend Clennon King and Reginald Carter, for president and vice-president and received 1,485 votes, all from the state of Alabama. After this election, it, too, faded from the scene.

In 1964, however, another national black party emerged, the Freedom Now party. This, along with the National Civil Rights party, was organized in 1963 after the March on Washington. That year it ran candidates in New York and Connecticut, though without success. In 1964, the party decided that, before it tried to establish itself in every state, it would concentrate on the state of Michigan. In Michigan the Freedom Now party placed thirty-nine black candidates in the field for positions ranging from the Wayne County drain commissioner to the United States Senate seat. The party chairman and gubernatorial candidate, the Reverend Albert B. Cleage, did much to promote the party throughout the state. His efforts proved in vain, however. The party pulled less than 1 percent of the black vote in Michigan and disappeared from the political scene.

By 1968, however, another black party attempted a rise to power: the Peace and Freedom party. Led by Black Panther Minister of Information Eldridge Cleaver and Douglas F. Dowd, an economics professor at Cornell, the party got on the ballot of more than nineteen states and received

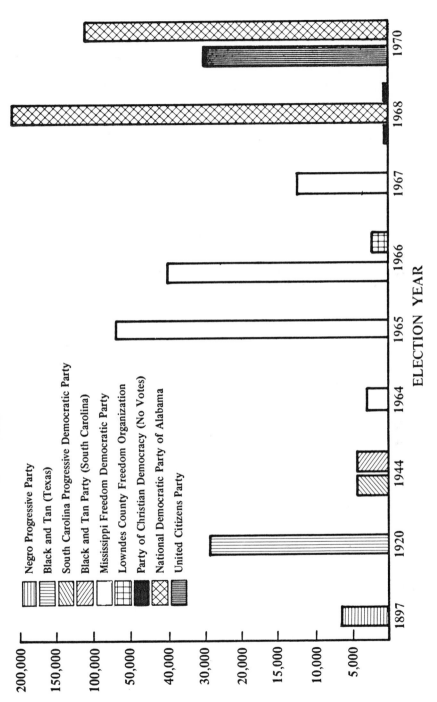

Figure 9. Votes Received by Black State Parties

Negro Progressive Party
Black and Tan (Texas)
South Carolina Progressive Democratic Party
Black and Tan Party (South Carolina)
Mississippi Freedom Democratic Party
Lowndes County Freedom Organization
Party of Christian Democracy (No Votes)
National Democratic Party of Alabama
United Citizens Party

ELECTION YEAR

Source: Hanes Walton, Jr., *Black Political Parties: A Historical and Political Analysis* (New York: Free Press, 1972).

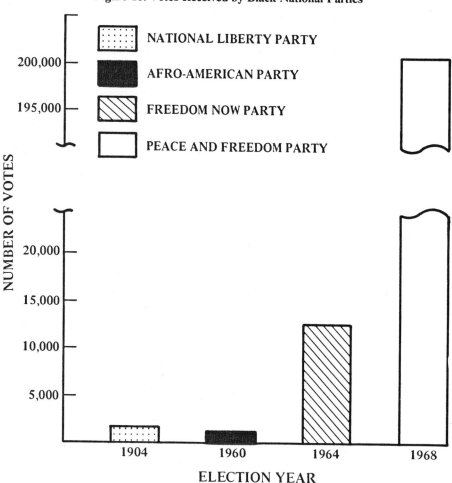

Figure 10. Votes Received by Black National Parties

Source: Hanes Walton, Jr., *Black Political Parties: A Historical and Political Analysis* (New York: Free Press, 1972).

some 195,135 votes.[10] This national black party differed from earlier ones in that it was a coalition between black militants and white liberals. Cleaver, the party's presidential candidate, justified this coalition on the grounds that black militants emphasized cultural nationalism because they were without a meaningful program for the black community. According to

[10] *Ibid.*, Hanes Walton, Jr., "Blacks and the 1968 Third Parties," *Negro Educational Review,* 21 (January, 1970), 22.

Cleaver, this cultural nationalism would do little to aid blacks in their problems of unemployment, slums, police brutality, etc. What blacks need, Cleaver argued, is a political revolution that would change the present economic and social system and bring a redistribution of wealth in which blacks would share equitably. In short, the black community needed a political, not a cultural revolution. Since many white liberals want the same thing, a union of some black militants with these white groups could bring the matter to fruition.

During the party's convention, Cleaver received 161 1/2 delegate votes to Dick Gregory's 54 to capture the party nomination. At age thirty-three, however, Cleaver was "two years below the United States Constitutional minimum age of thirty-five for a President,"[11] and even had he won, he could not have taken office. Nevertheless, his campaign attracted wide attention and a significant number of supporters. Part of this attention resulted from his numerous campaign speeches, from which the following is taken:

> America is up against the wall. This whole apparatus, this capitalistic system and its institutions and policies ... all need to be assigned to the garbage can of History and I don't give a——who does it ... The right to revolution can't be taken from the people ... we can go nowhere unless we have the right to defend ourselves against the Pig Cops. ...[12]

Cleaver's party lost the election, and Cleaver himself became an exiled fugitive from justice. The future of his party is unknown.

As Figure 9 indicates, black state parties have been much more numerous than black national parties (see Figure 10) and have lasted longer. Generally speaking, two types of black parties have emerged. There are the satellite and separatist parties.

For the most part, a black satellite party seeks both acceptance (i.e., by the national party affiliate) and the acquisition of power; the black separatist party, on the other hand, is concerned only with the latter. The satellite party seeks to persuade one of the national parties to recognize it as the authentic state party by arguing that the old state party is disloyal, or unrepresentative of the people, or repressive to certain ethnic groups within the state. In addition, the satellite parties mount seating challenges at national conventions and in Congress, and they call for expulsion of regular state party officials. If all this fails, the black satellite party seeks to acquire enough electoral victories within the state to convince the national party organization to accept it.

The black separatist party, on the other hand, seeks electoral victories

[11] J. Erroll Miller, "The Negro in National Politics in 1968," in P. W. Romero, ed., *In Black America* (Washington: United Publishing Corporation, 1969), pp. 5-6.
[12] *Ibid.*, p. 6.

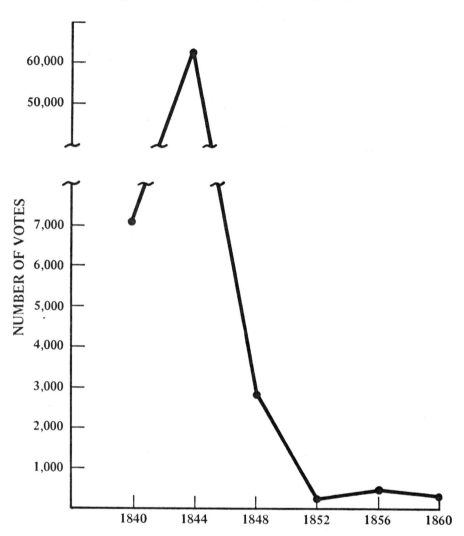

Figure 11. Votes Received by the Liberty Party

and tries to convince the voter that, if elected, it will effect meaningful changes. Winning, not recognition, is essential because it is from elected officials that the party expects the financial resources and policy spokesmen it will need in order to continue.

The parties also differ in that the black separatist party can exist on either the state, national, or local level, but the satellite party is limited to the state or regional level. The satellite party must always support the national party's presidential candidates, whereas the separate party can run or support anyone it pleases.

The similarities between the parties rest upon the fact that both are reformist organizations seeking to improve the political milieu, though from different approaches. Both are also similar in that they seek to raise the political power and attainments of black people.

To conclude, black parties have been third parties. Their function has been largely to protest the exclusion of blacks from the mainstream of American political life. Like third parties in general, they have disappeared almost as quickly as they have appeared. They will probably continue to appear as long as the racist factor in American politics makes them necessary.

BLACKS AND THIRD PARTIES

Blacks created their own parties, participated in the major parties, sought independence in political life, yet also participated in the third or minor parties in American political history.

Among the early third parties, for example, they participated in the Workingman parties in New York and cast votes for the anti-Masonic party in Pennsylvania.[13] Free blacks "expressed interest in and supported the first of the anti-slavery parties, the Liberty party, in its initial bid for power in 1840." Each year thereafter blacks participated in the convention of the Liberty party and supported it with declining votes and increasing oratory until it collapsed in 1860. The Liberty party responded to its black supporters by including resolutions in several of its conventions, by welcoming them into the party councils, giving them different leadership positions at the national convention, and by calling for the abolition of slavery in its political platforms. As Figure 11 indicates, however, support for the Liberty party was never enough to make it more than an organization of protest.

The Free Soilers continued the Liberty party's agitation against slavery, and blacks supported it and its banner of Free Soil, Free Speech, Free Labor, and Free Men. Like the Liberty party, the Free Soil party gave blacks the opportunity to participate in its political activities. Blacks returned the favor by supporting the party with their votes, newspapers and prayers. Unlike the Liberty party, however, the Free Soil party was successful and elected several men to public office, among them Charles Sumner, who went to Congress in 1841. He so angered congressmen with his exposes of the evils of slavery that he provoked a severe beating on the floor

[13] For a comprehensive account of blacks in the sundry third-party movements in the U.S., see Hanes Walton, Jr., *The Negro in Third Party Politics* (Philadelphia: Dorrance and Company, 1969). See also his "The Negro in the Early Third Party Movement," *Negro Educational Review,* 19 (April-July, 1968), 73-82.

of Congress by a representative from South Carolina. The beating impaired Sumner's health, but he was able to return to Congress and supported, along with Thaddeus Stevens, an old Anti-Masonic party leader, the Thirteenth, Fourteenth, and Fifteenth amendments.

These antislavery parties had their counterparts in proslavery parties in the South. Among these were the National Southern Rights party, the Nullification party, the National American party, and the Know Nothing party; in varying degrees, all supported slavery. It is on record, in fact, that from 1838 to 1860 blacks were *forced* to support the National American party in Rapides Parish, Louisiana.

After the Civil War blacks supported the Liberal Republican movement, the Equal Rights party, the Greenbackers, and the Prohibitionists. The support for the Liberal Republicans, the Equal Rights party, the Union Labor party and the Greenbacks was limited either because they were short-lived or because they were regional, but support for the Prohibition party, although small, was wider spread.[14] And if blacks were prohibitionists in many southern states, there were many antiprohibitionists.[15] In the different prohibitionist campaigns throughout the South, blacks opposed each other over the liquor issue. The point is that in both national and local elections, both prohibitionists and antiprohibitionists campaigned for the black vote.

The prohibitionists sought to reform America morally and spiritually by outlawing strong drink; the evangelism of the populists, on the other hand, was directed at the economic and agricultural sins of American society. The Populists sought to save the farmer, black and white, from despair, depression, and monopolistic tendencies in American society. Black populists began organizing in Houston County, Texas, in 1886. On February 22, 1892, at a Populist convention held in St. Louis, they merged with the white supremacy issue. All the black delegates who attended the convention, with the exception of the delegation from Georgia, supported the party's standard bearers, James B. Weaver and James C. Field. The Georgia delegation objected to the head of the black farmer alliance, a white Baptist missionary, R. M. Humphrey, casting a ballot for the colored alliance men, who favored a third party for blacks. In fact, the black delegation from Georgia was not angry with Humphrey so much as with the idea of a third party. Their walkout, however, had little effect on the national movement.

Once Weaver's campaign was launched, blacks turned out in large numbers to hear his speeches and support him. In Raleigh, North Carolina, the

[14] See Hanes Walton, Jr., "The Negro in the Prohibition Party: A Case Study of the Tennessee Prohibition Party Proceeding," ASNLH (Washington: Forthcoming); see also Hanes Walton, Jr., "Another Force for Disenfranchisement: Blacks and the Prohibitionists in Tennessee," *Journal of Human Relations,* 19 (Spring, 1971).

[15] Hanes Walton, Jr., and James Taylor, "The Negro in the Southern Prohibition Movement," *Negro History Bulletin,* January, 1971.

general was escorted to "Brookside Park by 300 white men and 50 Negroes." "When Weaver spoke at Waycross, Georgia, 3000 people, many of them Negroes, were gathered to hear him." In fact, throughout his campaign, blacks supported Weaver, and when national Populism failed electorally in 1892 and again in 1896, black Populism on the state and local levels continued.

In fact, blacks supported state Populist parties in many sections of the country even before the national movement began in 1892. In 1890, in Kansas, Benjamin Posts, a black Populist, won the post of state auditor by an overwhelming majority. In Arkansas, in the same year, a black minister, the Reverend I. P. Langlay, ran for Congress on the Populist ticket, and in Louisiana another black, E. A. Roachborough, ran on the same ticket for state treasurer.

In South Carolina, North Carolina, Alabama, Georgia, Texas, and Virginia, black Populists fused with white and black Republicans to win several state offices.[16] In North Carolina, in fact, this fusion technique enabled that state's black congressman, George E. White, to remain in the United States House of Representatives until 1901.

Black Populism died politically during the era of disfranchisement. White Populists, in many of the southern states, filled with prejudice and believing the myth that black voters had defeated them in nearly every election and had opposed their progressive measures, soon supported the movement to strip blacks of their voting rights.

Like the prohibitionists, the Populists could not overcome their race prejudice in order to promote progressive reforms instituted through a black and white coalition. They preferred to go it alone.

If the reformist-minded black Populists and black prohibitionists were forced from their respective movements, they found some comfort in the newly emerging Progressive party of 1912.

Black progressives were there from the beginning. Like the white progressives, numerous blacks had always believed that government should take positive action to improve society. In short, blacks too believed in progress. When Theodore Roosevelt took command of the Progressive movement of 1912, blacks joined the movement.

Roosevelt had attracted many black supporters during his first term in office when he appointed William Crum as custom collector in South Carolina, invited Booker T. Washington to the White House as a dinner guest, and announced his general concern for the welfare of the black race. During his second term, however, he lost many of these new black supporters by capitulating to "lilywhite Republicanism—dishonorably discharging

[16] Helen Edmonds, *The Negro and Fusion Politics in North Carolina* (Chapel Hill: University of North Carolina Press, 1951), pp. 2-28. See also William A. Mabry, *The Negro in North Carolina Politics since Reconstruction* (Durham: Duke University Press, 1940), pp. 31-56.

three companies of Negro soldiers for participating in the Brownsville riots and offering a quasi-defense of Negro lynching."[17]

In 1912, he appealed personally to blacks to join with him in the new party, and this caused "many Negroes both in the North and in the South to take him as their deliverer and they hastened to join the Progressive ranks."[18] Before the national convention, however, Roosevelt announced that his party would accept northern blacks as members, but because of southern traditions would not accept southern blacks. As the Brownsville affair had eroded black support of Roosevelt earlier, so did this new policy in the Progressive party.[19] Not all blacks withdrew from the Progressive party in 1912, however, despite Roosevelt's capitulation to Lily White Progressivism in the South. In March, a Negro Roosevelt headquarters opened in Chicago, which in April staged a Roosevelt Progressive Colored Republican race meeting to increase black support for the colonel. In Minnesota, Charles Sumner Smith, editor of the *Twin City Star*, and 390 other blacks formed "the Negro Independent Progressive Club of Hennepin County." In Baltimore, Maryland, a straw vote taken in the black community indicated that blacks favored Roosevelt twenty to one.

Moreover, "John R. Gleed, chairman of the Colored Bureau for the Progressives canvassed Negro voters in a far-reaching mailing campaign which sought their support and explained to them voting procedures."[20] The Bureau served as a distribution center for campaign letters and leaflets, and passed out a thousand copies of two black newspapers, the Cambridge *Advocate* and the Baltimore *Afro-American Ledger*, both of which endorsed Roosevelt.

In addition, "Gleed's Bureau supplied Negro speakers for Progressive rallies." Black orators went to the major cities of Delaware, New Jersey, Pennsylvania, and Connecticut. One, the Reverend William H. Mixon of Selma, Alabama, who edited the *Selma News*, covered more ground than any other black speaker on Roosevelt's behalf and employed the following punch line to help northern blacks accept Roosevelt's southern Lily White policy: "I have come 1,400 miles to tell you that the best Negroes of the South approve of Roosevelt's letter to Julian Harris" endorsing Lily White Progressivism. Mixon came under heavy criticism, for he was something of a political chameleon and was being paid for his services at the rate of fifty dollars a week, but he continued his speeches in Roosevelt's behalf. As Figure 7 reveals, the Progressives received a sizable number of black votes, but failed in their bid for power.

[17] Walton, *Third Parties, op. cit.*, p. 49.

[18] James Haynes, "Why the Negro Should Be a Progressive," *Crisis*, November, 1912, p. 42.

[19] Emma Lou Thornbrough, "The Brownville Episode and the Negro Vote," *Mississippi Valley Historical Review*, December, 1957.

[20] Douglas C. Strange, "The Making of a President, 1912: The Northern Negroes' View," *Negro History Bulletin*, 31 (November, 1968), 19.

The Progressive party of 1912 failed, but the vision of reform and the genuine concern for the downtrodden that it engendered continued. The party almost totally ignored the black problem in America, however. At its national convention in 1912, it had refused to adopt a resolution demanding full equality for blacks, and at its 1924 national convention sidestepped the black issue completely. Even under pressure, the Progressives and their presidential candidates would only commit themselves to the statement that "the Negro is an American citizen and is included in all that the Progressives seek for the American citizen."[21] In fact, not until October did La Follette change his position in regard to the black problem in America and begin to discuss it in his campaign. He went so far as to establish a Black Progressive Bureau. Only a few blacks—James Weldon Johnson, W. E. B. Du Bois, and William Pickens—actively supported the Progressive movement in the 1924 election, in which the party once again met defeat.

Twenty-four years later, another Progressive party emerged. This, headed by Henry A. Wallace in 1948, made a strong appeal for black support in both action and deed. Black supporters were welcomed, several blacks received high party appointments, and the presidential candidates espoused throughout the South a strong call for black civil rights. Under Truman, however, the Democrats outpleaded the Progressives on civil rights and won most of the black vote.

In Chicago, in William Dawson's district, the Progressives received only 5,000 votes to Dawson's 92,000. In Pittsburgh only 2 percent of black votes supported Wallace. "In Harlem, Wallace received 21,000 votes; Dawson, 25,000; and Truman, 90,000." In the South Wallace received less than a thousand black votes. Black Progressivism came to an end in 1948, although the party survived until 1956.

For the most part, the earlier Progressive party had ignored the black man. Its philosophical and ideological position did not include him. When the party finally decided to include blacks forthrightly, however, it was outdone by a major party.

Blacks have also been involved with the more doctrinaire third parties, and when socialism came to America it found some blacks waiting for it. Even before the turn of the century, black socialists, such as Peter H. Clark, propagated socialist doctrines in the black community.[22] When the Socialist Unity Convention met in 1901, three black delegates were present and had the convention pass a resolution that emphasized the socialist interest in the black cause. By 1904, a black newspaper, *The Voice of the Negro*, editorialized that socialism "is a splendid field for negotiations for

[21] Quoted in Walton, *op. cit.*, p. 54.
[22] Herbert C. Gulman, "Peter H. Clark: Pioneer Negro Socialist, 1877," *Journal of Negro Education*, Fall, 1965, pp. 413-418.

the Negro in these days when the Republican party has forsook him to the persecution of the Democrats."

This black enthusiasm for and participation in the prewar Socialist party was strongly curtailed, however, by race prejudice on the part of many Socialist leaders. Victor Berger, editor of the *Social Democratic Herald*, declared that "there can be no doubt the Negroes and mulattos constitute a lower race." Pleas by Eugene V. Debs notwithstanding, the best socialism could offer blacks was its claim to be an exclusively economic movement, and had nothing to do with social equality. But despite the socialist stand on the black question, a leader such as W. E. B. Du Bois[23] joined the local Socialist party in New York in 1912 (although he later joined the Democratic party that year), and when the Socialist National Convention met in Indianapolis in May, 1912, the only Negro delegate, S. C. Garrison of Montpelier, Indiana, prodded the party into inviting blacks to membership and offering a platform which appealed to them.

Even after World War I, however, and under Norman Thomas's tutelage, Socialists advocated only that blacks should join the party and vote their way to emancipation. Many Socialists imagined that once socialism was achieved, the two races would live in separate cities and have separate factories, separate schools, etc. For despite Thomas's appeal to the black community, socialism had nothing meaningful to offer the black electorate. It assumed that the uplift of the white worker would automatically aid the black worker. Nevertheless, several blacks ran for office on the Socialist party ticket. Frank Crosswaith was the party's candidate for lieutenant governor of New York several times. A. Philip Randolph and Chandler Owen also gave the party strong backing from time to time.

To this day, the Socialist party continues to make appeals to black people. In 1968, the Socialist Workers party ran a Newark black, Paul Boutelle, for vice president. The party's platform that year stressed black control of black communities, black people's right to self-defense and black noninvolvement in Vietnam. Still, the party received only a token number of black votes that year.

Communism also tried to win the loyalty of black Americans. As early as 1928, the Communist party was advancing the idea of a black nation in America that should revolt, declare its independence, and receive foreign aid from the home of communism—Russia.[24] When this idea failed to win many black supporters, the party changed its tactics. By 1930 the party was denouncing general discrimination against blacks in American life and tried to prove to blacks that they were defenders of minority rights by

[23] Du Bois, later as senatorial candidate, ran on the American Liberal party ticket in New York in 1950.

[24] See Wilson Record, *The Negro and the Communist Party* (Chapel Hill, N.C.: University of North Carolina Press, 1952), and William Nolen, *Communism vs. the Negro* (Chicago: Henry Regnery Company, 1951).

snatching from the NAACP the Scottsboro case.[25] When this also proved futile, the party ran a black, James Ford, for the vice presidency in 1932, 1936, and 1940. Each year the vote for the party dropped from the 1932 figure of 102,791 votes. Electioneering with black candidates continued on the local level, however, from time to time. In Chicago, black and white Communists waged a battle against black and white landlords, slumism, unemployment, etc. Finally, the party turned to electioneering and ran a black candidate, Gordon Ewen, for Congress in 1924. He received 32 votes. The party's black candidate in 1928, Edward L. Doty, received 100 out of 51,227 votes cast, and in 1932 Herbert Newton received 843 out of 61,467 votes. Elsewhere also, in Norfolk, Virginia, for example, a black Communist candidate received less than 500 votes.

Not all of these black Communists failed, however. Benjamin J. Davis became "the first Black Communist to be elected to the legislative office in the United States." He was elected to the New York City Council for six years, from 1944 until 1949.[26] Following his years as a councilman, Davis was indicted under the Smith Act and placed in a federal penitentiary. After his release, however, he campaigned on the People party's ticket in New York for state senator. During that campaign, he died.

In 1968, the Communists continued their tactic of trying to influence members of the black community by running a black woman, Charlene Mitchell, for president. During the campaign Mrs. Mitchell, who joined the party when she was sixteen and had been a member of the party's national committee since 1958, stated that racism was the number one issue in the United States. She argued that police should be disarmed and should reside in the communities in which they work. In her view, the U. S. involvement in Vietnam was bad; the U.S.S.R.'s action in Czechoslovakia she regarded as "regrettable but necessary." She also protested that the federal government refused her Secret Service protection and a briefing in international affairs. She received only 1,000 votes, but it is possible that the party will continue its policy of trying to attract blacks.

The doctrinal parties have shown as much prejudice and racism as the splinter and reformists parties. They too have used the race issue to try to advance their cause.

In the past and at present, the conservative and anti-civil rights minor parties have, like their predecessors, sought the black vote in an ambiguous or covert fashion. The racist Union party of 1936 appealed to blacks for support. The Dixiecrat movement in 1948 emerged because the Democratic

[25] See Wilson Record, *Race and Radicalism: The NAACP and the Communist Party in Conflict* (Ithaca, N.Y.: Cornell University Press, 1963), and Dan Carter, *Scottsboro: A Tragedy of the American South* (Baton Rouge: Louisiana State University Press, 1969).

[26] Benjamin Davis, *Communist Councilman from Harlem* (New York: International Publishers, 1969), p. 7.

party's civil rights platform encouraged black supporters. George Wallace's American Independent party of 1968 either ignored potential and actual black supporters or did little to encourage them. In fact, Wallace's platform, which was for law and order and against civil rights, was such as to preclude any appeal, either overt or covert, for black support. Nevertheless, there were blacks who supported him.

In retrospect, blacks have vigorously participated in the many third parties in American political history. Like the major parties, third parties have been handicapped by the racial issues in American life. Even in the most progressive of the third parties, some elements of racial discrimination have been present, and this factor has resulted in the loss of black support over a period of time.

BLACK POLITICAL INNOVATIONS

Black political participation in third parties and black creation of independent and satellite political parties do not constitute the whole political innovation by blacks in this country, and black political ingenuity in America will doubtless continue. Black people have consistently created new political tactics and devices in order to institute their policy preferences in America and to express their political opinions.

A notable example of black political innovation came in the spring of 1968 when Congressman John Conyers, Jr. (D.-Mich.), Bayard Rustin, and Mayor Richard Hatcher sent out several thousand letters urging blacks to join an organization that "would evaluate Presidential candidates and serve as a vehicle for political information in the black community."[27]

By June, 1968, the organization that evolved from this idea—the National Committee of Inquiry—held its first organizational meeting with about two hundred individuals participating in the deliberations. Conyers, who served as temporary chairman, stated after its initial meeting that this new organization would act primarily as a "jury to find the candidate" who most merited the backing of "Black America."[28] "We specifically intend to interview every candidate [even George Wallace]." After these interviews, a final report of the findings would be released to the black electorate prior to the November election.

At the initial meeting area chairmen were established according to functional and geographical need. The major idea embraced at the founding meeting was that black Americans had always been too divided, too fragmented, and needed to show unity and an organized force in politics. With a show of strength, black people had a chance to eliminate undesirable

[27] Miller, *op. cit.*, p. 32.
[28] *Ibid.*

political candidates. At the next strategy meeting on August 26, NCI reached two major decisions: (1) "to support all challenges by black delegates for convention seats, and (2) to push for a commitment from each of the major Democratic Presidential candidates to support the recommendations of the National Commission on Civil Disorders."[29] After several other sessions, the NCI decided, after a long and heated discussion, to endorse the Reverend Channing Philips of the District of Columbia as the favorite-son candidate for president and Julian Bond of Georgia for vice president. (They were the first blacks so nominated at a national convention of a major party). Bond withdrew, however, because he did not meet the age requirement, but Dr. Philips received 46 1/2 votes from seventeen state delegations and 21 of the 23 District of Columbia votes—for a total of 67 1/2 votes.

The committee failed to achieve its main purpose of uniting black people on one candidate, but their attempt to make objective "investigations of candidates for public office and evaluations of needed or impending party or governmental policies of direct concern to a particular segment of our population is a laudable and much needed effort."

Another notable example of black political innovation was Dick Gregory's independent campaign for the presidency. In some states, Gregory was endorsed by the Peace and Freedom party, and in others by the Freedom and Peace party; his campaign, however, was strictly personal. He emphasized the problem of "moral fallout"—i.e., "the spreading [of] cruelty and corruption, the disrespect for the dignity of any individual of any color, and the political decay that leads to immoral and illegal wars." He called for an improvement in the plight of American Indians and for placing sanctions against Rhodesia by "executive order" which would limit American exports there to "nothing except tuna fish, cranberry sauce, cigarettes, and color tv sets." In regard to his convictions about the Indians, Gregory held a fish-in with some Indians in the Nisqually River to protest an 1854 treaty that the U. S. broke because it guaranteed the Indians that in return for their land the fish and game would belong to them "for as long as the sun shall shine and the grass shall grow and the mountains shall stand." For this action, Gregory drew a ninety-day jail sentence that was upheld by the Supreme Court. Gregory continued his dramatic acts by distributing money-size bills bearing his picture and a dove instead of George Washington and an eagle. In New York and Nashville these handbills were seized when several found their way into automatic money changers. His colorful acts won Gregory 148,622 votes. After his defeat, he was inaugurated as president-in-exile and drew up plans for a Black House to be built across from the White House.

[29] *Ibid.*, p. 33.

IX

Black Pressure Groups

The American political scientist David B. Truman defines an interest group as "any group that, on the basis of one or more shared attitudes, makes certain claims upon other groups in the society for the establishment, maintenance, or enhancement of forms of behavior that are implied by the shared attitudes."[1] In this sense, "an interest group is a categoric group whose members are to some extent conscious of their common characteristics, regard themselves as having a common value or 'interest' arising from these characteristics, and to some extent direct their behavior to advance their common interest."[2]

Since the antagonists in political contests are groups of human beings, not isolated individuals acting without reference to or support from other individuals, political pressure groups become one means by which an organized interest group may pursue its objectives. The political interest group uses "pressure politics" to obtain governmental policies that will help it achieve what it wants or hinder opposing groups from achieving what they want. A pressure group, therefore, differs from a political party; the former seeks to influence public policy, but the latter seeks to gain control of the decision-making process. Parties are a device whereby one can institute his policy preferences in the American political system; pressure groups are another. Blacks have used both.

THE NATURE OF BLACK PRESSURE GROUPS

Like most black organizations in America, black pressure groups have differed from other such groups in America. The tactics and techniques they have employed have differed not only in kind, but also in degree from those of white pressure groups. Likewise, their success or failure has been determined by factors different from those that have affected other such groups.

[1] David B. Truman, *The Governmental Process* (New York: Alfred A. Knopf, 1951), p. 33.
[2] Austin Ranney, *The Governing of Men* (New York: Holt, Rinehart and Winston, 1966), p. 11.

140

Blacks have resorted to "pressure politics," either individually or collectively, whenever the ordinary avenues of political expression have been closed to them. In fact, blacks have had to protest even for the right to protest that the First Amendment supposedly guarantees every American.

In Alabama in 1958 the NAACP was barred on the supposed legal ground that it was a foreign corporation and did not comply with state law, but in actuality it was barred because the organization would give blacks the right to protest against the age-old system of segregation.[3] Blacks in the state, in effect, had to protest for the right to associate with each other in order to protest. Even famed civil rights leader Dr. Martin Luther King, Jr., argued that it was necessary for blacks to go outside of the law and disobey it, just to protest its unjust basis.[4]

To understand black pressure politics in America one muct understand blacks and their will to power. Blacks have continually entered the American political arena, even when doors to that arena were closed to them. The problems facing blacks, however, were altogether different from those facing any other group in the nation, and black pressure groups have accordingly been different also.[5] To begin with, white pressure groups generally represent a particular segment of the white community, for example, business, agriculture, or labor. Black pressure groups, on the other hand, must of necessity be concerned with the needs of the black community as a whole, for the problems that face blacks face all blacks, not just some of them. This means, of course, that black pressure groups must concern themselves even with those members of the black community who do not support their particular aims. White pressure groups, on the other hand, need concern themselves only with that segment of the white community that shares their views.

Black pressure groups generally seek ambiguous, intangible goals; white pressure groups tried to seek tangible rewards. The goals of black organizations have been abstract and symbolic—equality, freedom, dignity, pride, legal rights, etc. Even when these are granted in a tangible way, i.e., through legislation, they remain intangible because their principal effect is psychological.[6]

Still another difference is that whites have sought to influence public

[3] See *NAACP* v. *Alabama,* 357 U. S. 449, 1958; *NAACP* v. *Alabama,* 377 U. S. 288, 1964.

[4] Hanes Walton, Jr., *The Political Philosophy of Martin Luther King, Jr.* (Westport, Conn.: Negro Universities Press, 1971), chap. 3.

[5] Although there is little data on the nature and significance of black pressure groups, one should consult the following articles: Ralph Bunche, "A Critical Analysis of the Tactics and Programs of Minority Groups," *Journal of Negro Education,* 4 (July, 1935), and his "The Programs of Organizations Devoted to the Improvement of the Status of the American Negro," *Journal of Negro Education,* 8 (July, 1939), and Oliver C. Cox, "The Programs of Negro Civil Rights Organizations," *Journal of Negro Education,* 20 (Summer, 1951), 354–366.

[6] Roscoe E. Lewis, "The Role of Pressure Groups in Maintaining Morale among Negroes," *Journal of Negro Education,* 12 (Summer, 1943), 464.

policy that pertains to them in this country, but black groups have had to decide whether to pursue a policy of integration or separatism. Since the concern for abstract rights takes precedence over tangible benefits among black pressure groups, their attainment of rights in this country through integration or black separatism has set black and white pressure groups apart in terms of end-goals.

Finally, there are stylistic differences. When black pressure groups were denied access to agencies, or when governmental agencies were not responsive to their pressure—as during the first and second decades of this century—they turned to broader bases for support, such as the public at large.

The principal tactic of black pressure groups, and one that serves to distinguish them from most other such groups, is their appeal to the conscience of the people against the denial of justice in the broadest sense. The chief concern of black groups has been the attainment of rights that can only be had either through force, concern, or morality. Neither of the first two would prove effective, so the third had to be tried. From this there derives an important distinction. Most white pressure groups sought to promote their self interest in terms of economic benefits, or battled special types of *basic rights*. Black self-interest became one of rights, while white self-interest could dispense with this elementary concern and move into narrower spheres. And in this way, the heavy emphasis on convincing one group to grant another group its basic rights through appeals to moral principles embodied in the Declaration of Independence, the Constitution, the law of God or nature, could easily be dropped for much more sophisticated political activities concerned with more special aspects of one's interests.

In sum, black pressure groups have differed from white groups in terms of (1) their basic nature, (2) their focus and concern, (3) their goals, and (4) their style and choice of weapons. Such has been the case in the past, such is still the case now, and such will probably remain the case.

EARLY BLACK PRESSURE ACTIVITY

When suffrage rights were withdrawn from blacks in South Carolina because their voting in the 1701 and 1703 gubernatorial elections drew the ire of whites, they reentered state politics via pressure group activity. In January, 1791, a group of free blacks in Charleston petitioned the state legislature for a relief of legal disabilities placed upon them by the "Negro Act" (act for the better ordering the governing of Negroes and Slaves in this province) of 1740. The petition was rejected.

In fact, all during the colonial period blacks, slave and free, pressured state legislatures, North and South, for relief from legal disabilities placed upon their freedom (in the case of slaves), equal educational facilities, removal of unequal poll taxes, etc. In some cases pressure activities, such as issuing petitions, presenting memorials, praying, orating, staging violent revolts, quiet vigilances, and persuading influential whites to speak in their behalf, proved successful. At other times they failed. The point is that the annals of colonial America are replete with repeated efforts on the part of blacks to affect public policy on the state level.

In colonial America blacks, individually and collectively, brought what pressures they could upon local and colonial assemblies. After the creation of the national government these pressure activities were carried not only to the state level but also to the president and Congress on the national level. Black pressure activity expanded with the growth of the nation.

Eight years after the creation of the national government in 1789, free blacks from North Carolina residing fugitively in Philadelphia, petitioned the president and Congress through Representative John Swanwicks of Pennsylvania to void a law that North Carolina passed in 1788 declaring that all illegally manumitted slaves be returned to slavery. This petition was debated in Congress on procedural grounds (whether a petition from fugitive slaves was to be considered) and voted down.[7]

Three years later in 1800 another petition was sent to Congress by free blacks living in Philadelphia through representative Robert Waln. This petition called for a halt to the slave trade, a repeal of the fugitive slave act of 1793, and the abolition of the institution of slavery. It provoked such a long and heated debate in the House that it was referred to a committee, where it was quietly buried.[8]

Though unsuccessful, both these petitions prefigured future black pressure activity on the national level. With the budding of antislavery movements, black abolitionists continued to pressure Congress and the president through memorials and petitions to release their southern brothers from bondage. In fact, such a barrage of petitions from northern blacks and white abolitionists hit Congress that in 1836 the House of Representatives enacted a "gag rule" to table all measures relating to slavery rather than assigning them to a committee. John Quincy Adams fought this measure on the grounds that it breached a basic constitutional right by continually reading all petitions sent or given to him, "despite threats of his House colleagues to censure or expel him." When petitioning slowed, white abolitionists increased their activity; blacks did likewise, with a steady stream of petitions being laid at Congress's door even after the "gag rule" was repealed in 1844.

[7] *Annals of Congress of the United States,* 4th Congress, 2nd Session, VI (Washington, 1849), pp. 2015-2018.

[8] *Annals of Congress of the United States,* 6th Congress, X (Washington, 1851), pp. 229-230.

THE RISE OF BLACK PROTEST "ORG"

One factor had been discernible among the early black pressure activities: they lacked organization. One looks in vain for a permanent organization in colonial America promoting black interests; the few organizations there were, were temporary.

With the budding of the antislavery movement and the increasing disabilities being placed on free blacks and slaves alike, black pressure organizations began to appear. On September 20, 1830, in Philadelphia, delegates from seven states met to consider what should be done about their plight. One proposal adopted called for the establishment of a permanent national Negro convention with permanent state and local auxiliary units to consider programs and policies to aid or change the black man's condition in America. Regional offices were set up in each state, and these, in turn, elected delegates to state conventions at which a permanent state governing body was elected to consider how best to solve the problems facing blacks in the state. The state delegates also elected a delegation to go to the national body to discuss their problems and work out some kind of overall national strategy to eliminate the problems facing blacks. These delegations elected for a one-year term a national president, secretary, and other officers, to attend to the national organization and business for that particular year.

In addition, the national body had roving secretariats to work with state and local areas that did not have organizations or could not afford to establish them. Blacks felt that such an organization would provide them with a greater opportunity to affect the policies and decisions of local, state, or national governing bodies. Moreover, the black national convention movement was in tune with the times. There were conventions for women's rights, colonization, church supremacy, and peace. Each of these different conventions sought to reform certain social evils. None were pressure groups in the modern use of the word; they were their earlier counterpart in both word and deed.

The first annual national black convention met in 1831 and four more times during the 1830s, three times in the 1840s, twice in the 1850s; in the sixties it reorganized itself into the National Equal Rights League.[9] Although the meetings of the national organization were only occasional, those of many of its subsidiaries were regular.

There are many reasons why the national organization was irregular. From first to last, it could never agree on goals or strategies. The various delegations could not decide, for example, whether or not to remain in the United States. Moreover, those who wanted to leave could not decide

[9] See H. Bell, "The Negro Convention Movement, 1830—New Perspective," *Negro History Bulletin,* February, 1951, pp. 104-123.

where to go—Canada, Haiti, or Liberia. Those who wanted to stay could not decide whether to accept segregation or work for its abolition. They even differed over the question of what to do about slavery.

Given such confusion over goals, there was understandably confusion over techniques. In the 1840s, for instance, the national convention had a difficult time deciding whether to employ moral suasion or political action in opposing slavery.[10] This was after the convention had a difficult time deciding that slavery should be abolished.

In addition to these problems of goals and tactics were those of factionalism, jealousy, religion, and leadership, which finally impaired the effectiveness of the national organization.

Although the national organization did issue petitions, addresses, and prayers in trying to pressure Congress, little if anything was accomplished by the organization. Moreover, with so much internal strife that it was unable to control its state and local auxiliaries, the national organization could not even issue orders to its supposedly subordinate members. Several state organizations, like the Ohio branch, pulled away from the parent organization and pursued independent policies and activities because little that was meaningful was forthcoming from the national body. Comparatively speaking, many of the state and local auxiliaries had more success in pressuring governmental bodies than the parent organizations had. These groups felt that it was not necessary to take directions from the national body.

Organizational nomenclature was not the only problem facing the National Black Convention Movement. Another was leadership. The national convention never appointed a leader with enough administrative ability to pull the organization together and give it direction.

Finally, the political environment itself, affected as it was by racial prejudice, limited alike the national, state, and local conventions. These groups could count on few allies.

In terms of specific results, organized black pressure group activity accomplished nothing on the national level and little on the local level. In regard to general results, however, these organized black pressure groups actively led to intersectional strife.

During the Civil War the National Equal Rights League was created out of remnants of the old Convention Movement. This league sought to achieve suffrage rights for all blacks after the war was over and employed tactics similar to those of the Convention Movement. State, local, and national politicians were pressured and petitioned by the NERL. The league president, Frederick Douglass, met with President Andrew Johnson

[10] See Howard Bell, "National Negro Convention of the Middle 1840's: Moral Suasion vs. Political Action," *Journal of Negro History*, 22 (October, 1937), 247–260.

and presented his demands, but they were rejected. After the meeting, the group met with a group of congressmen who put the proposal in effect after the 1866 election. The league sought an alliance with the women's suffrage movement, but the antiblack prejudice of the suffragettes prevented this from taking place. Here again, the national body and its state and local auxiliaries worked almost independently of each other. The organization also suffered from poor leadership and problems over tactics. For the most part, however, it had overcome the problem of goals, which was resolved for it by the Civil War.

On the whole, after the passage of the Fifteenth Amendment, most national black pressure groups declined. A few state and local groups existed here and there; their raison d'être had been taken away by the three Reconstruction amendments and the promise of better things to come. With the end of Reconstruction, however, and the rise of the era of disfranchisement, black protest organizations began to reappear. Old state and local organizations were reactivated, and on the national level the National Afro-American League, patterned after the National Negro Convention and the National Equal Rights League, was formed in 1890.[11] Like its predecessors, however, and due largely to the same reasons, it died.

It was reactivated in 1898 as the National Afro-American Council, but it had little success in bringing about a change in the national policy of segregation and discrimination. The league and council failed basically because of the restrictive political environment that condoned this policy. In retrospect, it is hard to see what tactics the league or council could have used to change public policy toward blacks in this society.

Following the collapse of the council, several other black pressure groups emerged, such as the National Negro-American Political League, the Niagara Movement, etc. They issued a few protest statements and resolutions and then disappeared. For the most part, successful black pressure groups on the national level did not get started until the second decade of the twentieth century.

PRESENT-DAY BLACK PRESSURE GROUPS

If early black pressure groups suffered because they were organized from the bottom upward, with hordes of diverse people trying to give the organization meaning and direction, the present-day groups have largely overcome this tendency. Moreover, if the problem of goals and tactics plagued the earlier pressure groups, then the present-day black pressure groups have to some extent overcome that problem by concentration either on

[11] See Emma Lou Thornbrough, "The National Afro-American League, 1887-1908," *Journal of Southern History,* 27 (November, 1961), 498.

separation or integration. Numerous pressure organizations have advocated separation or escapism or a nonpolitical position—like Marcus Garvey's Back to Africa movement, the Forty-nine Staters, and Father Divine's Peace Movement—but we shall primarily concentrate on those major black organizations that pressure the American system for either inclusion or modification.

The Politics of the NAACP

Organized in 1910 from a coalition of black intellectuals and white
liberals, the NAACP set out to acquire for all black citizens the rights and
privileges enumerated in the Constitution. In order to achieve this goal, the
organization decided to rely chiefly upon legal proceedings in order to
make the courts declare that blacks were entitled to enjoy all those rights
spelled out in the Constitution and especially in the Fourteenth and Fifteenth amendments. In other words, the NAACP organizer felt the Constitution and justice to be color-blind in terms of fair play and equality before
the law, and felt that the courts would support this contention.[12]

If the major goals of the NAACP were to prove that blacks were entitled
to all the rights and privileges of other Americans, then the corollary to
that goal was that blacks also deserved and merited these rights. Thus,
coupled with legal proceedings was the use of education and propaganda to
promote the outstanding achievements of the race. Finally, the NAACP
relied upon moral suasion to convince people to accept and grant blacks
those rights that the courts decreed they had. Otherwise, public apathy
would nullify the court decisions.

The NAACP began its fight against state-supported segregation and
discrimination in America by exerting pressure on the public legislators,
decision-makers, and the courts. It expanded as membership grew by
establishing regional offices, state conferences, and youth councils and
college chapters. It grew rapidly but remained strongly centralized. Major
policy formulations were made at the highest level, with day-to-day decisions left to the discretion of the local officials.[13] Since its inception, the
NAACP's use of pressure tactics has obtained both success and failure for
it. Since, however, the NAACP has spent more than half a century in the
political arena, we shall focus upon a few examples to illustrate the organization in action.

A pertinent example of how the NAACP exercised its influence in the

[12] See Clement E. Vose, "Litigation as a Form of Pressure Group Activity," *Annals of the
Academy of Political and Social Science,* September, 1958, pp. 20–31.
[13] See Warren D. St. James, *The National Association for the Advancement of Colored
People: A Case Study in Pressure Groups* (New York: Exposition Press, 1958), pp. 103–104.
See also Robert A. Anglin, "A Sociological Analysis of the NAACP," Ph.D. dissertation,
Indiana University.

political arena[14] was the nomination of Judge John J. Parker for a Supreme Court vacancy. In 1930, when Supreme Court Justice Sanford died, President Hoover nominated Parker, a U.S. Circuit Court judge and native of North Carolina, as his successor. Immediately the NAACP inquired into Parker's background to discern his racial leanings. From their inquiry, the association learned that Parker, as a Republican gubernatorial candidate in 1920, had advocated continued disfranchisement of black citizens and favored poll taxes and the grandfather clause. In addition, during the campaign Parker had asserted that:

> The Negro as a class does not desire to enter politics. The Republican party of North Carolina does not desire him to do so. We recognize the fact that he has not yet reached that stage in his development when he can share the burdens and responsibilities of government ... I say it deliberately, there is no more dangerous or contemptible enemy of the state than men who for personal or political advantage will attempt to kindle the flame of racial prejudice or hatred ... the participation of Negroes in politics is a source of evil and danger to both races and is not desired by the wise men in either race or by the Republican party of North Carolina.[15]

After securing these data on the overt racism of Parker's campaign, the association contacted him for verification and his present view. When he refused to answer the association's request, the national office directed the association and its field officers "to oppose as vigorously as possible" Judge Parker's confirmation.

Immediately a protest was filed with President Hoover urging him to withdraw the nomination in accordance with a precedent set by President Taft, who had withdrawn a judge's nomination in 1912 when it was publicly proved that he had an antiblack record. President Hoover rejected the association's request, whereupon the association presented its case to the Senate subcommittee that was holding hearings on the nomination. The subcommittee, however, gave more consideration to organized labor's protest of Parker's antilabor stance. During the hearing "the American Federation of Labor avoided all contact with the association for fear it might appear they were allies."[16]

When the hearing proved fruitless, the association carried its case to the public. All branches of the association, especially in states where blacks

[14] *Ibid.*, pp. 121-126. See also Richard L. Watson, Jr., "The Defeat of Judge Parker: A Study in Pressure Groups and Politics," *Mississippi Valley Historical Review,* 50 (September, 1963), 213-234, and Gilbert Ware, "Lobbying as a Means of Protest: The NAACP as an Agent of Equality," *Journal of Negro Education,* 33 (Spring, 1964), 103-110.

[15] Quoted in Walton, White, "The Negro and the Supreme Court," *Harper's Magazine,* CLXII (1931), 239.

[16] St. James, *op. cit.,* p. 123.

voted in significant numbers, urged the entire black community and its fraternal, civic, educational, social, and other organizations to telegram protest to senators from those states. Alliances were formed with sympathetic white liberals and other national black groups such as the National Council of Colored Women. All of the important black newspapers (over 200) were enlisted to give the case front page and editorial coverage. Moreover, a white newspaper chain, Scripps-Howard, aided the campaign in its columns. In addition, white newspaper columnists kept the association aware of secret meetings and the numerous bribes made to senators to support the confirmation. The dissemination of this information produced an avalanche of telegrams, telephone messages, letters, petitions, declarations, and personal visits that engulfed the senators from both northern and southern states. This shotgun technique stirred complacent senators to action.

Unfortunately, in creating this flurry of activity the association set its own opposition in motion. In Washington, southerners lobbied in behalf of Parker; at home, they used economic reprisals, violence, and threats of violence against black communities in order to pressure them to stop their anti-Parker campaign. Moreover, several conservative black leaders were enlisted by whites to issue statements in support of Parker and to repudiate the association.

To these counterpressures the NAACP responded by appealing to northern Democratic senators that a vote for Parker's confirmation would help Hoover reward North Carolina for going Republican in the 1928 election. It asked the governor of North Carolina to take all necessary steps to insure the safety of the black citizenry. Finally, it published the past records of those conservative black leaders who denounced it in order to demonstrate their uselessness to the black community.

In response to the association's and other endeavors, the Senate Judiciary Committee voted ten to six against Parker's confirmation. Hoover, however, arranged to have a full Senate vote on the nomination, whereupon the NAACP held simultaneous mass meetings in many cities throughout the country. Telegraph blanks were given to those in attendance to write their senators and to once more urge the rejection of the Parker nomination. With over two thousand telegrams from Chicago alone, the Senate voted on May 7 to reject the nomination; the vote was 41 to 39.

The NAACP's tactics had proved successful, and it continued to employ them even after the vote. A list of senators who voted for Parker's nomination and who were up for reelection in September was sent to all the association branches, which, in conjunction with the national office, campaigned for their defeat. The association was instrumental in securing the defeat of eleven of the thirty-nine senators who had voted for Judge Parker's nomination.

A recent parallel of the Parker case can be seen in the 1969 struggle for the confirmation of Clement Haynesworth and G. Harrold Carswell. President Richard Nixon, apparently to repay a political debt to Republican Senator Strom Thurmond, nominated Haynesworth, a federal judge, for a vacancy to the United States Supreme Court created by Abe Fortas's resignation.

Haynesworth was a native of South Carolina, and immediately upon his nomination, the NAACP checked his record and found him to be of the segregationist persuasion. Moreover, in several racial cases that had come before his court, there was evidence that his judgments were partial to the whites involved. Organized labor came out against Haynesworth also, who had seemingly favored the antilabor interests in his state. Finally, one case that came before him was alleged to involve a conflict of interest on his part.

Like Hoover, Nixon refused to retract the nomination. At the hearing more attention was given to labor's protest, with a difference—labor and the NAACP coalesced and their alliance proved effective; the final vote denied confirmation of the Haynesworth appointment.

After the defeat of Haynesworth's nomination, Nixon nominated another southerner, G. Harrold Carswell of Florida, for the same post. Immediately, the NAACP found that Carswell had made several racist statements when he had run for a seat in the state House of Representatives of Georgia in 1948. Carswell argued that his position had changed considerably in the intervening twenty years, but then newspapers brought to light a connection between him and a private golf club that excluded blacks. In opposing the appointment, the NAACP was without major allies. That the confirmation was denied is therefore indicative of the organization's strength.

Nevertheless, if the NAACP's tactics have succeeded in some instances, they have failed in others. For example, the NAACP tried persistently but futilely from 1922 until 1940 to secure a federal antilynching bill,[17] which was badly needed, because a child victimized by educational discrimination could survive until litigation secured him his rights, but the victims of lynchings could not wait that long. Therefore, in 1913 when the association developed a systematic campaign to pressure the national government into taking some action on lynching and its cruelties, the association adopted what it felt to be the most persuasive tactics. These "techniques included the investigation of mob violence, the compilation and publication of statistics, the sponsoring of conferences and mass meetings and a generalized program of public education on the causes, enactments, and subse-

[17] See Robert L. Zangrando, "The NAACP and a Federal Antilynching Bill, 1934-1940," *Journal of Negro History,* 50 (April, 1965), 106-117.

quent minimal prosecution characteristics of lynchings." Despite the thoroughness of the tactics, however, this and later efforts failed.

In 1933, for instance, the NAACP drafted an antilynching bill and got Colorado's Edward Costigan and New York's Robert Wagner to act as cosponsors. In 1934, when the bill came before the Senate Judiciary Subcommittee for hearing, the NAACP personnel presented staggering statistics of lynchings in this country since 1882, the mob violence attendant upon them, the urgent need of blacks for protection, and numerous articles, editorials, and endorsements from state governors and other distinguished persons favoring the measure. Next, the subcommittee was told of the ineffective state laws and the possible constitutional sources of power that Congress could use to enact the bill. This testimony proved so effective that the Judiciary Committee reported the bill out in less than a month. The association then turned its attention to drumming up support among the senators. To do this the NAACP sent every congressman an open letter describing the urgent need for such legislation. Attached to the letter were signatures of outstanding authors, scholars, governors, ex-governors, mayors, bishops, college presidents, lawyers, jurists, etc. (a typical endorsement tactic of the NAACP). Moreover, a similar list was sent to President Roosevelt.

The public also was prepared. Newspapers, pamphlets, letters, booklets, parades, periodicals, etc.—even art exhibits on lynching which were attended by famous white and black artists—called upon the public to demand that their congressmen take positive action on the bill before them. Once again, however, the association's action caused southern opposition to increase.

In the House, the chairman of the House Judiciary Committee brought to the floor a weaker federal antilynching bill sponsored by the only black congressman, Arthur Mitchell from Chicago. A feud between Arthur Mitchell and the association ensued with the latter informing all House members of this "southern trick." Their endeavors worked; a discharge petition failed to bring the Mitchell bill to the House floor.

In the Senate, however, southern opposition in the form of a six-week filibuster in 1938 killed the antilynching bill. The first vote for cloture failed and the NAACP's efforts to petition senators to change their minds before the second vote for cloture also failed. Therefore, the Senate moved to other pressing matters and the bill was "unlamentedly buried."

Other efforts came in 1939 and 1940, but they too failed. At present the association has not been able to secure that piece of legislation.

These are just two examples of the NAACP's many efforts to end segregation. In other areas, such as the campaign against the poll tax which heavily discriminated against the black community, the association's efforts failed until the passage of the Anti-Poll Tax Amendment in the 1960s. In regard to the white primary case, victories and setbacks were intertwined until final victory came in 1944 with *Smith* v. *Allwright,* some two decades after the initial legal proceedings had started.

In 1954 the association finally won a major battle against segregated education. In 1965 it won the right for blacks in the area of public accommodations when the Supreme Court upheld the 1964 Civil Rights law. Here again, the victory came after many victories and defeats. In fact, on the national level, the association had an impressive record of thirty-four victories out of thirty-eight cases it had presented before the Supreme Court. Its court record on the local level, however, especially in the South, is less impressive. But here again the association's goal was to seek to get the federal government, if possible, to uphold Supreme Court declarations in order to forego the necessity for instituting individual cases on the local and state level. Unfortunately, the inability to secure federal support in the political arena to give general application to the Supreme Court's edicts was one of the association's weaknesses.

To begin with the NAACP has had some problems in the formation of its goals. When the association organizers saw that they could get the courts to declare a law valid or a right legally applicable, it was felt that this would be sufficient. In short, who would disobey the law of the land? The reverse of the statement is what should have been asked. Who would obey the law of the land? Furthermore, how rigorously would the federal government enforce the law of the land? For the NAACP has found that a right declared valid by the Supreme Court may not be a right in fact. To the association's disillusionment, folkways and mores, both North and South, have continued to defy the declared law of the land, which the federal government for political reasons has failed in many cases to support vigorously. The organization has suffered, in effect, from its most successful technique—legalism. Legal proceedings have proved both costly and time-consuming; they involve only a few people at a time, and depend upon the attitude and philosophy of the courts (i.e., a liberal as opposed to a conservative court).

Still another problem has been overcentralization and a tendency toward oligarchical control. In many instances, the local and regional bodies have little autonomy and flexibility. In addition, the organization has failed to include the black masses. It has had a tendency toward favoring the black middle class and its problems, which are mainly the lack of status goals, while those of the black masses call for a radical socioeconomic program or welfare goals that legalism cannot institute.

Moreover, a national black organization like the NAACP suffers from conflicting and overlapping membership. Blacks who belong to this group also belong to others and have therefore had difficulties in deciding which group to support. As a result, the association has not always been able to command loyalty from its own members, much less the rest of the black community. This has been reflected by poor financial support from time to time.

Finally, by attacking only the symptoms and effects of segregation—i.e., statutes—and seeking to remove them, little can be achieved in terms of socioeconomic programs in the black community, such as better housing, jobs, and wages. The NAACP thus far has not been able to move black interests from the abstract questions of racial justice to the more specific problems of economic interests.

The National Urban League

The Urban League was organized in 1916 out of a merger of three earlier organizations; it was composed of philanthropists, social workers, and professionals, who took as their motto the idea "that the Negro needs not alm but opportunity—opportunity to work at the job for which the Negro was best fitted, with equal pay for equal work, and equal opportunity for advancement. With this in mind, the organization chose educational and adjustmental tactics to carry out its program.

Although local branches were established throughout the country, with this goal the league tended primarily to aid the adjustment of the millions of southern rural blacks who were migrating to the northern cities. In stressing the improvement of black life rather than integration or political action, the league functioned as a giant social welfare agency for black people. While the national league took over this larger function, the local leagues all functioned primarily as employment agencies.

Thus the league had to contact employers and trade union officers and try to sell or persuade them to hire black labor, impressing upon them that black workers are efficient, satisfactory, good, and faithful. Then, blacks with good records were sent to the employer for the possible vacancy. The league also tried to keep avenues of vocational training open to black youths and to encourage these youths to take advantage of them. In addition, the league watched civil service boards in order to prevent discrimination, and encouraged blacks to take competitive examinations for civil service positions. The league also pressured for such community projects as playgrounds, housing projects, schools, and other public facilities. From time to time the league staged economic boycotts—i.e., "don't buy where you can't work" campaigns.

Taking Chicago as an example, one can realize the difficulties the league faced. From 1916 until 1921 it had to work in a limited and narrowly defined area, because it received only moderate financial support and had to struggle incessantly to maintain interracial goodwill and to find white supporters. When a race riot occurred in Chicago in 1919, whites ran to the agency for assistance "not in resolving the fundamental problems but in restoring a delicate race relations balance."[18] When the league failed in this momentous task, it was reduced to little more than a charity organization. From 1925 to 1956 it tried mightily to regain white supporters and the black community's faith. The whites grew conservative, however, and sought "sane" black leaders, and the black community became more militant and articulate. The league had to walk a tightrope. By 1965 its budget had just reached the half-million-dollar mark. Today, it is reorganized, hoping to become a force in the black community; it faces the same problems it did in 1916, only they have become worse.

Lately, under the leadership of the late Whitney M. Young, Jr., it has pressured the federal government for massive federal aid to the poor, and a basic compensatory program to help poverty-stricken, ghetto-bound blacks catch up with middle-class America.[19] As time continues, the problems of poverty-stricken blacks continue, and the plight of the Urban League in being unable to solve them intensifies.

As a pressure group, the National Urban League has no members. Its connections with the black community are somewhat nebulous. In fact, it is a pressure group with an informal organization that seldom communicates effectively with all the members of its categorical group—especially the poverty-stricken blacks.

Tactically, personal and interracial goodwill is its ultimate weapon. Moreover, its use of community chests and contributions from foundations and individuals often ameliorates these conciliatory tactics, for at times the money comes with strings attached. Furthermore, with a lack of steady funds, the organization has not been able to develop a meaningful program for black and white labor-solidarity and for the economic elevation of the black masses. In fact, in regard to the latter, the problem has been so great that it has simply been ignored.

Finally, the organization's goal—to make the most out of racial separation—was ideal but impractical as one looks at the gigantic problem facing the poverty-stricken black communities of the sixties and seventies. Even the federal antipoverty agencies have not had much success in eliminating the massive problems of the ghetto. Thus, as a black pressure group, the Urban League remains on the periphery.

Congress of Racial Equality (CORE)

CORE was born in 1943, when the Chicago committee of the Fellowship of Reconciliation (FOR), a separate committee on racial equality, and the national FOR organizations cooperated to form the new organization. The

[18] Arvach E. Strickland, *History of Chicago Urban League* (Urbana: University of Illinois Press, 1966), p. 260.
[19] See Whitney M. Young, Jr., *To Be Equal* (New York: McGraw-Hill Book Company, 1964), and his *Beyond Racism* (New York: McGraw-Hill Book Company, 1969).

major impetus for the formation of the organization came from the Chicago Committee on Racial Equality, which had employed two blacks, James Farmer and Bayard Rustin. These blacks conducted one-man campaigns of nonviolent action against segregation during 1942. Later that year the group coalesced with other members in the Chicago chapter and integrated a white restaurant in the Loop area. From this experience, Farmer, who became the first chairman of CORE, turned his attention to creating a national organization that would employ direct action and nonviolent tactics to combat segregation.

From 1942 until 1961, the first period of CORE's existence, small-scale direct action tactics were successfully employed in both the North and the upper South. The first freedom riders were introduced in 1946, as a result of a court decision integrating buses in Virginia. On the whole, however, small-scale direct action granted only small-scale victories.

In CORE's second period, 1961-1964, the era of mass direct action initiated by the second Freedom Ride of 1961, their pressure tactics proved vastly successful, because they put specific pressure on specific targets and did not simply rely on interracial goodwill to win over majorities.

The organization mushroomed during this period and used the single pressure tactic of direct action as a cohesive device more and more often.[20] But the tactic of direct action (street demonstrations, sit-ins, ride-ins, etc.) soon spent itself. As the thrust of rising expectations drew the members of CORE forward faster than its white allies and liberals could permit, opposition set in. Soon the direct action pressure tactic came to be thought of as lawlessness and violence and was looked down upon. In fact, its users were punished under the guise of "law and order," and its financial and fair weather allies withdrew from it.

If opposition and reaction to nonviolent direct action developed in the white community, however, it also developed in the black community when the 1964 major race riots occurred. It became evident to CORE that the pressure tactic had only aided the black middle class; the black masses were still outside.

In its present and third period, CORE has made a goal reversal from integration to black separatism, and its single pressure tactic has changed from direct action to black power—i.e., primarily electioneering and organizing the black community.

The Southern Christian Leadership Conference (SCLC)

SCLC was a direct outgrowth of the Montgomery bus boycott. From its inception it was inextricably bound up with one man and one philosophy

[20] See Marvin Rich, "The Congress of Racial Equality and its Strategy," in H. R. Manshood, ed., *Pressure Groups in American Politics* (New York: Charles Scribner's Sons, 1967), pp. 197-204.

and one pressure tactic. For all intents and purposes, to the loose confederation of local southern branches, the Reverend Dr. Martin Luther King, Jr., was SCLC. The basic goal of the organization—to achieve full integration of the black man into American life—also originated with King. The tactical strategy of nonviolent civil disobedience was likewise a device of the organization's leader. Furthermore, its finances, prestige, and victories rested with the same man.

King's pressure tactic of mass nonviolent civil disobedience demonstrations sought to create a crisis situation in which blacks could negotiate for better policies or force upon themselves reprisals that would cause the federal government to move in and enforce civil rights laws or enact them where none were present. As with CORE, the reliance upon a single tactic hindered the organization. It did not overwhelm it, but it did cause a shift in emphasis, a move not only toward integration, but also toward the self-improvement of the black community.[21] In addition, SCLC became increasingly concerned with the black masses after the riots in 1964, and shifted its forces from a primarily direct action against legal segregation to one against economic injustice and poverty. This culminated in the massive Poor People's Campaign, which King never led: he was assassinated in Memphis in April, 1968. Deprived of his charismatic leadership, SCLC went into a decline.

The Student Non-Violent Coordinating Committee (SNCC)

Organized in a conference at Shaw University in 1960 under King's auspices, SNCC ("Snick") by 1961 struck out on its own independent path. The decisive manifestation of the direct action technique—i.e., the sit-in at places of public accommodation—revolutionized the whole civil rights movement.

As the spearhead of the Black Revolution of the 1960s, however, SNCC soon developed a disdain for the pressure tactics of nonviolence and shifted its focus away from integration.[22] The brute realities of racism crushed the youthful idealism of the SNCC workers.

By 1964 Snick's pressure tactic of direct action quickly gave way to voter registration and political action. When the 1964 Democratic National Convention rejected the SNCC-led Mississippi Freedom Democratic party, Snick withdrew from its policy of coalition with whites and the goal of an integrated community. Although the shift was gradual, after the decision to create the separate Black Panther party in December, 1965, the pace of the tendency toward black separatism quickened and culminated with the cry

[21] Martin Luther King, Jr., *Chaos or Community: Where Do We Go from Here?* (New York: Harper and Row, 1969).

[22] For an earlier history, see Howard Zinn, *SNCC: The New Abolitionists* (Boston: Beacon Press, 1964).

for black power in the summer of 1966. Within the next few months community organizations and political tactics, rather than demonstrations and direct action, became the principal techniques of SNCC. With the shift in tactic came a shift from reconciliation and brotherhood to black power and self-defense. It was the articulation of this new idealism that snapped the back of SNCC—not the ideology itself but white Americans' reaction to it and to ideologues like Rap Brown and Stokely Carmichael. The new policy caused an intense rift and disarray, financial support dried up, and leaders were jailed for their new militancy. SNCC became the Student Coordinating Committee and nearly ceased to exist as a black pressure group.

In sum, SNCC, like CORE, used basically one tactic and the use of this tactic brought it success and led the organization to become alienated, and distrustful of whites. It not only retreated from the goal of integration, but from the larger American society. SNCC's new policy and goals irritated and antagonized the power structure. When Snick switched its pressure tactic from that of influencing public *policy* to abrupt change of the entire policy-making *structure,* the structure through its agencies, both federal and state, crushed SNCC and its attempt to rebuild American society. In short, Americans would not permit a political revolution.

The Politics of Other Black Pressure Groups

The civil rights "orgs" are not the only black pressure groups. In a larger sense, the entire black community is a pressure group, at least potentially. The black community, however, has produced groups that have sought not only their particular interest but those of the larger group also. Separate black organizations have flourished since colonial America. These organizations have ranged from black farmer associations to black bankers, realtors, and insurance associations. In fact, for almost every white organization, black America has something of a counterpart. Moreover, these black community organizations have from time to time entered the political arena in one fashion or another.

For instance, black doctors set up their own National Medical Association, since the white American Medical Association would not admit blacks. However, the NMA has never developed into a meaningful protest organization in the political arena. It has done little else than call attention to itself as a racially separate organization. Verbalism and alliance with the civil rights "org" has for the most part been the extent of its pressure activities.

Black educators likewise developed a separate organization for the same reason. Not only did these organizations exist on the state and local level, but a National Negro Educational organization was created in 1904.[23] Although in 1937 the group changed its name from the National Association of Teachers in Colored Schools to the American Teachers Association, the group as a whole never brought any meaningful pressure on the federal government. Its state and local associations did, however. During the period of 1904-1954 numerous pressure tactics were employed by various state and local black educational associations to get black teachers for black schools, equal pay, and better schools. Since 1954 these associations have pressed, primarily through courts or in conjunction with the NAACP, for a speedup in integration of both students and teachers.

When desegregation increased, however, and black teachers, especially in the South, were removed, fired, or demoted to get revenge for the Supreme Court's decision in May, 1954, the tactic of these organizations changed. In most states lobbying activities secured effective teacher tenure laws and retirement laws, placed blacks on the boards of education, and introduced black studies into the curricula. In addition to lobby activities, legalism was employed. The success of either weapon depended on the locality and the circumstances involved—i.e., the degree of racism prevalent in the local political process.

Although the appearance of more black legislators and public officials on the state and local level promised to help the lobbying activities of these groups, the "forced merger" tactic of the National Education Association (NEA) or the nonrecognition of separate local or state organizations means the eventual decrease of black educational pressure groups.

Examples of other black pressure groups—state, local, and regional— include the National Baptist Association, a nonpolitical religious group; "US," a militant black group in California; the paramilitary Black Panther party; numerous black labor groups and unions; several black farmer organizations, etc. Each has its own tactic. Some are nonpolitical, while others are political but lack the resources or leadership to do very much. Throughout the country there are numerous local black voters leagues, but they have had little political influence or effect. The least studied groups in the black communities have been the social clubs, fraternities and sororities. From time to time one can observe in black newspapers their plans to pressure for some particular community or social welfare project. Like the other black pressure groups, these groups also, mainly for operational, financial, and tactical reasons, work with the larger civil rights "org," because at the root of their particular professional or social problems is always the lack of civil rights. In other words, a black banker has trouble raising funds because he is black. Because of color prejudice, black organi-

---

[23] Sadly no systematic study has been made of their goals, history, or acknowledgment. For a short review of two, see Hanes Walton, Jr., "The Politics of Negro Educational Association," *Negro Educational Review*, 20 (January, 1969), 34-41.

zations must in the final analysis ally themselves to whichever civil rights organization they feel suits their degree of militancy and social philosophy. On such points coalitions grow or decline continuously.

TOWARD A THEORY OF BLACK PRESSURE GROUPS

From the foregoing analysis, it can be generalized that black pressure groups are basically one-tactic pressure groups. The NAACP uses legalism; CORE, SNCC, and SCLC use direct action. Although other tactics like lobbying, mass propaganda, violence, electioneering, working inside political parties, strikes, nonviolence, etc., are employed, each group is inclined to place its chief reliance upon one technique. Moreover, concomitant with the one-tactic stance of black pressure groups are efforts at public persuasion. All black pressure groups have had to seek not only to influence the particular governmental agency involved, but in most cases white society as a whole. In short, black pressure groups have been most effective when they have attained majority support from the white community. Without this support many of the victories won or advances made would have been in name only. For instance, rights won in the courts had to be won almost individually over and over again where majoritarian consensus was not attained.

In the long run the success of a black pressure group depends less on its size, location, social status, cohesion, or leadership (although these do affect them) and more on the politico-governmental environment—i.e., the attitude of white America. The one-tactic black pressure groups are a functional expression the liberal-conservative attitudes of white America. When the majority of America approves, then black pressure achieves success; when it disapproves, success is curtailed. For example, even when black leadership reaches the charismatic level of Martin Luther King, Jr., it is still dependent upon this attitude. King's political ideology was acceptable, his methods tolerated, and his philosophy agreeable, but in the final analysis these leadership attributes had to await support from the larger white community. When that support was withdrawn, his leadership proved somewhat ineffective. In other words, King's personality traits were enhanced by the situation but the situation itself was of more importance. No one yet can answer the baffling question of why the arrest of Mrs. Rosa Parks overnight unified the black community or why four black students suddenly decided to sit in at Greensboro, North Carolina, in 1960, which, when evaluated, lends still more credence to the situational thesis. Moreover, look at CORE and SNCC, or for that matter, King's own SCLC. They have almost all vanished in a conservative milieu. Organizational collapse due mainly to external pressure is imminent for each one, with SNCC and CORE being the hardest hit.

In addition, all three of these organizations were for the most part situationally created. Historically speaking, in fact, all black pressure groups have been situationally created. They arose not to promote but to protect or advance. The National Negro Convention Movement was created by the oppressive situation in which free blacks found themselves. The postwar black pressure organizations arose with the black man's deteriorating situation in the South after 1877, and the NAACP grew out of the lynching that took place in Springfield, Illinois, in 1909. Thus, the black man's situation has been a spur to black interest groups just as pressure groups generally arise out of a desire or need to promote their own interests.

White pressure groups (for example the American Civil Liberties Union) have no need to pressure a governmental agency to make good on past promises of constitutional and egalitarian commitments. Thus, no clash takes place. With black groups, however, either the agency's or the nation's integrity is at stake plus feelings of default and basic unfairness so that a clash sooner or later takes place not only between the agency, the executive, or congressional branches of government, but also in the judicial branch. To a lesser extent, the conservative or liberal philosophy, as we have seen from our analysis of the NAACP's legal proceedings, causes the black pressure group to clash with the conservative courts and even at times liberal courts, depending on their legal views.

In sum, black pressure groups are basically reformist in nature. They seek to reform the governmental agencies, legislation, and in some cases, society at large at the same time. If the governmental agency perceives the reforming attempt to be destructive, the black pressure group is crushed rather than given access to influence. Even if a clash is subtly avoided, reformist legislation can be either denied, delayed, or so weakened that it has no meaning, which forces the black pressure group either to dissolve or to become extremist, revolutionary, or a mere paper facade existing as a possible control mechanism in case of a race crisis.

At present, conservative white majority opinion has badly crippled several of the major black reform pressure groups like CORE, SNCC, and SCLC, and even the NUL and NAACP. Such pressure groups will dissolve completely when it is no longer possible or necessary to reform America in regard to color or racial belief. For the present, however, black pressure groups will remain situationally one-tactic reformist organizations. Although black politicians can help get reform legislation, they cannot do the job alone.

X

Blacks
and the
Federal Government

It goes without saying that the federal government and its different branches, as well as the state governments and their divisions, has had a tremendous impact upon the nature, scope, and significance of black politics (electoral and nonelectoral). However, the converse of this statement is just as true. Black politics (electoral and nonelectoral) has had a significant impact upon federal and state governments, their branches, leaders, and policies. The intensity and strength of this influence may have fluctuated and been less than the influence of the governments, but it has occurred from colonial America to the present directly and indirectly, minimally and maximally.

BLACKS AND PRESIDENTIAL POLITICS

Despite the limitations of his office and the constitutional restraints upon his power, the American chief executive is in a position to affect the lives and life-styles of black Americans. The best proof of this is the significant advances that black Americans have made under some presidents and the equally significant reverses that they have had under others.[1] Different men have used the same office to effect both positive and negative results in the black community.

When the Founding Fathers at Philadelphia required "the executive power shall be vested in a President" and that "he shall take care that the laws be faithfully executed," they clearly gave the executive branch of the government the right to oversee "the execution of the laws of the land," as

[1] Louis W. Koenig, *The Chief Executive*, rev. ed. (New York: Harcourt, Brace and World, 1968), pp. 317-328.

161

established by the Constitution and by legislative acts and upheld by the Supreme Court. But original intent in the political arena does not necessarily determine the functions of governmental institutions over time. In the growth of the presidency, the effective application of original intent has depended on the personality of the man in the office, the nature of the times, and the political fortunes of society. But despite its flux and change over time, the presidency remains an office in which the hopes and aspirations of minorities may receive some sympathetic response. This results primarily from the numerous roles that the chief executive assumes in carrying out his presidential duties.

The president as party chief is definitely in a position of influence. He can manipulate party resources such as funds and organization, and can take advantage of events and circumstances, in order to reap "impressive political harvests." In this way the president can foster meaningful legislation for any group. Being party leader, he is by his very nature a chief politician and can therefore persuade political leaders and the people to work in his behalf. Moreover, since the party puts him in touch with the people, he can make much of the opportunities that party campaigns and rallies afford. Nevertheless, though these powers are significant, they are not stabilized qualities of the office and depend in large part on the personal skills of a leader.

Moreover, a president's ability as party leader does not necessarily lead to success as legislative leader. As legislative leader the president can sponsor bills that will bring about social justice. He cannot control altogether what Congress does to his legislative program; situations sometimes affect congressional behavior to the point at which it will accept presidential leadership. As Professor Koenig has pointed out, Congress has a tendency to follow presidential leadership in three kinds of situations: during a crisis—when the social system or nation is at stake—when national opinion demands, and when the president's initiative is expected and desired. If this is true, then it is also true that the chief executive can advance the cause of social justice. To be a meaningful legislative leader, however, the president has to take the initiative. His success depends upon his commitment and abilities. In fact, the president as party and legislative leader depends upon his public leadership qualities. To affect the flow of legislation and its acceptance, the chief executive must rally public sentiment behind his policies. Moreover, in our political system the chief executive enjoys "impressive resources for reaching the public and rallying public opinion."

The mass media reach nearly all of the nooks and crannies of the nation. Presidential press conferences, major addresses, and speeches reach more living rooms than any other media program. Generally speaking, the president is carried simultaneously by all the major networks. In addition to his management of the news he can even create news. He is constantly molding, shaping, and directing public opinion. Kennedy and Johnson's use of the news media to get public support for their policies is well known. Kennedy's use of television to make steel magnates back away from price increases was a major step in presidential use of the news media.

He has other means at his disposal also, such as whistle stop tours. In short, the political potency of the presidency can be felt by the lowest man on the totem pole. In conjunction with the grand tour and the mass media is the availability of mass communication experts, the image-makers who can sell almost anything to the public.[2] The professional public relations firm can sell the president to the public, if not his policies. In fact, the president can go over the heads of Congress directly to the people for support, who in turn can force Congress to go along. In this sense, the president can discern the nature of public opinion and act on it in accordance with his own desires and abilities. As in his other roles, however, this role likewise calls for a man with dynamism and charismatic power.

The role in which the chief executive can successfully affect the black community is that of a value-committed individual with goals of social justice and the political astuteness to move toward these goals through the morass of politics. In other words, an effective chief executive is one who has the charisma, personal magnitude, and dynamism to move the people and Congress in the direction he wants them to go; he must also have a passionate concern for social justice in the racial sector of this country. Although the laws of political survival indicate that the chief executive "no matter how lofty the cause or how intense . . . he must win the next election . . . ,"[3] it is necessary for the chief executive at times to make an act of conscience and risk political fortunes. Kennedy's "stand on civil rights appeared to alienate millions of white voters, yet to have refused to take it would have alienated millions of Negroes and damaged his country in the eyes of the world."[4] In short, a characteristic of a great president is conviction and his willingness to operate on the basis of it despite its political outcome. As Professor Bailey asserts, making enemies of the unsavory sort by standing up for principles can be a distinct political asset.

However, if there are roles and dispositions that a chief executive can take to aid the black community, then there are some electoral and nonelectoral political activities that blacks can pursue to influence the presidency.

In influencing the presidential candidate, the power of the black elector-

[2] See Stanley Kelly, Jr., *Professional Public Relations and Political Power* (Baltimore: Johns Hopkins Press, 1956).

[3] Thomas Bailey, *Presidential Greatness* (New York: Appleton-Century-Crofts, 1968), p. 142.

[4] *Ibid.*

ate can be instrumental, generally speaking, prior to the campaign and during the election. For example, during the latter part of the nineteenth century and the first three decades of the twentieth, Republican presidential candidates used the "Black and Tan" factions of the Republican party in the South to help secure their nominations. Theodore Roosevelt's attention to blacks during his first term in office led his rival prior to the 1904 presidential nomination to automatically gain support of the white supremacist-lily-white southern Republican delegates. For counterweight, therefore, Roosevelt had to enlist the Black and Tan Republicans.

This is no longer possible today, even though rival delegations still contest each other at the national conventions. Presidential candidates nowadays can win black support by taking a meaningful stand on civil rights or a rights-related issue. No matter how flimsy it may seem, it is still a preconvention strategic option. And with more and more blacks now in state delegations, it is becoming an even more crucial issue to face.

In terms of the national convention itself, here again the number of blacks in each state delegation can affect not only the candidate's behavior, in that he might make secret convention deals, but if he wins the nomination, his platform and address will certainly take more notice of the crucial issue facing the black community. As the comparison of the number of black delegates to the political convention reveals, the larger the number of delegates attending the Republican convention, the more concern was given to the black problem. As the number increased in the Democratic conventions, so did the influence on party platforms and policy desires that blacks had. Republican concern came during the nineteenth century, and the Democratic party has exhibited concern most clearly since 1948.

It is during a national election, however, that blacks can truly affect the behavior of the presidential candidate. This is due to the fact that the northward migration of blacks has placed them in all of the key cities, in the large industrial states with large electoral votes, and carrying these states gives a candidate enough strength to offset the votes in nearly two-thirds of the other states. In this situation, a black vote under certain circumstances can become a balance of power factor and produce the desired margin of victory. In 1948 the black vote did just that. Truman could not have won without it. He received it because of his civil rights speech at the beginning of the campaign; he never mentioned the issue again until the end of his campaign in New York's Harlem.

In 1960 a similar situation occurred when Kennedy's phone call helped get the black civil rights hero, Martin Luther King, out of jail. The black electorate helped to provide Kennedy with his wafer-thin margin of victory.

It was even influential in 1964 when Johnson's landslide proved that he could have won even without the major states that carry the large black population. The failure of the Democratic party to win in 1968 with the black vote proved that it is not—i.e., the balance of power—operative at all times and under all circumstances; only when there is a particular type of division among the white electorate does its potential increase. Here again the myth is more effective for blacks than is reality. As long as political analysts believe black presidential votes are effective at all times, it becomes so to those candidates which seek them.

The influence of the electoral power of the black community on the chief executive decreases when he is in office because the man has a four-year term either to seek or create other sources and sections of support or only make concessions to the black community at the last minute. For instance, when John Kennedy called a leadership conference on civil rights in 1961 to discover black leadership views and convey the administration's intentions as well as the political realities, black leaders hoped for one thing and received another. When Roy Wilkins began reading the black statement (a sixty-one-page memorandum), Theodore Sorensen, the president's special counsel, let out the bitter news "that the administration would not push civil rights legislation at least in its first years."[5] In short, civil rights were to be held in abeyance so that other pressing projects could get through Congress despite the fact that the black vote had been crucial to Kennedy's election. Woodrow Wilson, who made a skillful and sophisticated appeal for black electoral support in 1912, completely forgot about black support once in office and rigidly segregated the civil service in Washington, D.C.[6] Thus, black nonelectoral politics becomes more important in influencing the chief executive before or after he takes office.

This can definitely be seen in the pressure of Martin Luther King during the Kennedy administration. As Professor Lubell asserts, "the aim of this strategy ... [was] to demonstrate that segregation can no longer be enforced in the South except by constant police repression." An immediate objective is to force negotiations that will bring some change in racial practice. Always in the thinking of the demonstration is the desire to embarrass our national leader, to assail the national conscience, and, if possible, to bring on federal intervention, to force the hand of the man in the White House, so that the slow pace of action on civil rights would be stepped up. And this King did again and again forcing Kennedy as well as Johnson to act on civil rights. Before the 1960s, the action and pressure tactics of A. Philip Randolph had the same effect upon Franklin D. Roosevelt and Harry Truman. And if nonelectoral politics can cause presidents to act positively for blacks, it can also provoke negative actions such as those of the Black Panthers. Black nonelectoral politics can cause the

[5] Koenig, *op. cit.*, p. 323.
[6] Harold C. Fleming, "The Federal Executive and Civil Rights: 1951-1965," *Daedalus*, 94 (Fall, 1965), 931-935.

government to act positively or negatively; it can also cause the government to respond in an insignificant fashion. A good example of this is the early pressure put on Kennedy by blacks to pass an open housing act; he did so through an executive order, which turned out to be too weak.[6] Although blacks have received some support from chief executives via the executive order, a major weakness of this instrument is that a presidential executive order is not binding on the next president and does not have to be enforced by him. But despite this inherent weakness, it is a device that can be used to bring some advancement in black aspirations.

In sum, both the chief executive and the black community can influence each other. But the *"President, as the principal elected officer of American democratic society, has made no enduring and unqualified commitment to either the advantaged or the disadvantaged."*[7] Some have been committed to one side or the other; others have remained neutral, indifferent, or even distracted. Black civil rights have frequently been ignored by the chief executive.

Lincoln's Emancipation Proclamation set the stage, but eight other presidents—five of them during the age of Reconstruction—followed a hands-off policy.

Theodore Roosevelt became the first president after Lincoln to act in a positive fashion. Even he, however, showed signs of ambiguity; during his second term in office he took a strong antiblack position, especially with regard to blacks in the South.

After Roosevelt, five other presidents failed to help during the lynchings of the 1920s and the despair of the depression in the 1930s. Franklin Delano Roosevelt's New Deal became the first significant presidential support for blacks in the twentieth century. Roosevelt was followed by Truman whose comments on race relations since he has been out of office have not been in keeping with those he exhibited in office.

Eisenhower's only major effort was Little Rock in 1957 and 1960; he did little otherwise. The civil rights bills passed during his administration were weak and ineffective.[8] Kennedy's actions during the last part of his tenure in office were most notable, as were the actions taken by his brother Robert Kennedy, the attorney general.

Probably the most active president on the question of civil rights since Lincoln was Lyndon Johnson, who secured the passage of several key civil rights laws and made major black appointments—to the Supreme Court, to the Cabinet, and to the United States Information Agency. The main high level appointments by Johnson went to Thurgood Marshall, Robert Weaver (HUD), and Carl T. Rowan.

[7] Koenig, *op. cit.*, p. 295.
[8] Strong, *Negroes, Ballots, and Judges*, chap. 1.

Excluding Kennedy and Johnson, historians have listed two presidents who actively supported black advancement (Lincoln and Franklin D. Roosevelt) among our greatest presidents and Truman and Theodore Roosevelt as near greats.[9] When a new assessment is made, it seems quite possible that Kennedy and Johnson will fall into one of the two categories.

If the great presidents have advanced the cause of blacks, one need not look at those who reversed it. Nevertheless, among the present-day black community Rutherford B. Hayes (designated as an average president) is probably considered one of the worst because of his compromise with the South in 1877 to withdraw the remaining federal troops from the South and leave the black problem to the "redeemer" state governments.

The strong, activist, conviction-oriented chief executive has for the most part fostered and promoted social justice in favor of the black American. Although black electoral or nonelectoral politics can influence the chief executive, not until recently has the nonelectoral technique been the most rewarding to the black community. In the future, however, the need for a president's commitment to social justice will become more and more apparent as new phases and intensities of racial relationship in America make it increasingly necessary.

BLACKS AND CONGRESSIONAL POLITICS

The office of the chief executive has not been the only target of black politics, and neither has the chief executive been the only figure of the federal government to affect the black community. The legislative branch has also had its impact and blacks have also had their influence on Congress.

When the Founding Fathers created a bicameral body to "make the laws of the land," they established a powerful branch of government in the federal system. Although Congress is curtailed somewhat in taking the initiative in the domestic scene, Congress can slow down, hamper, and even halt the progress of the black community by its legislative behavior.

Congressional action on civil rights bills and fiscal matters obviously has had significant meaning for the black community. For instance, when a civil rights bill is modified, killed, or passed, legal rights for black people are increased, denied, or meagerly granted. In fiscal terms funds to improve the black community can likewise be cut, denied, or granted. Thus, the legislative behavior of Congress on legislation can have meaningful effects in the black community. The political activities of numerous black individuals and organizations have been directed toward urging congressmen to pass civil rights bills. At times black pressure tactics have been successful,

[9] Bailey, *op. cit.*, pp. 24-25.

and at other times they have not. One can think of the numerous futile attempts by black "orgs," notably the NAACP, to have a federal anti-lynching bill passed or one can view the pressure applied successfully by the organizations to have civil rights laws passed—like voting rights legislation—and the outcomes of each. The history of both measures indicates the successes and failures of black pressure tactics.

One important factor is the composition of Congress itself. Certain congressional structures can facilitate the passage of bills pertinent to black people. For instance, taking Professor Randall B. Ripley's typologies of Congress—i.e., (1) truncated majorities when the House, the Senate, and the executive are not controlled by the same party, (2) presidential partisan majority, (3) presidential bipartisan majority and (4) a congressional majority.[10] The presidential partisan majority is the most successful in gaining new and curative legislation for the social ills in society. In fact, under this model, the president can take strong legislative leadership and with the aid of innovative leaders in Congress can enjoy something of a "honeymoon" with the legislative branch of government.

There is, however, one additional element required for effectiveness in civil rights improvements when the presidential partisan majority structure is in operation, and that is the presence of a national consensus favoring strong civil rights legislation. When there is no national consensus favoring civil rights, the presidential partisan structure can only aid blacks indirectly. When the national consensus exists, then legislation can be passed without much trouble. Two presidents, Roosevelt and Johnson, furnish examples of this phenomenon. Franklin Delano Roosevelt was one of the presidents who led a partisan majority in Congress. During his tenure he introduced the New Deal, which, especially in an economic sense, became meaningful to the black community. And although several southern senators objected that the New Deal was solely a disguised program to aid blacks, it did assist many blacks as part of its general program effectiveness. Moreover, FDR's Congress did not pass any civil rights legislation. He had to use legislative powers inherent in the executive order to get significant action. Lyndon Johnson's partisan majority, on the other hand, aided blacks legislatively, with the passage of four major civil rights bills. In both instances, black pressure activity was stronger than during other administrations.

A presidential partisan majority Congress structure seems to be the more helpful to the black community and more responsive to black pressure politics than other types of congressional majorities. If this is a generalization on Congress as a whole, then patterns for the individual houses would tend to differ because of the marked difference between the two houses.

[10] See Randall B. Ripley, *Majority Party Leadership in Congress* (Boston: Little, Brown and Company, 1969).

Prior to the decade 1956-1965, civil rights legislation in the Senate suffered from the institutional and personal power of conservative southern senators.[11] Bills have to negotiate at least two major hurdles in the Senate, and proponents of civil rights legislation had to negotiate both; antagonists needed only to block it at one point. "This is why defensive strength is generally more powerful than offensive strength in the legislative process."[12] The two hurdles in the Senate are (1) the Judiciary Committee which, if it is in the hands of a senator unfriendly to civil rights, can be detrimental to such legislation and (2) the Senate floor stage—the filibuster. If pro-civil rights forces bypass the Senate Judiciary Committee or overpower it, then the first line of defense of the anti-civil rights forces has been defeated. The second line—unlimited debate—has killed many proposed pieces of civil rights legislation. If cloture can be secured, the filibuster can be stopped and the bill can then move to the Senate floor. Prior to 1967, however, these two hurdles in the Senate proved insurmountable.

After the Senate has been conquered, the hurdles in the House must be negotiated. The three hurdles in the House are (1) the legislative committee stage in the House—the House Judiciary Committee (generally chaired by a northern liberal), (2) the Rules Committee in the House (earlier chaired by a southern conservative), and (3) the floor stage in the House where amendments can be added to the bill which can render the measure completely ineffectual. Although the House Judiciary Committee in recent years has generally been chaired by a liberal northerner, the procivil rights forces face tough hurdles with a Rules Committee chaired by a southern conservative or when numerous amendments are proposed from the floor to amend the measure. When the bill is held by the Rules Committee, a discharge petition with a majority of congressmen's names on it can bring the bill to the House floor for action. Getting enough signatures for a discharge petition is difficult, however, because this invites the wrath of the Rules Committee.

At the floor stage in the House, effective lobbying is carried on by the Leadership Conference on Civil Rights, an association of seventy-nine civil rights, labor, church, and other affiliated organizations. For the House debate, the LCCR assigns a member to every congressman, and when he is missing, a phone call goes to a friendly congressman's office close to him where two other members of the LCCR pay a visit or call on the absent representative asking him to return for crucial votes. These lobbying tactics, along with the advice given representatives by members of the attorney general's office, got the civil rights bill through the House without further trouble.

[11] Stephen K. Bailey, *The New Congress* (New York: St. Martin's Press, 1966), pp. 66-78.
[12] *Ibid.*, p. 66.

By 1965, the Judiciary Committee, the Rules Committee, and the floor of the House had become friendlier to civil rights proposals. In the Senate the power of the conservative anti-civil rights bloc had been undermined.

Structurally speaking then, conservative southern chairmen of key committees generally need to be replaced with liberal chairmen if significant or meaningful civil rights legislation is to be passed. If this is impossible, a presidential coalition with a partisan majority can force through civil rights legislation with procedural and political maneuvers used in conjunction with black pressures and a national consensus backing civil rights legislation. The latter structure is generally the most difficult since it depends upon dominating both the legislative and the executive bodies by one party, and furthermore requires an executive committed to the basic issue of social justice for black Americans. In addition, a presidential coalition must almost of necessity await either the emergence of a national consensus favoring civil rights legislation or the total collapse of the southern defense in order to pass meaningful bills.

Although black pressure activity, internally or externally, can aid Congress in passing effective measures, until the mid-sixties internal black power was not important because only a few blacks had been elected to Congress and these men lacked major personal and institutional power in either congressional body.

BLACKS IN CONGRESS

The first blacks—J. H. Rainey of South Carolina and J. F. Long of Georgia—took their seats in the House of Representatives, and H. R. Revels of Mississippi took his seat in the Senate in the 41st Congress which lasted from 1869 to 1871.[13] In fact, during the period from 1871 to 1901, twenty-two blacks (twenty representatives and two senators) held membership in Congress. Neither of the black senators was reelected, but ten of the representatives served more than one term.

When George White (R.-N.C.) left Congress in 1901, no other black served in Congress until Oscar DePriest (R.-Ill.) was elected in 1929. Since DePriest, ten more blacks were elected to Congress in 1968 including Shirley Chisholm who was elected to the House of Representatives from New York. Thus, from the 41st Congress to the 95th only thirty-five blacks (three in the Senate and thirty-two in the House) have held seats in Congress.

Findings from Table IV indicate that only a few blacks have been reelected enough times to get seniority and a chairmanship of a congres-

---

[13] See Samuel D. Smith, *The Negro in Congress, 1870-1901* (New York: Kennikat Press, 1966), p. 5, and A. A. Taylor, "Negro Congressmen a Generation After," *Journal of Negro History,* 7 (April, 1922), 129-130.

sional committee. The two blacks who have received chairmanships have been William Dawson, who retired in 1968, who chaired the House Government Operations Committee, and Adam Clayton Powell, who chaired the House Committee on Education and Labor. Both men headed committees in the House; no blacks have ever headed committees in the Senate.

If, therefore, institutional power is acquired through certain key committee chairmanships, black congressmen are without this power and always have been. Even if personal power is developed from technical and political skills, black congressmen, with the exception of Dawson and Powell, are still without it. Furthermore Dawson used his institutional and personal power to enhance his political position and influence in Congress and did not serve blacks in general, while Powell, before losing his position, advanced black issues and legislation in only a minimal and rhetorical fashion.

Finally, black congressmen have not been conspicuously successful in sponsoring meaningful legislation. The earlier black congressmen—those between 1871 and 1901—sought to promote two kinds of legislation: local improvement and racial justice for the black race. Regardless of their merit, however, those measures "met in general one of three fates: they were either sidetracked in committee, reported adversely, or defeated after debate in open session."

The legislative measures of the latter-day black congressmen—1929-1970—have not been studied, but casual observation indicates that no significant piece of civil rights legislation authored by a black congressman has been passed. In fact, none of the civil rights bills since 1957 has been sponsored by black congressmen, and some black congressmen have even been absent from the chambers during crucial voting periods on some of the civil rights bills. One must conclude, therefore, that, because of their lack of power within Congress, black congressmen have contributed little to the black community. Even blacks like Dawson, who could have, failed to do so because of machine influence in their constituencies.

In short, blacks have not been very effective in causing Congress to act. Generally, black congressmen are only peripherally significant in the lawmaking body. They suffer not only from a lack of power, but from a lack of unity and a failure to demonstrate a broad concern for the black masses. We shall explore this concern, however, in the next chapter.

THE ROLE OF THE SUPREME COURT IN BLACK POLITICS

In the federal structure, the executive and Congress are only two of the forces that have been significant for black people and black politics. The third branch of government, the Supreme Court, has been at least equally important. The Supreme Court has, through numerous judicial decrees,

Table IV. Blacks in Congress, 1869-1973

Number of Congress	Date	Member	State	Number of Times Reelected
41	1869-71	J. H. Rainey	South Carolina	
		J. F. Long	Georgia	
		*H. R. Revels	Mississippi	
42	1871-73	J. T. Walls	Florida	
		B. S. Turner	Alabama	
		J. H. Rainey	South Carolina	
		R. B. Eliott	South Carolina	
43	1873-75	R. B. Elliott	South Carolina	1
		R. H. Cain	South Carolina	
		A. J. Ransier	South Carolina	
		J. H. Rainey	South Carolina	
		J. T. Rapier	Alabama	
		J. T. Walls	Florida	
		J. R. Lynch	Mississippi	
44	1875-77	J. R. Lynch	Mississippi	
		*B. K. Bruce	Mississippi	
		J. T. Walls	Florida	2
		Jeremiah Haralson	Alabama	
		J. A. Hyman	North Carolina	
		C. E. Nash	Louisiana	
		J. H. Rainey	South Carolina	
		R. Smalls	South Carolina	
45	1877-79	R. H. Cain	South Carolina	1
		J. H. Rainey	South Carolina	4
		R. Smalls	South Carolina	
		*B. K. Bruce	Mississippi	
46	1879-81	*B. K. Bruce	Mississippi	2
47	1881-83	R. Smalls	South Carolina	
		J. R. Lynch	Mississippi	2
48	1883-85	J. E. O'Hara	North Carolina	
		J. Smalls	South Carolina	
49	1885-87	R. Smalls	South Carolina	4
		J. E. O'Hara	North Carolina	1
51	1889-91	H. P. Cheatham	North Carolina	
		T. E. Miller	South Carolina	
		J. M. Langston	Virginia	
52	1891-93	H. P. Cheatham	North Carolina	1
53	1893-95	G. W. Murray	South Carolina	
54	1895-97	G. W. Murray	South Carolina	1
55	1897-99	G. H. White	North Carolina	
56	1899-1901	G. H. White	North Carolina	1
72	1929-33	O. DePriest	Illinois	
73	1933-35	O. DePriest	Illinois	1
74	1935-37	A. W. Mitchell	Illinois	
75	1937-39	A. W. Mitchell	Illinois	

Table IV. Blacks in Congress, 1869-1973 (Continued)

Number of Congress	Date	Member	State	Number of Times Reelected
76	1939–41	A. W. Mitchell	Illinois	
77	1941–43	A. W. Mitchell	Illinois	3
78	1943–45	W. L. Dawson	Illinois	
79	1945–47	W. L. Dawson	Illinois	
		A. C. Powell, Jr.	New York	
80	1947–49	W. L. Dawson	Illinois	
		A. C. Powell, Jr.	New York	
81	1949–51	W. L. Dawson	Illinois	
		A. C. Powell, Jr.	New York	
82	1951–53	W. L. Dawson	Illinois	
		A. C. Powell, Jr.	New York	
83	1953–55	W. L. Dawson	Illinois	
		A. C. Powell, Jr.	New York	
84	1955–57	W. L. Dawson	Illinois	
		A. C. Powell, Jr.	New York	
		C. C. Diggs	Michigan	
		R. N. C. Nix	Pennsylvania	
		A. Hawkins	California	
		J. Conyers, Jr.	Michigan	
		Edward Brooke	Massachusetts	
		Shirley Chisholm	New York	
		William Clay	Missouri	
		Louis Stokes	Ohio	
92	1971–73	C. C. Diggs, Jr.	Michigan	8
		R. N. C. Nix	Pennsylvania	6
		A. Hawkins	California	4
		J. Conyers, Jr.	Michigan	3
		*Edward Brooke	Massachusetts	2
		Shirley Chisholm	New York	1
		William Clay	Missouri	1
		Louis Stokes	Ohio	1
		Ronald V. Dellums	California	
		George W. Collins	Illinois	
		Ralph H. Metcalf	Illinois	
		Tarren J. Mitchell	Maryland	
		Charles B. Rangel	New York	

* Senator
Source: Samuel D. Smith, *The Negro in Congress, 1879-1901* (New York: Kenni-kat Press, 1966), p. 5.

kept blacks in the political process and has kept alive their faith in the political process. Moreover, in some cases it has made black politics meaningful. In addition to sustaining black forces in the political arena, it has also enlarged, continued, and enhanced the political posture of blacks as politicians. These roles of the Supreme Court are significant because it has been a continual problem of American society to define the black man's position in the normal American political community. Black rights and privileges in this society have continually changed, but the problem of defining these rights and privileges has fallen to the American court system, with the final definition left up to the Supreme Court. This is not to say, however, that the district or appeal or state courts have not been significant. On the contrary, many of these courts have played an extremely important role—almost similar to that of the Supreme Court—but their roles were for the most part dependent upon the final word of the Supreme Court. In other words, the party (black or antiblack) which lost in the lower courts usually appealed to the Supreme Court.

Thus, in a larger sense, blacks and their political activities first had to await definitions of their status, rights, and limits by state legislatures, city councils, individuals, groups, or local counties. Then there was a move to get a redefinition especially in the courts. There were also attempts to get redefinition via legislative action, on the local, state, or national level.

Generally speaking, there have been two basic forces seeking definition of black rights and privileges, whether in the political, social, educational, economic, religious, or cultural communities. One force, broadly defined, consisted of pro-black groups, which seek acknowledgment of blacks as normal American citizens entitled to all the rights, privileges, and immunities guaranteed to all citizens by the constitution of the United States. Although this force has been somewhat vague in its composition and techniques, and at times its goals have been obscure (i.e., some who sought the extension and protection of civil liberties instead of black rights specifically can be included in this group), it has been a significant force despite its loose association of individuals and humanitarians.

The other loose grouping of forces, the constitutional restrictive antiblack forces, basically sought to have the rights, privileges and immunities of blacks restricted. It even sought to withhold from the black community the full privileges of citizenship. Although this group, like its counterpart, has not always been continuous, well formed, or highly organized, it has nonetheless been a recurring loose association of individuals or groups on the local, state, or national level, and at times has prevented blacks from achieving their constitutional rights and privileges.[14]

[14] See Helen Catterall, ed., *Judicial Cases Concerning American Slavery and the Negro* (Washington, D.C., 1929).

The struggle between the constitutional pro-black forces and the constitutional antiblack forces has been recurring and sporadic, but the struggle has covered the entire spectrum of rights and privileges in this country, running from a definition of citizenship rights to voting privilege and running for public offices. Although these forces have sought court definitions of black rights in the social, economic, religious, cultural, and educational spheres, only the political sphere—i.e., voting privileges and political involvement—will receive our chief attention. The other areas have been amply covered by numerous authors dealing with blacks and the Supreme Court.[15]

The struggle between these two forces began before the antebellum period. Then the problem was not so much defining the position of black slaves in American society as it was defining that of free blacks, North and South, in American society. In fact, the existence of this free black population, an anomaly in a generally slave society, was bound to raise great legal questions as to what rights and privileges should be accorded these people in light of those given to whites or, for that matter, to black slaves.

When the constitutional pro-black forces sought to aid the free blacks and get a clear declaration of their rights, they suffered continual losses in the lower and state courts. For instance, in North Carolina the State Supreme Court in *State* v. *Manuel* declared that free blacks were not entitled to the right to vote, although they had exercised suffrage rights in that state for significant periods of time.

In Philadelphia, in *Hobbs* v. *Fogg*, another state court found a new law that denied suffrage rights to free blacks to be fair and within the scope of the state constitution. In fact, in several other northern states the loss or restriction of suffrage rights by blacks was found to be legal and acceptable by state courts.[16]

In regard to full rights and privileges in all spheres, the free blacks, North and South, found that they were not allowed to enjoy these as whites could. Free blacks had limited rights at best, and even these limited rights could easily be denied or withdrawn without the courts returning them.

In the Dred Scott case, a major pre-Civil War Supreme Court decision, the antiblack forces won a major victory when the Supreme Court declared that blacks, slaves or free, had no rights that society was obliged to recognize. Blacks were not to be "thought of or spoken of except as property."[17]

[15] See Loren Miller, *The Petitioners: The Story of the Supreme Court of the United States and the Negro* (New York: Pantheon Books, 1966). See also Leon Friedman, ed., *Southern Justice* (Cleveland: Meridian Books, 1967), and Joseph Tussman, ed., *The Supreme Court on Racial Discrimination* (New York: Oxford University Press, 1967), and Jacobus Ten Broek, *Equal under Law* (New York: Collier Books, 1965).

[16] Litwack, *op. cit.,* pp. 64-112.

[17] Joseph Tussman, ed., *The Supreme Court on Racial Discrimination* (New York: Oxford University Press, 1963), p. 1.

In short, the Supreme Court defined blacks before the Civil War as basically devoid of rights, and several state and local courts granted blacks a
narrow and restrictive place in society and politics. After the Civil War, the
Emancipation Proclamation, and the Thirteenth, Fourteenth, and Fifteenth
amendments, blacks became citizens with full voting rights. The Compromise of 1877, however, enabled the southern states to withdraw these rights
and enabled the northern states to grant blacks second-class citizenship.
Blacks in both regions suffered from second-class status; those in the South
lost in addition almost all their political rights and privileges.

The move for disfranchisement was followed almost immediately by the
takeover of southern government from blacks and their Republican allies
by Bourbon forces. Although this action in many states took the form of
minor restraint, major action took place in the 1890s. These major restraints on black participation in southern political life had help from the
constitutional antiblack forces who had prevailed upon the Supreme Court
and had had that body establish whether there is any connection between
citizenship and suffrage. In *Minor* v. *Happersett* (1875), the antiblack
forces won a major victory because the Supreme Court declared that "the
right to vote was not one of the privileges and immunities of citizens of the
United States which the states were forbidden by the recently adopted
Fourteenth Amendment to abridge."[18] The Court further declared that the
states still retained their rights to establish qualifications for the suffrage
and that the amendment did not enfranchise any classes of citizens who
had previously been denied the right to vote.

Nine years later in *Ex Parte Yarbough*, the Court held vaguely that
United States citizens had a right to vote for federal officers and that this
right could be protected, but it did not reverse itself on its previous ruling
that states could set up qualifications for the right to vote. Since federal
elections fall on the same day on which state elections take place, one must
of necessity be qualified by the state for either state or federal officers.

Thus, with the right to establish voting qualifications that could discriminate in fact, if not in principle, the southern states enacted one discriminatory measure after another to keep blacks out of the political arena and the
two constitutional forces prevailed upon the Supreme Court to have their
positions verified.

First came the reading and interpretation test in which blacks had to
read and interpret sections of the state constitution to the satisfaction of a
local white registrar. Tied to the reading and interpretation test was the poll
tax which required blacks to pay a cumulative poll tax and the display of a
receipt indicating payment of this tax at each election.[19] Next was the

---

[18] R. E. Cushman and R. F. Cushman, *Cases in Constitutional Law*, 3rd ed. (New York:
Appleton-Century-Crofts, 1968), p. 1076.

[19] For information on groups seeking to abolish the poll tax see W. M. Brewer, "The Poll
Tax and the Poll Taxers," *Journal of Negro History*, 9 (July, 1924), 260-269, and G. C.

grandfather clause, which stipulated that blacks had to prove that they or their forefathers voted prior to 1860. By 1914 the white primary device went into practice. This device excluded blacks from participation in primary elections, which in a one-party system meant exclusion from meaningful participation in the electoral process. After the collapse of the white primary came variations of these restraints, such as the preprimary election.[20] Private club regulation of the primary,[21] and new reading and interpretation devices.[22] When these new devices proved useless, whites introduced racial gerrymandering.[23] But the Court destroyed these devices and other discriminatory acts on the part of local elections officials to keep qualified blacks from voting in *South Carolina* v. *Katzenrich* by upholding the Voting Rights Act of 1965.

Thus, from 1875 to 1965 the pro- and antiblack constitutional forces fought each other in court with the antiforces taking the greatest number of reverses to date. In fact, the pro-black constitutional forces have not only sustained, enlarged, and extended black voting rights, but have also won significant victories in nearly every area of society.

The pro-black groups have based their pleas and arguments on the Constitution and have sought a basic libertarian decision, but the antiblack forces have mainly relied upon a conservative court membership and a strict interpretation of the Constitution in light of states' rights. In the face of repeated reverses, the antiblack forces have shifted to supporting conservative judicial nominees for the Supreme Court. So far, two of President Nixon's nominees have been conservative southerners with alleged backgrounds of white supremacy, who have been offered for confirmation as a repayment of a political debt to the southern states for their support of his nomination for and election to the presidency. Whether this policy of trying to get conservative southerners on the Supreme Court can reverse the trend of the Court over the last sixty years of enlarging the rights and privileges of blacks remains to be seen. It is a possibility, however, that a conservative court could redefine black rights. The precedent is that in 1896—*Plessy* v. *Ferguson*—the Court held separate but equal to be constitutional and in 1954, fifty-nine years later in *Brown* v. *Topeka Board of Education*, the Court completely reversed itself and declared separate but equal to be unconstitutional. Hence, the relative political status of blacks.

Professor Samuel Cook, in summing up the Court from a historical

Stoney, "Suffrage in the South, part I, The Poll Tax," *Survey Graphic,* 29 (January, 1940), 5-9, 41, 33. Robert E. Martin, "War on the Poll Tax Front." *Opportunity,* 23 (April, 1945), 100.

[20] *Terry* v. *Adams.*
[21] *Rice* v. *Elmore.*
[22] *Schell* v. *Davis.*
[23] *Gomillian* v. *Lightfoot.*

perspective, states that:

> Until recent decades, the Supreme Court twisted and emasculated and
> nullified the privileges, rights, and immunities of Negroes and placed great
> power, prestige, and moral authority behind the incubus of racism. It justified
> the relegation of Negroes to an inferior order of existence in conformity with
> the dogma of white supremacy and therefore contributed mightily to their
> dehumanization. It did all this by insisting that the supervision and protec-
> tion of civil rights is the responsibility of the states—thereby succumbing to
> the infamous and, so far as Negroes were concerned, fatal doctrine of states'
> rights.[24]

He concluded, therefore, that in light of the unknowns of history, the
Supreme Court does not deserve total allegiance from black people.

In sum, the Supreme Court has gradually, but not always consistently
enlarged and expanded rights and privileges that blacks can exercise in
American society. The pro-black constitutional forces can point to these
increases as victories, but the antiblack forces have had some victories in
the Court's delays, temporary stalls, and momentary setbacks. In the matter of educational rights, victory is still not final, though, for example, the
Supreme Court's decision in 1970 for immediate integration has caused a
new wave of suits. Based upon the history of this conflict, it is doubtful if
either side will disappear no matter who gets a victory in this area of
disputed rights.

In regard to black politics, the Supreme Court has sustained the essence
of it—the black voter. Even when the president and Congress have failed,
the Supreme Court has carried the burden and problem confronting the
black electorate throughout the South. At present, the freedom and privileges that the black voter enjoys, he enjoys not because of the warmheart-
edness of election officials, but because of the consistent Supreme Court
decisions in this area. To paraphrase Professor Robert Martin, the relative
political status of blacks in the United States has been due primarily to, if
not totally to, favorable Supreme Court decisions in the area of suffrage
rights.[25] The tragedy, however, is that if Professor Martin's insights are
correct, the Supreme Court could also turn black electoral politics back to
a state of insignificance. Black political activity would once again have to
rely upon a nonelectoral or pressure group position. Hence, black politics
cannot do without the sustaining role of the Supreme Court. Not until the
politics of racism is dead will the role of the Supreme Court in black
politics become unnecessary or useless.

[24] Samuel D. Cook, Review of *The Petitioners* by Loren Miller, *Journal of Negro History*,
July, 1966, p. 221.
[25] See Robert E. Martin, "The Relative Political Status of the Negro in the United States,"
in Bailey, *op. cit.*, pp. 19-26.

BLACKS AND THE POLITICS OF THE REGULATORY AGENCIES

The regulatory agencies of the federal government have not been particularly involved in the race problem. The Securities and Exchange Commission has not been involved in the problem of race relations nor have the Federal Power Commission, the Food and Drug Administration, the Atomic Energy Commission, etc.

However, if these agencies have evaded the problem, others have been less fortunate. For instance, the Interstate Commerce Commission had few problems with race and racial discrimination until the freedom rides occurred during February, 1961. Although numerous freedom rides and sit-ins and protests about discrimination in interstate travel had taken place, little was done before President Kennedy and Attorney General Robert Kennedy had the agency ban discrimination in interstate commerce. Even after the agency issued the order, it left enforcement up to the attorney general's office and the president to carry it out and enforce compliance.

Since this major act, there have been only one or two instances in which the ICC has helped an individual black start a small trucking business in order to overcome the discriminatory obstacles placed in his path by the larger trucking firms. Otherwise, the ICC, like many of its federal counterparts, has not been concerned with or responded to black political activities.

Like the ICC, the Federal Communications Commission is another of the few regulatory agencies that have been dragged into the political arena of racism.[26] Since the FCC regulates radio and television through licensing and programming procedures and requirements, it was obvious that if a radio or television station adopted editorial policies of white supremacy, trouble would appear for the agency. Such a problem arose when a segregationist owner refused to allow the civil rights forces to present their point of view. Such behavior fails to give the other side equal time and goes directly against the "fairness doctrine" of the commission which declares that radio or television broadcasting should permit not only equal time to political aspirants but should also give equal time to opposing viewpoints and political ideologies. Segregationist-owned radio stations, however, rarely permit civil rights workers to air their views or give them equal time. In fact, their positions are generally slanted and they are pictured as anarchists or just plain old disturbers of the peace. Like the ICC, the FCC was prodded into action. A crisis brought each regulatory agency to take a stand, develop a policy and implement a program.

For instance, on December 31, 1964, Ben M. Herbster, president of the United Church of Christ, wrote a letter to the *New York Times* advocating

[26] Hanes Walton, Jr., *Political Theory and Political Broadcasting* (New York, 1971), chap. 6.

that the Federal Communications Commission deny renewal of licenses to a Mississippi television station "on the grounds ... that they are not serving the interest of 40 percent of the population there through refusal to present the view of the Negro.[27] This letter followed a petition that had been filed on April 15 with the FCC requesting that the commission deny the renewal of the temporary licenses of the two television stations in Jackson, Mississippi, because of their discriminatory programming. The letter expressed the hope that some action would be taken since more than a half-year had passed without the commission setting a hearing to determine the rights of blacks to have their side heard. In Herbster's thoughts, this correct aiming might stimulate concern and generate a good deal of reform within the state.

All Herbster's letter got was another reply from a reader who thought that the coercion Herbster called for would violate the First Amendment, and that such regulation should be left up to the moral conscience of the station.

However, after the local communication division of the United Church of Christ and a local council of the AFL-CIO instituted a suit seeking a court order requesting the FCC to give blacks a hearing on the charges that the stations had discriminatory programming, the United States Court of Appeals ruled that the FCC had to grant blacks a hearing.[28]

Complying with the court order, the FCC held a hearing and voted 4-2 to order the Lamar Broadcasting Company, which owned both stations, to end racial discrimination in programming. The FCC renewed the station license for one year only on condition that it do so. The commission also gave full licenses to five other stations in the area which had also been accused of bias in programming.

Several months later, in order to obtain a second one-year renewal, the segregationist owners agreed to end racial discrimination in their programming. The major stockholder, however, Lamar Life Insurance Company, got the FCC to go along with purchase of 80 percent of the Lamar Radio Station stock in order to insure an end to racially discriminatory programming. This move prevented other conflicts with the FCC. It did not, however, end the problem of the misrepresentation of blacks and their demands in other localities throughout the South.

On the national level, all major television networks, including National Education Television (NET), provide instructive programs on black life and history—e.g., CBS's "On Black America" and NET's Black Journal and NBC's Black History series—aimed at giving blacks a more favorable image.[29] In addition, several blacks were given shows, ranging from mild

[27] Ben M. Herbster, "FCC Ban Eyed in Mississippi," New York Times, December 31, 1964, p. 18.

[28] Martin W. Cooper, Letter to the Editor, New York Times, January 14, 1965, p. 34. For the complete discussion see Racial Justice in Broadcasting (New York: Office of Communications, United Church of Christ, 1970), pp. 3-4.

[29] On this point see Joseph Pentecoste, "The New Black Television—A White Strategy: A Commentary," Inner City Issues, October, 1969, pp. 4-11.

militancy to the fairyland of NBC's "Julia."

In retrospect, the case of WLBF-TV in Jackson is just one of the many in which southern stations have either distorted the black man's image, demands, and culture or left him out altogether. The regulatory agency in this situation had to be prodded into action by a court suit, just as the ICC was prodded into action by the crisis situation created via the Freedom rides.[30] The federal regulatory agencies as a rule follow change: they do not promote it.

In conclusion, the federal government has not always moved in unison to aid or ensure the black rights. If the president took action, Congress and the courts were silent. If the Supreme Court took the lead, the president and the Congress were silent. For the past sixty years, it has been mainly the Supreme Court that has sustained and responded to black politics. Though Presidents Roosevelt, Truman, Kennedy, and Johnson took the initiative in responding to the black community, several presidents have not responded at all.

Thus, black politics—electoral and nonelectoral—has been significant in getting one or more branches of the federal government to respond to black demands. Both have succeeded in persuading the chief executive to respond to the needs of the black community, but nonelectoral politics has been more meaningful in getting the Supreme Court and regulatory agencies to act. The federal government has yet to establish a consistent policy toward the black community. It has and it will probably remain this way until each branch formulates a consistent policy toward blacks and the black community.

BLACKS, PUBLIC POLICY, AND THE FEDERAL GOVERNMENT

Public policy consists of those rules, regulations, laws, treaties, judicial decisions, executive orders, administrative decisions, local ordinances, or legal enactments that have the enforcing power of the political system behind them. When instituted, these policies or decisions are considered "authoritatively binding upon all members of the society." Since public policy is so significant, black Americans have tried incessantly to influence the making of public policy in America.

Black political organizations have also been concerned with policy adoption, policy application, and policy adjudication. It would be futile, however, to think that all blacks want only one kind of policy output—i.e., legislation that would achieve integration and social justice. On the contrary, many black leaders have sought policy outputs that were concerned with achieving separatism and/or colonization. Black policy leadership,

[30] For recent information see John H. Britton, "Threat of Challenges Broke Complacency of Broadcasters: How Blacks Won TV-Radio Fight in Atlanta," *Jet*, April 30, 1970, pp. 14–22.

therefore, falls basically into two broad categories: (1) black integrationist policy leadership and (2) black separatist policy leadership.

THE INTEGRATIONIST LEADERSHIP: CONCERNS AND FOCUS

Black integrationists have primarily sought legislation that would enable them to acquire an equal place in American society and remove all discrimination and prejudice based on color. This group has been active since colonial times. At that time, the group consisted mostly of free blacks, though there were some slaves who petitioned for their freedom. After the Revolutionary War, the focus of black integrationist policy leadership became the national government, and the techniques include petitioning and protesting. The drive for meaningful public policy in this period, however, was fragmentary, individualistic, and uncoordinated.

By the 1830s, black organizations began to appear on the state, local and national levels. For instance, the National Negro Convention Movement with state and local auxiliaries tried until the Civil war to persuade the federal and state governments to aid the plight of free and slave blacks. Although the organization was ineffective, the Civil War brought partial solutions. The events following the war such as the passage of three major amendments, and other legislative enactments, caused most black policy groups to dissolve. The events of 1877, however, and the rise of Jim Crowism ushered in a new wave of black organizations seeking to recapture the "promise of the American dream." These different black groups have from time to time, however, been able to achieve at least some significant legislation or policy enactment fostering integration. As Table V reveals, each branch, the presidency, Congress, and the Supreme Court, has made major policy decisions in favor of the black community.

Moreover, as is revealed in the graph (Figure 12), a comparison of policy outputs reveals that the Supreme Court has made more than any other branch. This indicates that policy adjudication has been for the most part easier to achieve than policy adoption or policy application. In fact, to get Congress to pass civil rights bills is a tremendous task, as was revealed earlier. Even less policy adoption has taken place via the presidency, which could indicate either his noncommitment or his rather limited power in the area.

The major problems for black integrationist leadership in policy achievement have been policy application and enforcement. The Supreme Court's *Brown* v. *Board of Education* decision is a perfect example. Although declared unlawful in 1954, segregated education for blacks is still a reality in many American educational districts. Black integrationist policy leadership must continually pressure for more and better laws in order to achieve full enforcement or compliance.

Table V. Policy Outputs to the Black Community

Presidential Executive Orders

Year	Number
1863	Emancipation Proclamation
1941	8802
1948	9981
1961	10925
1962	11063
1963	11114

Supreme Court Decisions

Year	Case
1915	Guinn vs. United States (V)
1917	Buchanan vs. Warley (RC)
1921	Newberry vs. United States (V)
1926	Corrigan vs. Buckley (RC)
1927	Nixon vs. Herndon (V)
1932	Nixon vs. Condon (V)
1935	Grovey vs. Toronsend (V)
	Norris vs. Alabama (J)
1938	Missouri Ex rel Gaines vs. Canada (E)
1939	Lane vs. Wilson (V)
1940	Allston vs. School Board (E)
1944	Smith vs. Allwright (V)
1948	Sipuel vs. University of Oklahoma (E)
	Shelley vs. Kraemer (RC)
	Rice vs. Elmore (V)
1950	Sweatt vs. Painter (E)
	McLaurin vs. Oklahoma State Regents (E)
	Henderson vs. United States (E)
1954	Brown vs. Board of Education of Topeka (E)
	Bolling vs. Sharpe (E)
1957	Pennsylvania vs. Philadelphia (E)
1958	N.A.A.C.P. vs. Alabama (FA)
1960	Gomillian vs. Lightfoot (V)
1963	N.A.A.C.P. vs. Button (FA)
1964	Heart of Atlanta Motel vs. United States (CR)
	Katzenbach vs. McClung (CR)
	N.A.A.C.P. vs. Alabama (FA)
1966	South Carolina vs. Katzenbach (V)
1967	Loving vs. Virginia (M)

Civil Rights Legislation—Congress

Year	
1865	Thirteenth Amendment
1868	Fourteenth Amendment
1870	Fifteenth Amendment
1875	Civil Rights Act
1957	Civil Rights Act
1960	Civil Rights Bill
1964	Civil Rights Bill
1965	Voting Rights Act
1968	Housing Act
1970	Renewal, Voting Rights Bill

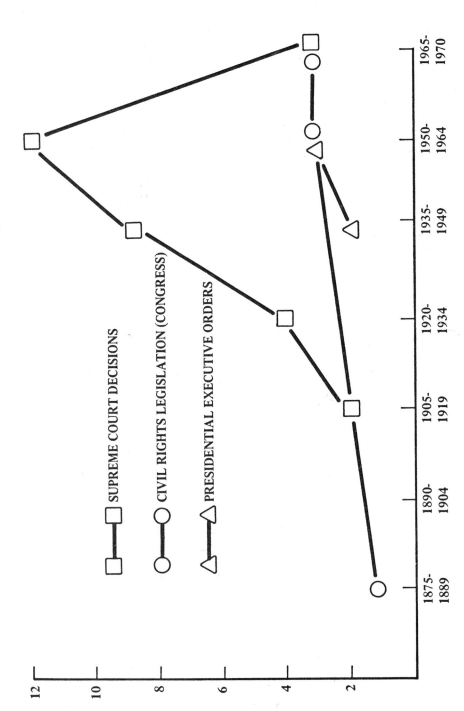

Figure 12. A Comparison of Policy Output from the Supreme Court, Congress, and the Executive to the Black Community

☐—☐ SUPREME COURT DECISIONS

○—○ CIVIL RIGHTS LEGISLATION (CONGRESS)

◁—◁ PRESIDENTIAL EXECUTIVE ORDERS

Figure 13. Black Integrationist Organizations: Tactics and Techniques, 1830-1970

Input

Memorials, Prayers, Petitions, 1680s–1860s

Violence, Insurrection, Riots, Runaways, Underground Railway, 1700s–1860

National Negro Convention, 1830–1860

State Auxiliaries, 1830s–1860

Equal Rights League, 1861–1867

National Afro American League (NAAL) and National Afro-American Council (NAAC), 1880s–1900

Niagara Movement and National Association for the Advancement of Colored People (NAACP), 1904–

National Negro Congress, 1939–1942

March on Washington, 1941–1946

Congress of Racial Equality (CORE), 1941–

Southern Christian Leadership Council (SCLC), 1957–

Student Non-violent Coordinating Committee (SNCC), 1961–

Decision-Makers

Local Government
State Government
National Government

Policy Output*

Abolition in the Northern States

Emancipation Proclamation, 1863

Civil War, 1861–1865

Thirteenth Amendment, 1865

Fourteenth Amendment, 1868

Fifteenth Amendment, 1870

Civil Rights Act, 1875

Civil Rights Act, 1957

Civil Rights Bill, 1960

Civil Rights Bill, 1964

Voting Rights Act, 1965

Housing Act, 1968

Renewal, Voting Rights Bill, 1970

*Policy output listed here does not include Supreme Court decisions and executive orders of the president; for information on these, see Table I and Table V.

Figure 14. Black Separatist Organizations: Tactics and Techniques, 1788-1970

Input

Negro Union of Freeport, 1788

Paul Cuffe, 1815

Black Emigrational Society, 1851

Black National Emigration Convention, 1854

Pop Singleton's Exodus, 1879

African Emigration Association, 1881

Marcus Garvey—Universal Negro Improvement Association (UNIA) 1914–1924

Pan African Congresses, 1919–1945

Father Divine and Daddy Grace, 1920–1940

Black Republic, 1924–1940

Forty-Ninth State, 1930–1939

Black Muslims, 1930–

Black Panthers, 1968–

Republic of New Africa, 1968–

Decision-Makers

| Local Government |
| State Government |
| National Government |

Policy Output

Congressional approval of $100,000 to American Colonization Society, 1819

Lincoln support of colonization projects, 1859–1861

Sen. Theodore Bilbo's resolutions supporting emigrationist projects, 1930s–1940s

Support of emigrationist projects from local white groups, 1920s–1970s

THE SEPARATIST LEADERSHIP: CONCERNS AND FOCUS

Because of the seemingly endless obstacles to integration some blacks have rejected the idea of integration and have sought elsewhere to achieve social justice. These leaders, referred to as black nationalists, have also petitioned the government for legislative enactment in this favor.

Some black separatists sought colonies within the United States, but others have wanted to leave the country. Both groups received some backing prior to the Civil War. As Figure 14 reveals, each group has had some success. However, the Civil War and subsequent events gave blacks hope of acquiring full citizenship within America so that they would not need to emigrate. Thus, black separatists since the Civil War have been unable to achieve anything substantial through public policy-makers. Only a few white organizations and private individuals have tried to attain legislative enactment for the removal of black Americans. During the late thirties and forties Senator Theodore Bilbo from Mississippi supported the separatists.

But even more revealing is the fact that since the Civil War, whites have supported only emigrationist projects, and have not encouraged those black separatists desiring to remain in the states. The most recent proposal to date is the proposal of the National States' Rights party of Savannah, Georgia, which urged the federal government to use the foreign aid money it gives to communist countries to help blacks leave the country and resettle elsewhere.

Black separatists presently, however, have withdrawn from pressuring the government for assistance and have developed their own self-help program—the black Muslims are a perfect example—to achieve their goals.

Concluding, then, the federal government is presently committed to a policy of integration; black groups of this nation perpetually seek to achieve policies and administrative actions that will fulfill their goals of first-class citizenship and equality.

XI

Black Public Officials and Public Policy

Except for the era of Reconstruction, blacks have never occupied or held as many major and minor public offices as they now hold. In the South alone, they now hold over seven hundred state and local offices, ranging from justice of the peace to mayorships of such southern cities as Chapel Hill, North Carolina, and Fayette, Mississippi.[1] Since Reconstruction, they have always held mayorships in the all-black towns in the South, but the capture of these new positions, plus the vice mayorship in Atlanta, demonstrates rising influence of the black electorate in the South. In the North, however, the rise of black politicians has also been remarkable. Blacks have captured the mayorships of Cleveland, Ohio, Gary, Indiana, and Flint, Michigan—to name a few. In New York, Shirley Chisholm became the first black woman elected to the House of Representatives and in Massachusetts, Edward Brooke became the first black elected to the United States Senate from the North and the first from anywhere since Reconstruction.

THE EMERGENCE OF BLACK POLITICIANS

In short, in both North and South and on both the state and municipal levels, black politicians are emerging. For the most part, these politicians have become prominent since the sixties. In the South until the 1920s blacks had seats as councilmen in Memphis, Atlanta, San Antonio, Knoxville, and Nashville; in the North, they held similar positions in New York City, Chicago, and Philadelphia. Still, they were a rarity. During the 1873–74 session of Congress, for example, seven black men had seats in the House; in the 1968–69 session there were nine black representatives and one black senator.

The black politicians of yesterday were mainly southern Republicans. Northern blacks held few offices, but those who did were also Republicans.

---

[1] Harold Rose, "The All-Negro Town: Its Evolution and Future," *Geographical Review,* July, 1965, pp. 362-381. See also "The Black Mayors," *Ebony,* February, 1970, pp. 76-84.

Today, however, black politicians are mainly Democrats and hold offices both North and South. Southern blacks may hold more local and state offices, but northern blacks hold more state and national offices. In fact, all of the national congressmen are from northern states. As Table VI indicates, the majority of state congressmen and top state officials are from the North, or hold offices in northern states; the southern blacks are mainly capturing the grass root posts and positions.

Many factors account for these differences. First, as was stated in Chapters IV and V, northern blacks were gradually absorved *into* the political structure of northern political parties. Southern blacks, on the other hand, though their votes were counted—in contrast to their preferences which were ignored—were forced *outside* the political structure. Blacks in the South were never permitted to join even a segregated party organization. While some localities permitted them to vote from time to time, they never entered the political arena except as voters. Black bosses and machines existed in the South as in the North, but the southern black machines were restrained by the prevailing ideology that "politics was white folks' business." In short, the number of southern blacks who could vote was kept small. In the North, however, white bosses encouraged a large black electorate. They enlisted as many black voters as possible and spurred them to vote for their political machine. In the South, however, black voters were somewhat anomalous. They voted because the segregated system here and there permitted them to, but never in large enough numbers to really control the white political machines. Moreover, the number of black voters was restricted in order that the white electorate and community would not become alarmed. In fact, white bosses, like Crump of Memphis, refused to acknowledge receiving black votes, though he secretly campaigned for the few of them that were left.

Elsewhere, the situation was generally the same. Electoral obstacles, ranging from legal to illegal devices, limited the black southern electorate prior to the 1960s, but in the North no hindrances were installed to curtail black voting. In fact, in the North, blacks were urged to vote. Furthermore, those southern blacks who were permitted to vote achieved the right either through sheer internal fortitude or as a token from the white community rewarding their "uncle tom" behavior. Those who had the right to vote in the South made it clear to other blacks that if they conformed to certain "Anglo-Saxon" characteristics, they too might acquire the vote. For a southern black the right to vote had mostly a prestige value. The black bosses enlisted only those middle-class blacks who exemplified the behavior that whites approved of.

The end result of this treatment of the black electorate was that northern blacks became wards of their political machines, and southern blacks lost interest in politics. In the North blacks were told how to vote; in the South

Table VI. Black Elected Officials in United States

	Total	U.S. Congress	State			County			City			Law Enforcement				School Board
			Senators	Representatives	Others	Commissioners, Supervisors	Election Commissioners	Others	Mayors	Councilmen Aldermen	Others	Judges, Magistrates	Constables, Marshals	Justices of Peace	Others	
Alabama	86					4		4	4	38	2		8	19		7
Alaska	1															1
Arizona	7		1	2												4
Arkansas	55								4	9	1			4		37
California	105	1	1	5		1			2	27	1	14				53
Colorado	7		1	2						2		1				1
Connecticut	31		1	4	1					17	1		3			4
Delaware	9		1	2		1				4						1
District of Columbia	8															8
Florida	36			1		1			2	27	1		2			2
Georgia	40		2	12		3			1	14		1				7
Hawaii	1									1						
Illinois	74	1	4	10					1	23	2	9				24
Indiana	30			3		1		1	1	8	2	2		1		11
Iowa	5			1								2				2
Kansas	6			3		1				1						1
Kentucky	41		1	2		1			1	22		4	4			6
Louisiana	64			1		5			3	26			13	7		9
Maryland	43		2	9					5	23		4				
Massachusetts	8	1*		2						2						3
Michigan	110	2	3	10		25		2	2	22		11	1			32
Minnesota	8			1							1	2				4
Mississippi	81			1		4	17	1	3	32			7	10	1	5
Missouri	65	1	2	13					2	23	4	5	1		1	13
Nebraska	2									1						2
Nevada	3			1						1		1				
New Jersey	73			4		3		1	3	33	1					28
New Mexico	3			1						2						
New York	74	2	3	9		4				10	2	20				25
North Carolina	62			1		1			5	44		1				10
Ohio	89	1	3	10		1			4	40	3	11	1			15
Oklahoma	36		1	4					2	10						19
Pennsylvania	49	1	1	10				1		13	1	9	4			9
Rhode Island	2			1						1						
South Carolina	38					2			2	27	1	4				2
Tennessee	38		2	6						9		11	3	1	2	4
Texas	29		1	2					1	15						10
Virginia	36		1	2		4		1		22				6		
Washington	4			1						1		2				
West Virginia	1															1
Wisconsin	7			1		2				3						1
Wyoming	1															1
Totals	1469	10	31	137	1	64	17	11	48	552	23	114	47	48	4	362

* U.S. Senator.
February, 1970.
Note: Nine states have no black elected officials: Idaho, Maine, Montana, New Hampshire, North Dakota, Oregon, South Dakota, Utah and Vermont.
Source: *National Roster of Black Elected Officials* (Washington: Metropolitan Applied Research Center, Inc., 1970).

they were encouraged or forced to stay out of politics altogether. In the North, however, as the black vote became more and more significant, it provided much of the machine's strength. Still only a few token blacks like Oscar DePriest, Arthur Mitchell, and William Dawson were given the opportunity to get minor political offices; the rest went to white.

Nevertheless, involvement in the political arena fostered in blacks a sense of political independence. As was pointed out in the chapter on "Blacks and the Republican Party," blacks slowly began to run independently and without the sanction of the political machines or even party endorsement. Such mavericks usually lost or were ostracized, but they blazed that path that many blacks would follow. Eventually, certain of the independent black candidates won, and their victories served to weaken party control over the black electorate.

These occasional victories by independent black candidates were complemented by—indeed, were symptomatic of—a general decline of machine politics. Eventually, political bosses and machines, either because of corruption, loss of power, or the growing welfare services of the cities, began to disintegrate their hold on the black masses. This decline took place in some cities before others, but the general effect was an increased number of black candidates, whose chances for victory, given a large and politically knowledgeable black electorate, were at least fair.

The white political machines in the North adopted one of two different attitudes toward the black community. They either sought black support only at election time and forgot about it afterwards, or else they ignored the black community altogether, leaving it to be organized by a subservient black boss who worked from the top down.

In time, with the collapse of the machine, emerged independent black politicians like Adam Clayton Powell, who built his political following precisely because Tammany Hall had left Harlem to black political bosses who still worked from the top to the bottom. Other gaps were filled by non-machine sources like the Communist party candidacy of Benjamin Davis, who captured a position on the New York City council because other parties would not sponsor blacks. The Communists were eager to do so, however, and they not only sponsored candidates, but organized the community as well. In short, rising political independence, a highly encouraged black electorate, the continued easing of party control, and certain politically ambitious groups helped the black politicians to emerge, and with the aid of the party machinery, blacks were able to obtain at least some national political offices. In the North a viable two-party system brought the kind of competition that prompted one party or the other to make certain concessions to the black electorate in order to win the election even if this meant granting blacks minor offices, local, state, or national. Such lively competition did not exist in the South.

In the South, the ideology of white supremacy according to which "politics was white folks' business" kept the blacks outside the party organization altogether. For a black to obtain the right to vote without white sanction was virtually impossible from about 1900 until 1960, during which time the achievement of the ballot was the sole political aim of the black community in the South. Moreover, even after the legal right to vote had been acquired, the white community employed extralegal devices in order to prevent blacks from exercising it. It was not until after the Voting Rights Act of 1965 that the right of blacks in the South became meaningful in a practical sense.

The southern one-party system also stymied the emergence there of black politics. Where a single party prevailed, its sole raison d'être was to eliminate the threat of black domination. Thus, no concession had to be made to the black electorate—for either it didn't exist in a meaningful way, it ran counter to prevailing folkways and mores, or in view of the doctrine of white supremacy, it was bad politics.

In a two-party system, the loss of a bloc vote usually means a disaster at the polls, but in the South the attachment of black voters could mean political defeat. Thus, it was not only good business not to have the black vote, but the race issue itself was a form of political capital that many southern demagogues used to success. In the North, loss of black support meant defeat; in the South it usually meant a victory.

Moreover, though black political independence in the North might mean ostracism and the loss of the right to participate in regular party affairs, in the South such independence often meant the loss of one's life as well. For a black merely to vote independently, much less run independently could prove fatal. The one-party system limited the number of candidates, their alternatives, and options, and tied white politicians to the prevailing white supremacy.

For more than two decades, the one-party system and its white primaries, poll taxes, literacy tests, and gerrymandering effectively eliminated the black voting in the South. Besides the external restraints operating to block black participation in the electoral and political process, there were internal restraints within the black community. The few blacks who had the ballot restrained other blacks from trying to seek office. To permit such would have brought down upon these few eligible black voters the wrath of the white community who would have taken away their privileges. As a result, black politicians refused to run for office even when they had a fair chance of winning. Blacks who could vote were therefore careful not to vote too often or else voted in such a way as not to precipitate revocation of their privilege. As a result, white politicians represented all-black districts and white minorities ran the local government. Such was the case in Tuskegee,

Alabama, where blacks had been restrained from taking part in the white man's business, politics.

Soon, however, legal assaults and new leadership began to undermine this ideological control. While legal victory came in 1944, segregation continued through informal rules and regulations. Despite legal victories the learned political behavior of blacks within the region kept blacks from venturing as actors into the political arena. Limited voting remained for nearly two more decades. In fact, despite the rise in the strength of the black electorate, prior to the Voting Rights Act of 1965 only 72 black elected officials existed in all of the eleven southern states.[2] The final blow to white supremacy and the one-party system which came in the civil rights movement stimulated blacks to seek public offices.

By eliminating all of the outward vestiges of support for white supremacy in everyday life, plus eliminating segregation in the areas of transportation, public accommodation, education, opportunities, employment, and voting, it was only a matter of time before segregation was eliminated in the area of politics. Many blacks ran for public office during the era of the sit-ins and nonviolent marches, but the black electorate was not large enough to sustain them. But as the black electorate grew following the Civil Rights Act of 1965 black politicians had the power which appeared to serve the enlarged electorate. Following the collapse of overt segregation black politicians fought for state legislative posts, mayoral posts, aldermatic posts, justice of the peace and school board positions. Blacks were no longer barred from the political process. Still, the southern blacks' entrance into the political arena was different from that of their northern counterparts.

In the North blacks rose to national political office through the regular political organizations.

In the South, however, blacks had to run as independents; they had to form separate or satellite parties or else go it alone. They suffered at nearly every turn because funds, information, and procedures were withheld from them repeatedly. These are only some of the measures instituted by whites to prevent blacks from winning office: (1) abolishing the office, (2) extending the term of the white incumbent, (3) making the elective office appointive, (4) raising filing fee, (5) withholding pertinent information on how to qualify for office, (6) withholding certification of the nominating petitioning black candidates, and (7) imposing barriers to halt successful black candidates from taking office.[3] Eventually, however, the civil rights movement overcame even these barriers. Blacks continued to take office, and as more obstacles were eliminated, more black politicians arose.

[2] John B. Morris, ed., *Black Elected Officials in the Southern States* (Atlanta: Southern Regional Council, 1969), p. 1.

[3] United States Commission on Civil Rights, *Political Participation* (Washington: Government Printing Office, 1968), p. 172.

Black migration since World War I and World War II has tremendously increased black involvement in party organizations. Moreover, the New Deal awakened blacks to their actual potential and the possibilities open to them in government and politics. More important, however, was the fact that the token political concessions the northern political parties had made during the New Deal to the increasing numbers of blacks in their ranks were destined to increase after the larger black migration brought in by World War II. After the war the northern black voters proved crucial in not only national contests, but also in state and local contests—so much so that more and more concessions were made to them.

In fact, in cities like Cleveland, Gary, St. Louis, New York, Chicago, etc., blacks provided so many votes to the Democratic organization and so dominated the central cities, that it was only a matter of time before party control over the northern black voter would collapse and blacks would take control of the organizations themselves.[4]

Since blacks only furnished votes while whites controlled the money, leadership, and organization, the fight for control at times forced blacks in the North, like their counterparts in the South, to go outside the regular party organization. Both Mayor Hatcher of Gary and Mayor Stokes of Cleveland were denied party funds and had to rely upon foundation support (Ford Foundation, Marshall Field Foundation, etc.) to finance their campaigns. They swept to power with the black vote, but their opponents still denied them entrance into the regular party machine. The party had to be built almost all over again. Moreover since these black mayors have been in office only a short while, it remains to be seen how long blacks can, with only voters and leadership, continue to control northern political organizations.

If the civil rights revolution released politically ambitious blacks in the South, in the North it released a new phase of white liberalism, which sought to prove its freedom from prejudice by sponsoring blacks for office; in Massachusetts whites elected the first black man to the Senate in almost a hundred years, over a staunch white civil rights advocate and liberal.

A kind of convergence was taking place. Blacks took control of the party organizations in the North at the same time southern blacks broke the long standing control of white supremacy and segregation.

BLACK POLITICIANS AND OFFICIALS

With the collapse of regular party control, black politicians arose almost simultaneously in both the North and South. In fact, all over the country blacks captured political offices. While the process has yet to stabilize itself,

[4] See Edward T. Clayton, *The Negro Politician: His Success and Failures* (Chicago: Johnson Publishing Company, 1964), pp. 157-168.

black political activity continues to rise, and in some states blacks are now seeking governorships, for the first time since the 1920s.

In the North, black politicians are mainly national politicians. All of the ten black congressmen are from the North. In the South, the majority of black politicians are municipal or state officers. While southern black politicians hold more positions than northern ones, northern blacks have more control over the dominant party organizations than southern ones. Although the northern black electorate is in a better position than ever, the southern black electorate is still forty percent under-registered and its position is tentative because of the possible expiration of the Voting Rights Bill, which is the main source of the new black voting strength.

In some future election, southern blacks may very well capture a congressional seat, but they will need a strong organization and significant liberal white support to do so. Because they have to operate outside the regular party organization, they must finance and organize campaigns by themselves. Because they are unsure of their electoral support, blacks in the South have tended to avoid expensive senatorial and gubernatorial campaigns and they have concentrated on local and minor offices.[5]

In the South, federal power was required to put the black man in the political arena, and unless federal power maintains him there—or the ideology of southern whites changes—he may not be able to stay there. The southern black politician and voter will remain on shaky ground until whites fully accept them as participants in the political arena. At present, unless federal power stays within reach, the black political position in several southern states will revert to lower stages of involvement.

In several of the black belt counties, blacks are in the majority and can therefore assume complete political control. In the North, however, no region approximates the black belt southern area. Nowhere in the North are blacks in a majority. Blacks nearly dominate the central cities, however, and there are more major cities in the northern counties than in the southern ones. Hence, nothern blacks can dominate larger political units. In the rural South, segregation forced them into their own enclaves, to which southern reapportionment has now given some political power.

In addition, the citywide election in the North tends to dilute black voting power, but the old system of district and ward election in the South has given blacks more political representation.

While population residential location and the district and ward electoral system have given blacks in the South more elected officials than northern blacks, party absorption and continued political participation have brought northern blacks a significant number of national elected officials. Thus

[5] Julian Bond, *Black Candidate: Southern Campaign Experiences* (Atlanta: Southern Regional Council, 1969), p. 50.

despite the factors inherent in the emergence of the black politicians—and the relative number of black politicians in either North or South—their true significance lies in their loci of power and the temporal element (i.e., time of emergence) present.

BLACK POLITICIANS: POWER AND TIME

What can the newly elected black politicians do for the black community? How can they best solve the problems (more than three hundred years of them) of the black population? Headlines that advertise that America has more than 1,500 elected black officials do grave injustice to the black community because they foster the myth that black politicians can solve all the problems that beset blacks: slumism, poverty, ignorance, political alienation, and unemployment. Such headlines imply that if the black politicians fail to eradicate these major problems, their failure is a failure of blackness and black people's agility, skill, and political sophistication. This tragic myth is born of heavy emphasis on the electoral approach to politics and has pushed the black masses to inhuman sacrifices and suffering to attain the ballot and elect their own officials, who were in turn supposed to solve their problems. Attaining the right to vote and electing black officials is not necessarily the answer, however. Politics is not always the art of the possible. Electing black officials may have some emotional and psychological satisfaction for the black community, but this satisfaction will give way increasingly to despair over the day-to-day lives of black people. In short, *black politicians without power, or outside the loci of power, are just as bad as no black politicians at all.* Because the increase in black officeholding creates an illusion of reality, it makes people feel that they have accomplished more than the reality indicates. One expectation can cause groups and individuals within the black community not only to disdain politics, but disbelieve and distrust black politicians, who are, in turn, frustrated and virtually powerless even in the arena of power.

Fifteen hundred new black politicians are indeed significant, but a close analysis reveals the limited nature of the offices held by blacks. As Table VII shows, the majority of blacks are school board members, city councilmen, state legislators, justices of the peace, and county officials. An even closer analysis reveals that the majority of southern black politicians hold positions in predominantly black belt regions, whose counties are the most underdeveloped in the country,[6] and thus lack the economic means for improving the welfare of blacks.

Beyond the nature of the counties, however, is the nature of the positions

[6] S. D. Cook, "The Tragic Myth of Black Power," *New South,* 21 (Summer, 1966), 61. See Table IX.

Table VII. Black Elected Officials in the Southern States

	Ala.	Ark.	Fla.	Ga.	La.	Miss.	N.C.	S.C.	Tenn.	Texas	Va.	Total
Legislators												
State Senate				2					2	1		5
State House				12	1	1	1	1	6	2	1	25
												30
City Officials												
Mayor	3	4	1		1	1						10
City Council	28	10	15	6	13	7	11	15	8	10	18	141
Civil Service Board			1									1
												152
County Officials												
County Governing Board	2		1	5	11	4	1	4	5		2	35
County Administration	1			1		1					1	4
Election Commission						15						15
												54
Law Enforcement Officials												
Judge, District Court							1					1
Sheriff	1											1
Coroner	1					1						2
Town Marshal					2							2
Magistrate								4	4			8
Constable	6		1		8	5			3			23
Justice of the Peace	20	3			8	10			1		2	44
												81
School Board Officials												
School Board Members	5	33		3	9	6	4	2	1	8		71
Totals	67	50	19	29	53	51	18	26	30	21	24	388

Chart prepared as of information on hand January 10, 1969.

In Tennessee one man serves both as State Representative & City Councilman.

Source: *Black Elected Officials in the Southern States* (Atlanta: Voter Education Project of Southern Regional Council, 1969), p. iii.

Table VIII. Number of Southern Counties with Black Majorities

States	Total Number of Counties	Black Majoritarian Counties	Percentage
Alabama	67	12	18%
Arkansas			
Florida	67	2	3%
Georgia	159	34	21%
Louisiana			
Mississippi	82	28	36%
North Carolina	100	8	8%
South Carolina	46	15	32%
Tennessee			
Texas	254	3	1%
Virginia	95	2	2%

in terms of power. Black politicians are mainly in positions that traditionally have been of very limited power. School board membership is significant only in states like New York and California, which have enough money to pay for the education of their young. Membership on boards within these states can of course become crucial in providing quality education in ghetto schools, if the black members can only expose discrimination, or act as gadflies. The southern states remain reluctant to integrate their public schools, and the number of segregated academies is increasing.[7] Moreover, white school board members make it difficult for black members to be really effective.

Black city councilmen also suffer from limited power. If they belong to a weak mayor-council form of city government, they may have not only ordinance-making powers but some budgetary or administrative powers. However, in a strong mayor-council form of government, their powers are lessened and confined somewhat to enacting ordinances.[8]

The next largest group of elected black officials is the state representatives. As legislators, their small numbers—as indicated in Table IX—render them all but helpless to enact significant legislation. In Iowa, for example, Mrs. A. June Franklin, the only black in the state legislature, but also minority house whip, has stated that "it gets to the point where you hate to go over there (State House) day after day" and see your legislation killed.[9] In Georgia, which is the state with the largest number of black legislators,

[7] "Segregation Academies Flourish in the South," South Today, 1 (October, 1969), 1-6.
[8] Henry A. Turner, American Democracy: State and Local Government (New York: Harper and Row, 1968), pp. 69-70.
[9] Judy Ann Miller, "The Representative is a Lady," The Black Politician, 1 (Fall, 1969), 17.

Table IX. The Number and Percentages of Blacks in State Legislatures

State	Legislature Membership		Blacks in Legislature		Blacks as Percent of Membership		Blacks as Percent of Population
	Senate	House	Senate	House	Senate	House	
Alabama	35	106	—	—	—	—	30.0
Alaska	20	40	—	—	—	—	2.9
Arizona	30	80	1	2	3.3	2.5	3.3
Arkansas	35	100	—	—	—	—	21.7
California	40	80	1	5	2.5	6.3	5.6
Colorado	35	65	1	2	2.8	3.0	2.2
Connecticut	36	177	1	4	2.7	2.2	4.2
Delaware	19	39	1	2	5.2	5.1	13.6
Florida	48	119	—	1	—	.8	17.7
Georgia	54	205	2	12	3.7	5.8	28.4
Hawaii	25	51	—	—	—	—	.7
Idaho	35	70	—	—	—	—	.2
Illinois	57	175	4	10	7.0	5.7	10.2
Indiana	50	100	—	3	—	3.0	5.7
Iowa	61	124	—	1	—	.8	.9
Kansas	40	125	—	3	—	2.4	4.1
Kentucky	38	100	1	2	2.6	2.0	7.1
Louisiana	39	105	—	1	—	.9	31.9
Maine	32	151	—	—	—	—	.3
Maryland	43	142	2	9	4.6	6.3	16.7
Massachusetts	40	240	—	2	—	.8	2.1
Michigan	38	110	3	10	7.8	9.0	9.1
Minnesota	67	135	—	1	—	.7	.6
Mississippi	52	122	—	1	—	.8	42.0
Missouri	34	163	2	13	5.8	7.9	9.0
Montana	55	104	—	—	—	—	.2
Nebraska	49		—	—	—	—	2.0
Nevada	20	40	—	1	—	2.5	4.7
New Hampshire	24	375	—	—	—	—	.3
New Jersey	40	80	—	4	—	5.0	8.4
New Mexico	42	70	—	1	—	1.4	1.7
New York	57	150	3	9	5.2	6.0	8.4
North Carolina	50	120	—	1	—	.8	24.4
North Dakota	49	98	—	—	—	—	.1
Ohio	33	99	3	10	9.0	10.0	8.0
Oklahoma	48	99	1	4	2.0	4.0	6.5
Oregon	30	60	—	—	—	—	1.0
Pennsylvania	50	203	1	10	2.0	4.9	7.5
Rhode Island	50	100	—	1	—	1.0	2.1
South Carolina	50	124	—	—	—	—	34.8
South Dakota	35	75	—	—	—	—	.1
Tennessee	33	99	2	6	6.0	6.0	16.4
Texas	31	150	1	2	3.2	1.3	12.3
Utah	28	69	—	—	—	—	.4
Vermont	30	150	—	—	—	—	.1
Virginia	40	100	1	2	2.5	2.0	20.5
Washington	49	99	—	1	—	1.0	1.7
West Virginia	34	100	—	—	—	—	4.8
Wisconsin	33	100	—	1	—	1.0	1.8
Wyoming	25	61	—	—	—	—	.6

Source: *The Black Politician* (Summer, 1970), p. 20.

the problem is much the same. Much of their jointly sponsored legislation is killed off. In short, black legislators and senators are numerically weak and lack institutional or personal power because of their positions as neophytes in these legislative halls. In fact, black politicians are not only novices, they are nearly powerless. They hold positions that traditionally have had only limited power. Moreover, as the problems of urbanism grow worse, and federal powers grow greater, these positions become increasingly insignificant. This brings us to another topic: time.

According to political observers like Pat Watters and Reese Cleghorn, black people are entering the political arena "at times when the American city, spilling over into amorphous suburbs and threatened with losing political coherence and identity, is beginning to take new direction."[10] The concentration of impoverished blacks in our major cities, which has resulted from Negro migration from the rural South, rapid growth of population, and the continuing movement of the white middle class to the suburbs, has increased at a time when the cities themselves are disintegrating.[11] This "continued in-migration of low income Negroes and out-migration of middle income whites . . . means further erosion of the city's tax base . . . as commerce and industry follow the more affluent whites to the suburbs."[12] Black politicians in city administrations will find that this continual concentration of poverty and unemployment puts an enormous strain on the city budgets with the result that there will not be sufficient funds to pay for welfare programs, housing programs, improved schools, union pay rates, control of violence and juvenile delinquency.[13] In the South, on the other hand, black politicians are gaining control in black majority counties that are the poorest "economically, educationally and otherwise in the poorest section of the country."[14] Southern black politicians will in effect be governing ghost towns. An excellent example is Fayette, Mississippi, which has just elected Charles Evers as mayor. Besides its fundamental problems of a lack of industry, low tax rolls, hostile whites, and heavy poverty, Fayette has a large deficit left by the outgoing white administration.

As Table X indicates, however, seven of the ten largest U. S. cities will have a black majority in terms of population in the next fifteen years, with the prospect also of more black officials. However, though blacks are beginning to dominate the central cities, their economic advancement is not "progressing rapidly enough so that they can hope to assume responsibility for rehabilitating the central city cares that are already badly suffer-

[10] Pat Watters and Reese Cleghorn, *Climbing Jacob's Ladder: The Arrival of Negroes in Southern Politics* (New York: Harcourt, Brace and World, 1967), p. 75.
[11] Urban Coalition, *One Year Later* (New York: Praeger, 1969), p. 2.
[12] Thomas R. Dye, *Politics in the States and Communities* (Englewood Cliffs, N.J.: Prentice-Hall, 1969), pp. 293, 357.
[13] *Ibid.*
[14] Cook, *op. cit.*, p. 61.

Table X. Predicted Date of 50% Black Population
in Central Cities

New Orleans, La.	1971
Richmond, Va.	1971
Baltimore, Md.	1972
Jacksonville, Fla.	1972
Gary, Ind.	1973
Cleveland, Ohio	1975
St. Louis, Mo.	1978
Detroit, Mich.	1979
Philadelphia, Pa.	1981
Oakland, Calif.	1983
Chicago, Ill.	1984

Source: *Report of the National Advisory Commission on Civil Disorders* (Washington, D. C.: Government Printing Office, 1968), p. 216.

ing from neglect."[15] Black officials will not be able to govern effectively unless federal and state aid increases and compensatory programs are instituted. The problems of urban blight, economic anemia, and physical decay cannot be solved by black politicians who at the same time are called upon to render more and better services to the inhabitants. In other words, depopulation of a city by the wealthy does not mean that city spending for education, police, fire protection, health, hospital, and welfare will decrease. In many instances, the cost of these services doubles.

Black politicians are coming to power at a time when the central city is falling apart. They are assuming positions that are losing power in view of the rising need for federal assistance to cities and states. They are coming to power just as the urban crisis is peaking. Not only are they expected to devise solutions and solve problems that will avert the impending crisis, they must also deal with the problem of black political coherence.

Before the changes of the 1960s, black bosses and machines had a fairly tight degree of control over the black population in the cities—North and South. There were only a few such bosses, but they commanded a fairly high degree of discipline. However, the increasing population in the central cities has decreased this discipline and tight control—because the black machines have never been organized well enough to maintain control over a sizable number of the black community. Nor do they have the economic resources to service the needs of such communities. Secondly, the civil rights revolution stimulated new leadership, and the old-style leaders have

[15] L. Masatti, J. K. Hadden, et al., *A Time to Burn* (Chicago: Rand McNally and Company, 1969), p. 84.

been dismissed, displaced, and disavowed. With them went the small compact leadership mantle. Today, there are many black leaders and the black electorate is breaking up into not one or two, but several blocs. This fragmentation of the black electorate means trouble for black politicians who, in order to get elected or to gain support for legislation, must bridge each bloc. This only adds to the problems that black politicians must face.

BLACKS AND PUBLIC POLICY

Ultimately, the chief concern of black administrators must be the formation and implementation of policy. These functions grow out of the needs of the black community—whether urban, rural, ghetto, or suburbs. The nature of racism in this country, which has black Americans in relation to native whites segregated on the average of 86 percent for all cities,[16] has forced the black community to concentrate on two main categories of policy: civil rights policy to grant blacks equal justice before the law and welfare policy to solve problems of dislocation, unemployment, poverty, housing, slumism, and education. Given these two main categories of policy, the question is how to implement them. White America has generally felt that to pass a law is to solve a problem, but laws that are meaningless on the local level actually create more frustration than they dispel, for people become aware eventually that the law, though enacted, is not being effectively executed. Yet the law exists and further legal action on the matter is made difficult. Though implementation is mainly a problem of emphasis, power, and concern, it is secondary to public policy-making. The law must be made or passed before policy can be implemented.

Policy-making and the introduction of legislation designed to make the implementation of earlier legislation easier and more meaningful must therefore be the first concern of the black politician. It has already become the first concern of the black community. In fact, it is one of the reasons behind the continual election of black officials, for it is felt that they will pursue public policies that will be both meaningful and effective. At this point, however, two major factors need examination: the first is the nature of the black community, and the second is black politicians themselves. Neither the community nor the politicians are monolithic, nor do they view public policy in the same manner. Since not all blacks want integration, not all black politicians will pursue a policy of integration. Some blacks, like those in RAM, want complete black control of society.[17] These divergent

[16] K. Tauber and A. Tauber, *Negroes in Cities* (Chicago: Aldine Publishing Company, 1965), pp. 36–37.

[17] For an analysis of the different black groups and ideologies in the black community see C. Eric Lincoln, "American Negro Protest Movements," in J. P. Davis, ed., *American Negro Reference Book* (Englewood Cliffs, N.J.: Prentice-Hall, 1966).

responses require black political representatives to take divergent policy positions to satisfy their particular desires and preferences. Moreover, black politicians, while the subordinate group, often coalesce with the dominant white group whenever their preferences are mutual. Since dominant groups have always "pursued certain policies to maintain their superordinate positions vis-à-vis their submissive counterpart, the subordinate group has pursued policies which were designed to maximize their positions or [significantly] alter their situations."[18]

As indicated in Figure 15 these are the goal patterns pursued in a dominant-subordinate group situation. There are basically four dimensions to the dominant-submissive group mode. "The first two involve intra-factional competition in each of the communities, the third involves competition across group lines, and the fourth is the synthesis of the other three."[19] The final policy outcome represents the synthesis.

Given these basic divergences in the black and white communities, as exhibited in Figure 16, the policy orientations of both groups become fairly clear. Black politicians are likely to pursue policies in these six areas in varying degrees in order to find some white support.

Black politicians who are integrationists and seek cultural assimilation constitute the largest group. They seek to initiate and support strong civil rights and welfare legislation designed to improve the conditions of the subordinate group as long as "these measures involve increased interaction with the dominant members" of society.

Black politicians of the S2 Accommodationist pattern will generally be concerned with legislation and policy that will gradually give blacks their freedom. In the meantime, they will accept legal protection. Their political enactments are generally not black-oriented, but are passed in the name of the greater good of society. If it happens to affect the black community, well and good. Civil rights in general will not be the major political enactment of this group.

On the other hand, the black politicians of the Black Consciousness (S3-cultural pluralism) strain obviously will pursue policies that "stress internal improvement within institutions already controlled by and neighborhoods densely populated with" black people. These black politicians' policy orientations will stress the need for an improved self-image—black control of black communities and development of all facets of black life, culture, and experience. Many black politicians get on platforms to articulate such

[18] For an excellent attempt to structure a frame of reference in which to view black politics see Mack Jones, "A Frame of Reference for Black Politics" (a paper presented at 1969 annual meeting of the Southern Political Science Association, Miami, Florida), p. 8. On this point see also H. Blalock, *Toward a Theory of Minority Group Relations* (New York: John Wiley and Sons, 1967). The foregoing charts were taken from Professor Jones' paper, and the discussion relies heavily upon his analysis.

[19] *Ibid.*, p. 9.

**Figure 15. Goal-Directed Patterns of Activity in the
American Dominant-Submissive Group Situation**

DOMINANT GROUP

PATTERN	POLICY

D1 Integrationist   Cultural assimilation (permitted)
                              ⌐ continued subjugation ⌐ *

D2 White Separatist   Legal protection
                              ⌐ continued subjugation ⌐

D3 Restrained White   Continued subjugation
    Supremacist

D4 White Terrorist   Extermination

SUBMISSIVE GROUP

PATTERN   POLICY

S1 Integrationist   Cultural assimilation (forced)

S2 Accommodationist   Legal protection

S3 Black Consciousness   Cultural pluralism

S4 Black Nationalist   Population transfer (peaceful)

S5 Revolutionist   Reversal of status

*The policy orientation "continued subjugation" is enclosed in broken lines to indicate that each dominant group faction, rhetoric notwithstanding, in varying degrees, tends toward continued domination of the submissive community.

Figure 16. Goal-Directed Patterns of Activity in General Dominant-Submissive Group Situations

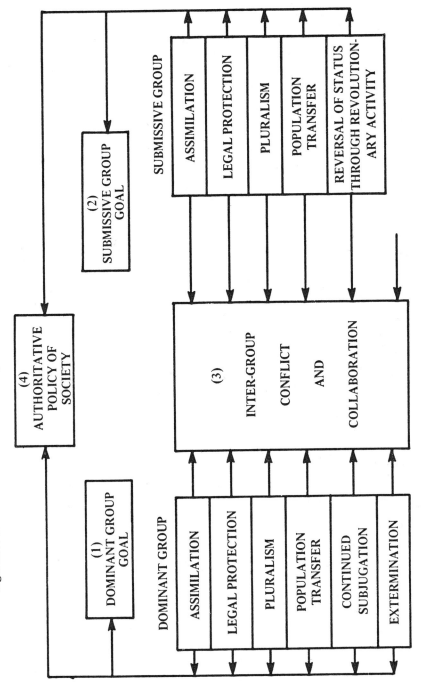

Note: As the directional arrows indicate, each pattern of activity seeks to have its policy orientation accepted as the goal of its respective group and the society at large, and at the same time each pattern attempts to influence patterns across group lines in a manner consistent with its goals.

concern, but their post-election policies cannot always reflect platform promises.

The black politicians of the S4 Black Nationalist orientation seek a removal of blacks to certain isolated black territories, black regions, black states, or outside of the country. "Population transfer is the basic policy orientation of this faction." It is generally pursued through legislation that seeks to create not only separate black institutions but separate black states.[20]

However, these politicians express the political dimension of black nationalism, whereas the politicians of the Black Consciousness strain express the economic and cultural dimensions of black nationalism. These dimensions are separate in theory, but they are not always so in practice, and there is a question whether land and a separate political entity that is all black can be achieved by a policy enactment.[21] Moreover, since it is easier to seek internal improvement than population transfer, there are not many black politicians of this strain.

The next segment of black politicians, designated S5—Revolutionist, seeks the institution of black domination. At present no revolutionists are in office; even if they were, it is doubtful that any of their policies would be enacted since no legislative system is going to permit its own destruction.

The paramilitary organization, the Black Panthers, is an example of the S5 group; their political tactics provoke many legislators to enact laws designed to suppress the organization. In fact, it is difficult for this group to achieve any of its political goals, because its ideology frightens society. Thus, the categories that have just been described are general ones that hopefully will help political analysts understand some of the policy orientations of black politicians and the black community. They also form a framework which helps one understand why black politicians of the black consciousness faction, whites of the white separatists, and white supremacists can sponsor or work jointly on the same kind of legislation. These factions can work together because they hold nearly similar views about each other's race and the relationship between the two.

Moreover, these general policy categories help one to understand the policy fights that occasionally break out among black politicians. For instance, black politicians of the S-3 strain often conflict with those of the S-1 group. The first group will seek separateness and exclusiveness, but the latter group, represented by "orgs" like the NAACP, will seek greater interracial contact and association. In addition, this general framework discloses blacks who seem totally disinterested in the black community or

[20] Jones, *op. cit.*, p. 15.

[21] For insight into the different dimensions of culture see J. Herman Blake, "Black Nationalism," in *Protest in the Sixties, The Annals,* no. 377-382 (March, 1969), pp. 16-20.

the black problem. In short, its categorizing of black politicians will in the main give some insight into what kinds of public policy they are most likely to seek.

A note of caution must be added, however, on the relationship between campaign tactics and policy-making. Black politicians may find a position of the Black Nationalist type effective for winning an election and yet pursue a largely different course in office.

A perfect example of black politicians who can divorce the two was William Dawson of Chicago. Dawson gained black support by declaring his interest in racial goals and hopes, proceeded to pursue other policies, policies that never mentioned blacks, because his machine gave his black electorate the immediate patronage they needed. In many instances policy-making cannot deliver the goods and rewards as fast as machines can. And this brings us to our next major point—implementation.

Black politicians, despite their policy goals or orientations, are plagued constantly by the needs of the black community. How long will the black community wait for its black politicians to deliver? How much longer can they wait for the badly needed, promised, and not forthcoming services?

In a sense, black politicians may find that policy enactment may be only another empty victory to the black community, for the implementation of such policy may be delayed either by lack of funds or by the bureaucracy set up to deliver the goods. Thus, in many ways, Dawson has been successful because his returns were immediate. As Professor Brian Crozier remarks in his little book, *The Morning After*,[22] the black community expects more from their newly installed black politicians than they can deliver immediately. This could cause not only more frustration and discontent, but some political repercussions. Hence, it may be useful for black politicians to become more concerned in the earlier stages of their political career with the *implementation of policy,* rather than with just policy enactment.

Black politicians represent areas that are badly in need of goods and services, and in many cases they become captives of the problems of policy implementation. They will also be more or less politically impotent until the communities' needs are systematically attained in some measurable way. In seeking to give the community what it needs, black politicians become either *machine politicians* (bosses), who can dispense tangible goods, *rhetoric politicians,* who can provide intangible goods (psychological needs), *activist politicians,* who seek to begin programs and opportunities that can enhance and improve the wants and desires of their constituency, or *accommodationists,* who seek to satisfy their white supporters.

"The Rhetorical black politicians seek to answer the needs of the black

[22] Brian Crozier, *The Morning After* (New York: Oxford University Press, 1963).

community with verbiage and promises."[23] They make promises and offer phrases and slogans to replace programs and actions they cannot carry out.

Black bossism has emerged from the efforts of black politicians to respond to the environmental needs of the black community. In this instance, black politicians create political *organizations* that reward their top leaders, usually black ministers and civic leaders, who in turn use their influence to keep voters coming to the organization.

The third political style is Black Activism. A black politician of this type combines rhetoric and organization with programs. "He will attempt to employ whatever programs the local, state, or national government agencies have created to help solve the pressing socioeconomic needs of his black constituency."

Another political style is represented by the Black Accommodationist. Elected by a predominantly white constituency, he will naturally assume an accommodationist posture, by which he will satisfy his white voters.

These styles will vary according to personalities and localities, but the major influence—the environmental need—will remain crucial.

SUMMARY

In conclusion, because of the need of their constituents for immediate rewards, some black politicians will become politicians who will grant these needs through machines and patronage politics (machine politics). Others will become politicians of rhetoric, who will retain their constituents by means of psychological and verbal rewards. The next group, of course, will be the activist politicians who seek to make already existing programs more meaningful, by expanding them and supplementing them. The accommodationist will coalesce with whites. It is possible, however, that some black politicians will fall into all these categories, since reelection is much more important than nonelection. It is conceivable that the desire for political security may cause some blacks to straddle all the categories at once. In the final analysis, this all depends upon the continuing state of race relations and racism in this country.

[23] For a complete and comprehensive analysis of black political styles, see Hanes Walton, Jr., and Leslie B. Mclemore, "Portrait of Black Political Styles," *The Black Politician,* 11 (October, 1970), 9-13.

XII

The Politics of Blackness in the Metropolis

Black urbanization has not only changed the lives, style, dreams, and politics of black Americans, it is also about to change urban America. Although this shift has come within the last fifty years, the impact of it has just begun to be felt. Moreover, future black migration from rural areas to urban America is likely to continue.

The roots of black urbanization lie in the black migrations that took place from the agricultural and caste-oriented South to the industrial North, basically for escapist reasons. The push and pull effects, which Professor Eli Ginzberg has noted, operated as the two major forces that brought blacks to American cities.[1] The push effect of southern segregation and its brutal manifestations and the pull effects—the lure of new jobs, new opportunities, and the promise of land—worked together in promoting this mass exodus.

Unfortunately, these blacks brought with them a poor education, unskilled labor, no financial resources, the psychological burdens of color, and deferred dreams. The promised land had no opportunities for such travelers. In fact, the land of opportunity was closed to all but a few of them. According to Claude Brown, "before the soreness of the cotton fields had left Mama's back, her knees were getting sore from scrubbing 'Goldberg's' floow."[2] Consequently they passed on to their children their disillusionment, disappointment, anger, and frustration. But "to add to their misery, they had little hope of deliverance. For where does one run to when he's already in the promised land?"[3]

There were additional problems. Not only did urbanism magnify all the problems that were inherent in small-town America, it also created new problems and new ways of life, mores, and customs. Urban America atomized the individual and isolated him. It created conformity, a quest for

[1] Eli Ginzberg, *op. cit.*, pp. 227–228.
[2] Claude Brown, *Manchild in the Promised Land* (New York: Signet Books, 1965), p. 8.
[3] *Ibid.*

209

community, more efficient use of time, conspicuous consumption, new social values, and a concern with "security, safety, and the opinions of others." These, of course, were problems confronting the individual as a result of urbanization. Confronting society as a whole were traffic congestion, slumism, a desire for skills, rise in crime, unemployment, inadequate housing, overt discrimination and prejudice, and a rise in the demand for goods, services, and welfare. This demand for new services overwhelmed most governments of the central cities, which could not provide the schools, water supply, parks, hospitals, utilities, local roads, and services needed to service a growing population.

Thus, urban America with its numerous and complex problems, with its enchantments and lure of a better life, had added to it a new element— black Americans—in increasing numbers that multiplied each problem and magnified racial tensions and antagonism.

BLACK POLITICS AND URBANISM

Among the chief features of urban America were the machine and the boss. It was due to the existence of these institutions that race relations in urban America, especially in the earlier stages, were less abrasive. In fact, machines and bosses, although they differed from city to city, helped in part to facilitate black accommodation to the promised land. The machines were sustained by the votes of the recent immigrants, whom they rewarded with a variety of social services needed to maintain at least a marginal existence in the urban society. This was as true of Irish, Poles, and Jews as it was of black Americans.

With their black submachines and bosses, the urban political machines accelerated the registration and voting of blacks, though, of course, black political leadership was intentionally discouraged. Almost all political machines made only those commitments, compromises, and concessions to blacks that they had to. In large measure, although black political involvement was high in urban America, black political rewards remained low, except for the black bosses and their top lieutenants. A reward gap soon developed—i.e., only the top blacks benefitted from the mass participation of the black electorate. As Figure 17 indicates, the black bosses and their lieutenants received significant tangible rewards for their participation in the politics of the city. They usually received one of the limited or token political appointments for their support of the white machines. In some cases, like that of Dawson in Chicago, the political reward was meaningful; it not only had some degree of permanency attached to it, but carried with it status, prestige, a substantial salary, and other side benefits.

On the other hand, the majority of the black electorate in urban America received nothing significant or substantial to improve their life or decrease

Figure 17. Political Rewards for Black Urbanites

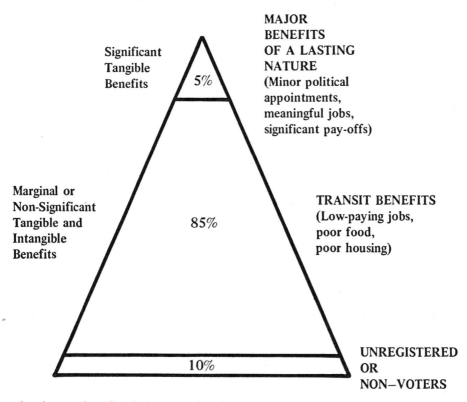

the day-to-day discrimination they had to encounter or endure. Generally speaking, the majority of the black electorate in urban America obtained from the white political machines or black submachines only the bare necessities to sustain them until the next election. In fact, they almost became wards of the political machine.

First, these new arriving black pilgrims needed housing, which machine workers directed them to—i.e., the black ghetto. Secondly, they needed to adjust to city life, and the machine provided them with some form of employment. Since the new black pilgrims lacked major skills, education, and training, the jobs they could obtain paid poorly and involved menial work.

The pay for these jobs was in most cases low, and rent for dilapidated houses was high. The cost of food was so high that the low-paying jobs could provide for only a small amount at best. When black submachines did give food supplements, they only did so on holidays. Clothing, like food supplements, was given once or twice a year in areas where the winters were severe or heat in poor or deteriorating buildings was lacking. Generally it was used and badly worn, and there was not much of it. Finally, other benefits from the machine for the majority of the black electorate—getting sons or daughters out of jail, or making small loans at high rates, or getting a ride to the hospital, or obtaining groceries on time—were just as transient and marginal as the others. The political machines never solved any of the major problems of the black electorate in terms of food, clothing, or shelter.

Apart from these tangible needs, the machines could not overlook the physical and psychological effects of discrimination and segregation in the ghetto. Here racism reached its greatest intensity. Police brutality, economic discrimination, landlord extortionism, etc., all worked against the poor, uneducated blacks who had nothing but a ballot and the handicap of their color. In such a situation of unemployment, low pay, transient jobs, poor housing, and general gloom and despair, the specter of escapism emerged. In the black ghetto, the escapism meant drug-peddling, the numbers racket, bootlegging, prostitution, gambling, etc. Generally, these vices, with their promises of quick success and avenues of escape, flourished in the ghetto. Instead of providing avenues of relief and escape, however, they became new devices for further exploiting the black arrivals. The worst part of this rise in crime and vice was that it went unregulated, unnoticed, or with the blessing of the political machine or its suboffice. Black politics in urban America, in the final analysis, was unable to aid the majority of the black electorate.

Black politics in the cities was dependent on a political structure that did not seek reform or improvement. The leaders of the political machine did not try to improve the ghettoes, nor did they try to improve or eradicate the cause of the problems under which the black masses labored. No programs for developing work skills among blacks were established, nor did wages improve, and the rackets and undergroundism intensified.[4] In many cases, the rackets and vices continued *because of* political or police connections.

In the words of Kenneth Clark, the dark ghettoes are social, political, educational, and—above all—economic colonies. Their inhabitants are subject peoples, victims of the greed, cruelty, insensitivity, guilt, and fear of their masters.[5] Politicians and the political system became almost dysfunctional for the black ghetto inhabitants. The pride of having a black state assemblyman, or a black congressman, or black councilman remained too much at the symbolic level to satisfy the increasing needs of the black ghetto. Pride in a symbol did not fix the house that leaked, or had not heat;

[4] See Roland L. Warren, "Politics and the Ghetto System," in R. L. Warren, ed., *Politics and the Ghettoes* (New York: Atherton Press, 1969), pp. 11–30. See also Norton E. Long, "Politics and the Ghetto Perpetuation," *ibid.*, pp. 31–43.
[5] Kenneth Clark, *Dark Ghetto* (New York: Harper and Row, 1965), p. 11.

it did not put food on the table or clothes on black backs, or pay bills and high interest rates. The white politicians were slow in learning that symbolic black political appointments did not solve the continuing and increasing problem of the black urbanites.

The lack of political independence because of reliance on the machine sapped the vitality of black politics in urban America. With the avenue of politics available and open, but dysfunctional, it was simply a matter of time before the desire to change or escape would take another form—violence. Before that happened, however, blacks made other behavioral adjustments to their oppression. Speaking collectively, some blacks accepted the ghetto; others organized in churches, lodges, groups, etc., and rebelled against it.[6] Still others suppressed their rage or directed it against themselves or their fellow blacks.[7] Finally, some blacks reacted individually or in a specified manner to "internal colonialism." In terms of typologies, black urbanites took one of the following seven responses: stoicism, defeat, exploitation, achievement, rebellion without a cause, activism, or revolution.[8]

The black stoic-urbanite is an individual who accepts the evil and the problems of the ghetto and resigns himself to them. Basically apathetic, this individual usually withdraws into a traditional black religion or a cultist religion like the black Muslims. Others drop their religious attitude and maintain a "cool" front of indifference to the problems of society. The defeated black urbanite generally seeks escapism or outlets for his miseries in drugs, alcohol, or psychotic delusions. On the other hand, the black exploiters—i.e., the numbers man, blockbuster, etc.—"accept the status quo and for economic reasons prefer society in its present form." They give lip service to civil rights and integration, but thrive on the caste system because they have a vested interest in segregation.[9]

Among the black achievers there is, first of all, the one who seeks to better his own position "but may have little concern for the collective" conditions of other blacks. Generally professionals, these blacks, are status-seekers and highly motivated. They almost always set high levels of aspirations for themselves and seek to realize them regardless of sacrifice and hardship. Ultimately, this "born achiever" feels that his accomplishments are the only contributions he needs to make to the black race.

The "rebel without a cause" rebels against the confines that society places upon him and takes out his own frustration upon other blacks.

[6] See W. McCord, John Howard, et al., *Life Styles in the* Black Ghetto (New York: W. W. Norton and Company, 1969), pp. 76-77.
[7] See P. Cobbs and Grier, *Black Rage* (New York: Basic Books, 1968).
[8] McCord et al., *op. cit.*, pp. 76-77.
[9] E. Franklin Frazier, "Human All to Human: The Negro's Vested Interest in Segregation," *Survey Graphic*, 36 (January, 1947).

These are the black criminals, whose major offenses are against black people. They are not working for long-term social reforms, but other rebels—i.e., the activists—are. These—exemplified by men like Roy Wilkins, the late Martin Luther King, Jr., the late Whitney M. Young, Jr., Jesse Jackson, and Ralph Abernathy—seek to reorganize and improve American society. They see the constitutional structure of America as basically sound, and they believe that problems arise "from a few anachronistic practices here and there (discrimination for example). The major goal of the activists is integration and full assimilation into American life. They believe that the problems of black people will disappear with the advent of integration, which may be utopian on their part. The black revolutionary, finally, seeks to create a new order, a new system, a new institutional structure, a better world. For him, reform is a new day with a new system. He sees the old system as corrupt and impossible to repair because of its inbred racism. To him, violence and the overthrow of the present order is the only way out, the only answer to the black problem in America.

These black ghetto life-styles, or reactions to urban ghetto oppression, have not been enough, however. Nor have the black bosses or white machines, which could not deliver payoffs to a black population standing in the need of all the rewards it could get, been enough. So, Watts came in 1964, although riots had occurred long before Watts.[10] Watts, Detroit, and Newark came to symbolize a "new day"—the rise of political violence.

THE POLITICS OF BLACK VIOLENCE

With the political participation of blacks in urban areas dysfunctional, with black life-styles and personal adaptation insufficient devices, and with the problem of the ghetto and urban areas increasing, it was obvious that new channels of access to change would emerge or be created. Finding themselves barred from legitimate access to the ladder of achievement and in a political, social, and economic structure that "effectively prevented them from utilizing not only legitimate channels of opportunity, but criminal and illegitimate channels as well," black urbanites resorted to acts of violence to achieve their needs.[11] According to Professor Lewis Coser, "violence equalizes and opens to the participants access to hitherto denied areas of achievement." Participation in violence offers opportunity to the oppressed and downtrodden . . . a chance for the first act of participation in the polity, for entry into the world of active citizenship." Revolutionary violence indeed announced the need for a new day.

[10] On this point see A. Grimshaw, ed., *Racial Violence in the United States* (Chicago: Aldine Publishing Company, 1969), and A. Washaw, *From Sit-in to Race Riot* (New York: Doubleday and Company, 1964).

[11] Lewis A. Coser, "Some Social Functions of Violence," *The Annals,* no. 362-367 (March, 1966), p. 10.

According to Professor H. L. Nieburg, the need for this new day arises from the unevenly distributed stress in society.[12] In his view this stress falls heaviest upon "groups without access to the formal process of values."[13] The main function of government is to allocate values; its inner function is to reallocate uneven stress. When government fails to distribute stress uniformly, groups with more than their share attempt to eliminate the problem themselves. Thus, "just as forms of direct action and political protest may be viewed as efforts to reallocate stress" on the part of blacks, so political violence became just another device to achieve this goal. Langston Hughes put it this way:

> Seems like what makes me crazy
> has no effect on you—
> I'm gonna keep on doing until
> you're crazy too.

Dick Gregory puts it another way: If the "white power structure" does not share its garbage trucks with us, "we gonna share our garbage with you!" Hence, black political violence became a new force in urban America.

If political violence—i.e., acts of disruption and destruction and injury—has had political significance in tending to modify the behavior of others in dealing with the black community, it has additional functions as a danger signal and a catalyst. The black rioting in urban areas during the 1960s indicated that numerous institutions were dysfunctional in regard to the black needs and community, since a "social dysfunction can, of course, be attended to only if it becomes visible if not to the total community at least to certain more sensitive and more powerful sectors of it."[14] Black violence spoke of severe maladies and defects in the body politic. It was merely one manifestation of a generally underlying condition that needed immediate attention.[15]

It also served as a catalytic agent in arousing community concern. The aim of this violence was to goad power holders into effecting a change in the conditions of stress rampant in the black ghetto. These violent acts were attention-getters, devices that brought focus, concern, and a review of priorities, and numerous studies of the needs of the ghetto complex. Whether the riots achieved their initial objective can be disputed, debated, and argued. The white response to black militancy—to punish the whole

[12] H. L. Nieburg, *Political Violence: The Behavioral Process* (New York: St. Martin's Press, 1969), p. 136.

[13] *Ibid.*

[14] Coser, *op. cit.*, pp. 12-13.

[15] See the Report of the National Advisory Committee on Civil Disorders (New York: Bantam Books, 1968).

community and treat all blacks alike—helped to unify the black community and gave rise to new paramilitary organizations like the Black Panthers, the Black Liberation Front, and a cry for black control of the ghetto. Although the more extreme tactics of these militant forces created new divisions within the black community, a new lull in programs for integration has become apparent, and attempts to create separate organizations and to establish self-rule and a collective identity are beginning to gain momentum.

The creation of black self-control is still far from reality, however, and black political violence has simply changed its forms. The earlier black riots, for instance, were mainly *expressive riots*—i.e., "violent confrontations that involved all segments of the Negro community in a diffuse form of protest." This Watts type of riot came to an end in the late sixties, and a new form of black political violence—urban guerrilla warfare—replaced the disrupting and seemingly pointless expressive riots.[16] Urban guerrilla warfare is "ideologically motivated attacks on highly selected targets of the white 'establishment.' "[17] Such activity has been initiated chiefly by the new black revolutionaries, who seek not reform, but a new society and a new day. Motivated by a concern for the black masses and their need for better ways of life as well as by the inherent racism of American society, these ideologues have learned a lesson from the black expressive riots. "They recognized their futility and, in place of mass riots, elected to emphasize selective acts of sabotage, destruction, and self-defense."[18] Operating in small, highly mobile, and localized groups, these black revolutionaries seek to concentrate on the enemy's weaknesses and to destroy the white man's control, at least over the black ghetto. The new revolutionaries lacked mass support and backing in the ghetto communities, but the earlier phases of the black power rhetoric are beginning to catch on.[19] The idea that blacks must assert their political and economic power by implementing black control of the cities or areas where blacks are in a majority has become meaningful in the dark ghetto.

BLACK CONTROL OF THE CITIES

With the emergence of more and more black politicians, it is difficult to deny the assertion that many blacks must feel that if the socioeconomic structure is to change, it will be necessary to exert black political power. Although blacks in the past have had little reason to expect tangible gains

[16] McCord, *op. cit.*; see also Martin Oppenheimer, *The Urban Guerrilla* (New York: Quadrangle Books, 1969).
[17] *Ibid.*
[18] *Ibid.*, p. 275.
[19] See Arthur L. Smith, *Rhetoric of Black Revolution* (Boston: Allyn and Bacon, 1969).

Table XI. Black Representation on City Councils of
Selected Non-Southern Cities (March, 1965)

	Total City Council	Black Councilmen	%Black on Council	% Population Black
High Representation				
Cleveland	19	10	30.3	28.6
St. Louis	29	6	20.7	28.6
Los Angeles	15	3	20.0	13.5
Chicago	50	7	14.0	22.9
Low Representation				
Detroit	9	0	0.0	8.9
Boston	9	0	0.0	9.1
New York	35	2	5.7	14.0
Cincinnati	9	1	11.1	21.6

Source: W. McCord et al., *Life Styles in the Black Ghetto* (New York: W. W. Norton and Company, 1969), p. 288.

from political participation, they have become politically socialized due to the black revolution of the sixties, and they accept politics, black politics, as a means to an end—equality and justice in America. Unfortunately, if black politicians are elected to solve the problems of black urbanites, they will soon fall into disrepute, like their white counterparts. As was clearly stated in Chapter XI, the problems of the dark ghetto and black people in general are beyond the scope and power of black politicians.

As Table XI indicates, in comparing the cities in which blacks are almost in control with those in which they are a minority, there are no major differences between the two in regard to improving the social and economic state of blacks within the cities. One would expect black mayors and councilmen to exert a "broad influence over a whole range of affairs, such as the allocation of community resources, municipal hiring practices, and the allocation of contracts," but the fact remains that the ghetto needs are so great that no city hall can make any noticeable changes. In fact, the condition of black urbanites tends to worsen as time proceeds, even with black political control firmly entrenched in the political structure.

Perhaps black control of the cities and the emergence of black politicians has come too late. Their emergence in the early sixties curbed the riots in some cities, but as time goes on and problems remain, new rioting and black political violence are bound to reoccur. Black control of the cities has come at a time when the cities are disintegrating and collapsing from problems nearly half a century old. In short, black politicians have inherited problems that have been ignored for decades and that may be insoluble. For advocates of black political violence, however, a quick payoff is expected soon.

In comparing the two sets of cities in Table XI, three of the four cities with high black representation had riots, and so did three of the four cities with low black political representation. Blacks in the ghetto rioted in spite of the black politicians in offices downtown. On the other hand, even with black representation, whether in Chicago, Cleveland, Detroit, or Cincinnati, black unemployment remained high, and welfare organizations tended to perpetuate rather than relieve conditions of poverty. Police brutality remained high, and slumism, poor housing, and transient jobs continued to characterize the black community. *In other words, it is not at all clear that there is any measurable difference in ghetto conditions between cities in which Negro representation on the city council is roughly proportional to their numbers in the population and those in which they are underrepresented.*[20] In short, the power of black officials is not enough to solve the problems of urban America, nor is the power of the local or municipal or state governments enough.

Nevertheless, despite their black officials' lack of power, black people have begun to regard their economic, social, and cultural deprivation as beyond the abilities of black politicians to solve. In a recent survey in a southern metropolis, a questionnaire was circulated in a completely black district. The purpose was to gain some knowledge of what the inhabitants desired, now that they had the first opportunity since Reconstruction to elect a black state representative. The result showed that they felt that a black elected official could bring them only about the same or less than a white official. This is only a sentiment actually recorded in one southern area—because pollsters have not yet raised this question, nor has it been adequately researched—but the actions of several black groups elsewhere suggest that they understand that black officials are powerless in the local, municipal, and state governments. These blacks have in the main called for complete control of their neighborhoods and the creation of neighborhood governments.

Neighborhood government in urban America simply means that inhabitants of any area that has both physical and social boundaries be "organized for the control of their institutions to serve their own rather than outside interest."[21] A classic example is the New York Ocean Hill Brownsville school district, which barred nineteen teachers and administrators sent from the central New York City Board of Education simply to reassert

[20] McCord, *op. cit.*, p. 289.
[21] Milton Kotler, *Neighborhood Government: The Local Foundations of Political Life* (Indianapolis: Bobbs-Merrill Company, 1969), p. 10. See also Alan Altshuler, *Community Control* (New York: Pegasus, 1970).

local control over the schools. The establishment of neighborhood governments will mean the emergence of a federated city in which the "so-called 'little man' can gather into his hands the power he needs to make and shape his life."[22] In other words, black neighborhood government would give the masses of black people a chance to solve their problems through self-help and a command of the direction in which the local neighborhood would move.

The first conscious attempts by blacks to establish such a neighborhood organization came in the spring and summer of 1960 in Chicago. Here blacks created the Woodlawn Organization (TWO) a federation of about nineteen representative black groups in the community, including churches, businessmen's associations, and an assortment of black clubs, neighborhood associations, social groups, etc. This organization, founded in a slum area south of the University of Chicago that contains between eighty and a hundred fifty thousand blacks, is the prototype of black neighborhood governments. The organizer of TWO called upon Samuel D. Alinsky, executive director of the Industrial Areas Foundations, to help the organization get started and become attuned to the problems of the area. And with its help, by 1963, TWO not only had a national impact, but also effected meaningful improvement within the black slum. Following TWO in Chicago, other black neighborhood governments began to develop, like FIGHT in Rochester, BUILD in Buffalo, and the West Side Organization (WSO) in Chicago.[23]

In the South, black neighborhood organizations are still in their infancy, but area economic cooperations for black farmers and workers are beginning to emerge in the rural counties of the South. Orzell Billingsley of Alabama has recently begun incorporating predominantly black areas as cities, and he applies for federal funds and private grants in order to rebuild them. This black attorney now advocates incorporation or the developing of neighborhood governments to solve some of the problems of blacks in the political milieu of our cities.[24]

These black neighborhood governments are still relatively new—in fact, the concept of neighborhood government itself is new—but some neighborhoods are headed toward this new political entity in urban America. The white rush to the suburbs and their refusal to let their suburbs be annexed are an example of white attempts to create neighborhood governments. In the South, the cry for local control of the schools is another trend in this general direction.

[22] Charles Silverman, *Crisis in Black and White* (New York: Vintage Books, 1964), p. 321.
[23] For a complete analysis of the West Side Organization see William W. Ellis, *White Ethics and Black Power* (Chicago: Aldine Publishing Company, 1969).
[24] Carlyle Douglas, "Incorporation: A New Tactic for Saving Black Areas," *Ebony*, August, 1970, pp. 100-105.

In regard to blacks, the quest for separateness and black control of their communities makes neighborhood government a possibility, though the problems of internal power, taxation, relationship to other spheres of law, and nomenclature for neighborhood government remain unsolved and unclear. In addition, black politicians "must be particularly careful to make links from neighborhood governments to higher levels of power." Because of a national tendency in the white community to encourage black separatism, black neighborhoods could become detached from the local and state governments; this would ultimately mean the collapse of the black sphere of power or else warfare between the two spheres of power.

BLACKNESS AND METROPOLITANISM

Since "American political institutions were originally designed for an agrarian society," urbanization and its problems have necessitated the creation of new political institutions. One new creation, "metropolitan government, many proponents hope, will solve our urban ills."[25]

Metro government derives its basis from the fact that numerous problems of local government cut across political boundaries and therefore cannot be effectively solved by local government. Coordination or joint action between the two separate political entities is needed, and metro government offers this kind of cooperation. The effects of local action (or inaction) that spread into other communities are known as spill-over. The residents of a central city, for example, may be taxed to provide service that is important for the suburbanites, but is inadequate for the city dweller's needs. Spill-overs, therefore, create the need for cooperative action.

Since the problems of urban America are of such magnitude that the local governments are unable to meet the needs of the metropolis, federal and state governments have taken on increasing responsibilities for metropolitan welfare. The state role is diversified, and ranges from financial assistance to direct state operations such as highway building, water supply, and port development; the federal role is to provide financial assistance to state and local programs.

Unfortunately, federal and state programs to aid the blighted metropolitan area complicate the already fragmented governmental scene. They complicate the coordination efforts, and they bring to the fore troublesome political and governmental issues. Moreover, with state and federal intervention, local governments can not only pass the buck to higher authorities, they can also lose control at the local level. Thus, poor coordination, conflict of interest, and loss of local control are just some of the weaknesses of metropolitanism in theory and in practice.

[25] *Ibid.*, p. 114.

Finally, this newly created political entity has another problem. "Race is the key to understanding the magnitude or our urban problems." The urban crisis is usually defined in terms of the massive concentration of impoverished blacks living in the deteriorating and decaying central cities while whites in suburbs enjoy unparalleled affluence and refuse to help the tax-burdened and strife-torn cities. Since the cities are deadlocked and the state governments are too weak financially to act, the federal government has to take a hand. The problem, however, arises not so much from federal intervention as from the impact of metropolitanism upon the new division of localism, central city and suburbia.

Some white and black political observers have warned that blacks will be losers in the new metropolis.[26] Their argument follows two major patterns. The first holds that metropolitanism will bring back a majority of white voters to add to those already in the central cities. Black political power will be sufficiently diluted to render it practically impotent or of limited effectiveness. The second argument has been developed only recently. It postulates that in order to retain its power and majorities, the national democratic administration has to find a way to hold together the conflict-ridden cities, but also has to retain the support of the suburbs and avert a political schism from occurring between them and the cities. To do this, the theory holds that the national Democrats, under the guise of metro government, have developed a metropolitan administrative apparatus to see to it that localities "comply with a comprehensive plan drawn up in accord with federal guidelines." This "plan" makes sure, as a condition for federal aid, that a wider planning by several localities has taken place, which the federal government argues is necessary for "orderly metropolitan growth."[27] Moreover, according to the theoreticians, the "plan" requires long-range commitments to interrelated projects. If a bridge is projected, it is linked to other projects—highways, airports, industrial parks—and to destroy a project is to destroy the entire scheme. In addition, each project brings in a chain of corporate interests—builders, construction unions, business, and real estate agents. Thus, by fashioning programs to meet the interests of numerous local groups, the national Democratic administration will retain its power.

In Piven and Cloward's view, "the black poor get a little public housing, a bit of relief from the 'model cities' programs; middle income whites get rather generous housing subsidies and housing and real estate interest receives substantial urban renewal funds."[28] Suburbanites get highways,

[26] Frances Fox Piven and Richard A. Cloward, "Black Control of Cities," in A. Shank, *op. cit.*, p. 316.
[27] *Ibid.*, p. 323.
[28] *Ibid.*, p. 321.

airports, sewage, water facilities, mortgage insurance, and tax write-offs for homeowners. This is how the Democratic urban coalition is maintained.

But metropolitan reorganization limits the traditional power of cities and nips rising black political power in the bud.

Even if the national administration became Republican, these theorists argue that the "trend toward consolidation wouldn't be reversed"—only the direction would be shifted, because Republicans must build their coalition on suburban and rural areas, rather than in the cities.

Not all criticism of metropolitanism has come from white observers, however. Numerous black leaders and politicians have also viewed the new political entity as a possible evil.[29] Mayor Richard Hatcher of Gary, Indiana, sees metro government—an enlargement of the metropolis—as a device that adds territory around the blacks, and deters and "weakens whatever momentum black political action can generate."

"Metro government," Hatcher feels, "is one more flanking maneuver— another way, however subtle, to offer oblique reaction to needs that require honest response." "To the ghetto," Hatcher asserts, metro government "still looks as if whitey is trying to mute black voices by diluting the vote of the new huddled masses."[30] Moreover he agrees with this view of the black ghetto, as do many other blacks.

These critics, whether black or white, do not go unanswered. The proponents of metro government argue that blacks have nothing to fear from metropolitanism.[31] They argue that the black populations in cities like Nashville and Miami have not lost their political influence.[32] On the contrary, the political power of the black populations there has been enhanced, and its effectiveness has been improved.[33] Likewise, the social service functions of government have been improved, and problems can now be solved with greater efficiency.

Finally, the proponents of metro government argue that consolidation will bring immediate relief to the impacted ghetto area. Metro government, these theorists say, is the answer to the problem of urban America.

While the debate between the opponents and proponents of metropolitanism continues, so also do the problems of the black urbanites. Even metro areas like Nashville, Miami, and Jacksonville still have their black

[29] Richard C. Hatcher, "The Black Role in Urban Politics," *Current History,* November, 1969, p. 287.

[30] *Ibid.,* p. 289.

[31] Daniel R. Grant, "Metro's Three Faces," in A. Shank, *op. cit.,* pp. 309-310.

[32] *Ibid.* See also Peter R. Moody, Jr., "The Effects of the Adoption of Metropolitan Government in Nashville and Davidson County Tennessee on Negro Political Influence" (unpublished senior honor thesis, Vanderbilt University, 1965).

[33] *Ibid.* See also Roslyn Allen, "The Impact of County and City Government Consolidation in Jacksonville Area on Black Political Power" (paper presented to state government class, Savannah State College, December, 1969). Her findings indicated that consolidation caused black representation on the city council to drop.

ghettoes, and research has begun to suggest that the metro government of Nashville is having trouble solving the problem of urban Nashville. Moreover, in 1970 an analysis of the proposed metropolitan form of government for the county of Charleston, South Carolina, revealed that the central city would have less representation in the new metro government board of aldermen than would the suburbs, even though more inhabitants and especially more blacks live there. This grant of fewer aldermanic positions to the central city is indicative of the fact that the commission set up to devise the metro plan of government not only needs black representation, which it does not have in Charleston, but also a possible black veto. Without such, metro government will be like urban renewal—i.e., a new name for segregation and discrimination.

One raises again the perennial question—Can American political institutions, new or old, with their ingrained racism, solve the problems of blacks in the metropolis? The final answer has not been made yet. Perhaps the question still has not been formulated correctly. Meanwhile, black urbanites continue to wait for viable solutions to their problems.

BLACK POLITICS AND THE PROMISE OF AMERICAN SOCIETY

The nature of black politics is inherent in the nature of white politics in America. Black politics is an outgrowth of racist politics in America. It is both colored by and colors American public policy. Blacks have, from the time of their entrance into the political arena, sought to gain the good life by means of American political devices. They have yet to achieve satisfaction; meanwhile, the politics of black America continues to grow, change, and reflect the general trend of larger American society, as well as the needs of the black community. It can readily be seen that black politics has constantly changed throughout American history. As racism has changed from locality to locality, the direction of black politics has shifted, but the larger trend has remained the same—i.e., to make politics meaningful to black Americans.

Black politics in its overall aspect, however, has been more than just a reaction to American racism, politics, and policies. It has in many cases led the field. Black politics has created reforms and motivations within the political system that have kept alive the ideas expressed in the Constitution and the Declaration of Independence. Finally, black politics has continued to effect a change in American politics. It has enlarged the area of civil liberties, modified the practices of political parties, forced national political conventions to equalize representation, caused both executive and bureaucratic innovation, enhanced the necessity of pressure group activity, and created new tactics for them. Black politics must be seen for what it has been and is, a changing force in American politics.

For centuries, blacks have fought to enter the political arena only to be removed, excluded, and isolated. The struggle has continued until now, after 300 years, black participation has reached its highest level in the country's history. Now that partial victory has been won, however, a new era in American politics has begun. Black politics has emerged at a time when American politics is undergoing a transformation. Old coalitions are collapsing, urbanization is creating new political entities, and the politics of race is taking on new forms. Black politics finds itself in a transitional period, one that will inevitably have some effect upon the politics of all Americans. No matter what the outcome is, the politics of black Americans will continue to maintain its ethnicity and inviolability as long as race remains a factor in American politics. Black politics will vary in America from locality to locality. Black politics will reflect not only the needs of blacks and the ambitions of black politicians, but also the shortcomings and ills of America in general. Black politics includes a strain of reformism, but it also includes a strain of reactionism and opportunism. In short, the nature of black politics is the nature of human enterprise, sharing its strengths and weaknesses, shortcomings and achievements, successes and failures. Black politics is American politics in microcosm—it differs only in that it includes a particular racial group—black Americans.

A Bibliography on
Black Politics

Presently there are no systematic and comprehensive bibliographies on black politics. Heretofore, bibliographies on black politics, like books on the subject, have mainly covered blacks in northern or southern politics, and basically from an electoral angle. Therefore, this bibliography, although not exhaustive, is both systematic and comprehensive in that it covers black politics from the colonial period to the present—and northern and southern politics at the same time.

General Approaches, Methodologies, and Theories of Black Politics

BENNETT, LERONE, JR. "The Politics of the Outsider." *Negro Digest,* 17 (July, 1963): 5–8.

CNUDDLE, CHARLES. "Consensus, Rules of the Game, and Democratic Politics: The Case of Race Politics in the South," chaps. 1–2. Ph.D. dissertation, University of North Carolina, 1967.

HOLLOWAY, HARRY. *The Politics of the Southern Negro: From Exclusion to Big City Organization,* chap. 1. New York: Random House, 1969.

JONES, MACK. "A Framework for the Study of Black Politics." Paper read at the Southern Political Science Convention, Miami, November 6–8, 1969.

LADD, EVERETT C., JR. *Negro Political Leadership in the South,* pp. 1–13. Ithaca, N.Y.: Cornell University Press, 1966.

MATTHEWS, DONALD R., and JAMES W. PROTHRO. *Negroes and the New Southern Politics,* chap. 2. New York: Harcourt, Brace and World, 1966.

MURAPA, RUKUDZO. "Race, Pride, and Black Political Thought." *Negro Digest,* 18 (May, 1969): 6–9.

PATTERSON, BEEMAN. "The Politics of Recognition: Negro Politics in Los Angeles," chap. 6. Ph.D. dissertation, University of California, 1969.

PRESTAGE, JEWEL. "Black Politics and the Kerner Report: Consensus and Directions." *Social Science Quarterly,* 49 (December, 1968): 462–464.

STRANGE, JOHN. "The Negro in Philadelphia Politics, 1963–1965," chap. 9. Ph.D. dissertation, Princeton University, 1966.

WALTON, HANES, JR. "The Negro in the Prohibition Party: A Case Study of the Tennessee Prohibition Party." *Papers and Proceedings of the 53rd Annual Meeting of the Association for the Study of Negro Life and History,* 8: 1–5.

Blacks and the American Political System

ADAMS, JAMES T. "Disfranchisement of Negroes in New England." *American Historical Review,* 30 (April, 1925): 543–547.

BELL, HOWARD H. "National Negro Conventions of the Middle 1840's: Moral Suasion vs. Political Action." *Journal of Negro History,* 42 (October, 1957): 247–260.

FOX, DIXON RYAN. "The Negro Vote in Old New York." *Political Science Quarterly,* 32 (June, 1917): 252–275.

GINZBERG, ELI, and ALFRED S. EICHNER. *The Troublesome Presence: American Democracy and the Negro,* chaps. 2–3. Glencoe, Ill.: Free Press of Glencoe, 1964.

GREENE, LORENZO JOHNSTON. *The Negro in Colonial New England, 1620–1776,* chap. 9. New York: Kennikat Press, 1966.

225

LITWACK, LEON F. "The Federal Government and the Free Negro, 1790–1860."
  Journal of Negro History, 43 (October, 1958): 261–278.
LITWACK, LEON F. *North of Slavery: The Negro in the Free States, 1790–1860,*
  chaps. 2–3. Chicago: University of Chicago Press, 1961.
QUARLES, BENJAMIN. *Black Abolitionists,* chap. 8. New York: Oxford University
  Press, 1969.
WALTON, HANES, JR. "The Negro in the Early Third-Party Movement." *Negro
  Educational Review,* 19 (April–July, 1968).
WESLEY, CHARLES H. "Negro Suffrage in the Period of Constitution Making, 1787–
  1865." In *Neglected History,* edited by C. H. Wesley, pp. 41–55. Ohio: Central
  State College Press, 1965.
WRIGHT, MARION THOMPSON. "Negro Suffrage in New Jersey, 1776–1875." *Journal
  of Negro History,* 33 (April, 1948): 168–224.
ZILVERSMITH, ARTHUR. *The First Emancipation,* chap. 1. Chicago: University of
  Chicago Press, 1967.

Black Electoral Politics

AIKIN, CHARLES, ed. *The Negro Voter.* San Francisco: Chandler Publishing Com-
  pany, 1962.
ALLSWANG, JOHN. "The Chicago Negro Voter and the Democratic Consensus: A
  Case Study, 1918–1936." In *The Negro in Depression and War,* edited by Bernard
  Sternsher, pp. 234–257. Chicago: Quadrangle Books, 1969.
BACOTE, C. A. "The Negro in Atlanta Politics." *Phylon,* 16 (fourth quarter, 1955):
  333–350.
BAKER, RAY STANNARD. "Negro Suffrage in a Democracy." *Atlantic Monthly,* 106
  (November, 1910): 612–619.
BETH, L. P. "The White Primary and the Judicial Function in the United States."
  Political Quarterly, 29 (October–December, 1958): 366–377.
BICKEL, ALEXANDER M. "The Voting Rights Bill Is Tough." *New Republic,* 152,
  April 3, 1965, pp. 16–18.
BLACKFORD, STAIGE. "The Twenty-fourth Amendment." *New South,* 19 (February,
  1964): 13–15.
BLAINE, JAMES G., et al. "Ought the Negro to Be Disfranchised, Ought He to Have
  Been Enfranchised?" *North American Review,* 128 (March, 1879): 226–228.
BREWER, WILLIAM M. "The Poll Tax and the Poll Taxers." *Journal of Negro
  History,* 29 (July, 1944): 260–299.
BRISBANE, R. H. "The Negro's Growing Political Power." *Nation,* September 27,
  1952, pp. 285–289.
BRISBANE, R. H. "The Negro Vote as a Balance of Power in the National Election."
  Quarterly Review of Higher Education among Negroes, 20 (July, 1952): 97–100.
BRITTAIN, J. M. "Some Reflections on Negro Suffrage in Alabama—Past and
  Present." *Journal of Negro History,* 47 (April, 1962): 127–138.
BRODER, DAVID S. "Negro Vote Upset Off-year Pattern." *New York Times,* No-
  vember 4, 1965.
CAFFEY, FRANCIS G. "Suffrage Limitations at the South." *Political Science Quarterly,*
  20 (March, 1905): 53–67.
CARLETON, WILLIAM G., and HUGH D. PRICE. "America's New Voter: A Florida
  Case Study." *Antioch Review,* 14 (1954): 441–457.
CARTER, DOUGLAS. "Atlanta: Smart Politics and Good Race Relations." *The Re-
  porter,* July 11, 1952, pp. 18–21.
COLLINGS, E. M. "Cincinnati Negroes and Presidential Politics." In *The Negro in
  Depression and War,* edited by Bernard Sternsher, pp. 258–265. Chicago: Quad-
  rangle Books, 1969.
DANIEL, JOHNIE. "Changes in Negro Political Mobilization and Its Relationship to
  Community Socio-economic Structure." *Journal of Social and Behavioral Science,*
  13 (Fall, 1968): 41–46.
"Deluge: Negro Registration in the South." *Newsweek,* 66, August 23, 1965, pp.
  17–18.
"Desegregation Resistance Slows Negro Registration." *New South,* October, 1959,
  pp. 3–5.
DOUGLAS, PAUL H. "Trends and Developments: The 1960 Voting Rights Bill: The
  Struggle, the Final Results, and the Reason." *Journal of Intergroup Relations,*
  1 (Summer, 1960): 86–88.

DOWD, D. F. "The Campaign in Fayette County." *Monthly Review*, April, 1964, pp. 675–679.

DUKE, PAUL. "Southern Politics and the Negro." In *American Party Politics*, edited by Donald G. Herzberg and Gerald M. Pomper, pp. 513–517. New York: Holt, Rinehart and Winston, 1966.

DYER, BRAINERD. "One Hundred Years of Negro Suffrage." *Pacific Historical Review*, 37 (February, 1968): 1–20.

FISHEL, LESLIE. "The Negro in Northern Politics, 1870–1900." *Mississippi Valley Historical Review*, 42 (December, 1955): 466–489.

FISHEL, LESLIE. "Wisconsin and Negro Suffrage." *Wisconsin Magazine of History*, 46 (Spring, 1963): 180–189.

FISHEL, LESLIE H., Jr. "Northern Prejudice and Negro Suffrage, 1865–1870." *Journal of Negro History*, 39 (January, 1954): 8–26.

FLEMING, G. JAMES. *An All-Negro Ticket in Baltimore*. New York: Holt, 1960.

FOSTER, VERA CHANDLER. "'Boswellianism': A Technique in the Restriction of Negro Voting." *Phylon*, 10 (first quarter, 1949): 26–37.

GAMAREKIEN, EDWARD. "A Report from the South on the Negro Voter." *The Reporter*, 16 (June 27, 1957), 9–12.

GATLIN, DOUGLAS S. "A Case Study of a Negro Voter's League: Political Studies Program—Research Report No. 2." University of North Carolina Department of Political Science, March, 1960.

GAUNLETT, JOHN H., and JOHN B. McCONAUGHY. "Some Observations on the Influence of the Income Factor on Urban Negro Voting in South Carolina." *Journal of Negro Education*, 31 (Winter, 1962): 78–82.

GAUNLETT, T., and J. B. McCONAUGHY. "Survey of Urban Negro Voting Behavior in South Carolina." *South Carolina Law Quarterly*, Spring, 1962, p. 365.

GILLETTE, WILLIAM. *The Right to Vote: Politics and the Passage of the Fifteenth Amendment*. Baltimore: Johns Hopkins Press, 1969.

GLANTZ, OSCAR. "Recent Negro Ballots in Philadelphia." *Journal of Negro Education*, 28 (Fall, 1959): 430–438.

GOMILLION, CHARLES G. "The Tuskegee Voting Story." *Freedomways*, Summer, 1962, pp. 231–236.

GOSNELL, HAROLD. "The Negro Vote in Northern Cities." *National Municipal Review*, 30 (May, 1941): 264–267.

GOSNELL, HAROLD F., and ROBERT E. MARTIN. "The Negro as Voters and Office Holders." *Journal of Negro Education*, 32 (Fall, 1963): 415–425.

HAINSWORTH, ROBERT W. "The Negro and the Texas Primaries." *Journal of Negro History*, 18 (October, 1933): 426–450.

HAMILTON, CHARLES V. "Race, Morality, and Political Solutions." *Phylon*, 20 (third quarter, 1959): 242–247.

HARRELL, JAMES A. "Negro Leadership in the Election Year 1936." *Journal of Southern History*, 34 (November, 1968): 546–564.

HENDERSON, ELMER. "Political Changes among Negroes in Chicago during the Depression." *Social Forces*, May, 1941.

HOFFMAN, EDWIN D. "The Genesis of the Modern Movement for Equal Rights in South Carolina, 1930–1939." *Journal of Negro History*, 44 (October, 1959): 346–369.

HOLLAND, LYNWOOD M., and JOSEPH L. BERND. "Recent Restrictions upon Negro Suffrage: The Case of Georgia." *Journal of Politics*, 21 (August, 1959): 487–513.

HOLLOWAY, HARRY. "The Negro and the Vote: The Case of Texas." *Journal of Politics*, 23 (August, 1961): 526–556.

HOLLOWAY, HARRY. "The Texas Negro as a Voter." *Phylon*, 24 (Summer, 1963): 135–145.

JACKSON, LUTHER P. "Race and Suffrage in the South since 1960." *New South*, June–July, 1948, entire issue.

JEWELL, MALCOLM. "State Legislatures in Southern Politics." *Journal of Politics*, 26 (February, 1964): 177–196.

JOHNSON, JAMES W. "How Should We Vote?" *Crisis*, 35 (November, 1928): 368, 386.

JOHNSON, JAMES W. "The Gentlemen's Agreement and the Negro Vote." *Crisis*, 28 (October, 1924): 160–164.

KEECH, W. R. "The Negro Vote as a Political Resource: The Case of Durham." Ph.D. dissertation, University of Wisconsin, 1966.

KYLE, KEITH. "Desegregation and the Negro Right to Vote." *Commentary,* 23 (July, 1957): 15–19.

LEGGETT, JOHN C. "Working, Class Consciousness, Race, and Political Choice." *American Journal of Sociology,* 69 (September, 1963): 171–176.

LEWINSON, PAUL. *Race, Class, and Party: A History of Negro Suffrage and White Politics in the South.* New York: Russell and Russell, 1963.

LEWIS, ANTHONY. "Negro Vote Curbs Exposed by the F.B.I." *New York Times,* August 4, 1957.

LEWIS, PIERCE F. "Impact of Negro Migration on the Electoral Geography of Flint, Michigan, 1932–1962: A Cartographic Analysis." *Annals of the Association of American Geographers,* 18 (March, 1965): 23–36.

LINK, ARTHUR S. "The Negro as a Factor in the Campaign of 1912." *Journal of Negro History,* 32 (January, 1947): 81–89.

LIPSKY, ROMA. "Electioneering among the Minorities." *Commentary,* 31 (May, 1961): 428–432.

LITCHFIELD, EDWARD. "A Case Study of Negro Political Behavior in Detroit." *Public Opinion Quarterly,* 5 (June, 1941): 267–274.

LLOYD, RAYMOND G. *White Supremacy in the United States.* Washington, D.C.: Public Affairs Press, 1952.

LOGAN, RAYFORD, ed. *The Attitudes of the Southern White Press toward Negro Suffrage, 1932–1940.* Washington Foundation Publishers, 1940.

MABRY, WILLIAM. *Studies in the Disfranchisement of the Negro in the South.* Durham, N.C.: Duke University Press, 1938.

MABRY, WILLIAM ALEXANDER. "White Supremacy and the North Carolina Suffrage Amendment." *North Carolina Historical Review,* 13 (January, 1936): 1–6.

MATTHEWS, DONALD, and JAMES W. PROTHRO. "Negro Voter Registration in the South." In *Change in the Contemporary South,* edited by Allan P. Sinder, pp. 119–149. Durham, N.C.: Duke University Press, 1963.

MATTHEWS, DONALD, and JAMES PROTHRO. "Southern Images of Political Parties: A Comparison of White and Negro Attitudes." *Journal of Politics,* 26 (February, 1964): 82–111.

MIDDLETON, RUSSELL. "The Civil Rights Issue and Presidential Voting among Southern Negroes and Whites." *Social Forces,* 40 (March, 1962): 209–215.

"The Mississippi Freedom Vote." *New South,* December, 1963, pp. 10–13.

MOON, HENRY LEE. *Balance of Power: The Negro Vote.* New York: Doubleday, 1948.

MOON, HENRY LEE. "The Negro Vote with South 1952." *The Nation,* 175 (September 27, 1952): 288.

MOON, HENRY LEE. "The Southern Scene." *Phylon,* 16 (fourth quarter, 1955): 351–358.

"The Negro in Louisiana Politics." *The Sepia Socialite,* April, 1942.

"The Negro Prefers Truman." *New Republic,* 119, November 22, 1948, p. 8.

"The Negro Vote in the South." *Journal of Negro Education,* 26 (September, 1957). See the entire issue for insight on the behavior of the black voter in all of the southern states.

"Negro Voter Registration Remains Constant in South." *New South,* January, 1959, pp. 8–9.

ODGEN, FREDERICK D. *The Poll Tax in the South.* University, Ala.: University of Alabama Press, 1958.

OLBRICH, EMIL. *The Development of Sentiment on Negro Suffrage to 1860.* Madison, Wis.: University of Wisconsin Press, 1912.

OVERACKER, LOUISE. "The Negro's Struggle for Participation in Primary Elections." *Journal of Negro History,* 30 (January, 1945): 54–61.

PORTER, KIRK. *A History of Suffrage in the United States.* Chicago: University of Chicago Press, 1919.

PRICE, MARGARET. *The Negro and the Ballot in the South.* Atlanta: Southern Regional Council, 1959.

PRICE, MARGARET. *The Negro Voter in the South.* Atlanta: Southern Regional Council, 1957.

PRICE, MARGARET. "The Negro Voter in the South." *New South,* September, 1957.

ROSE, JOHN C. "Negro Suffrage: The Constitutional Point of View." *American Political Science Review,* 1 (November, 1906): 17–43.

Rowan, Carl. "Who Gets the Negro Vote." *Look*, 20, November 13, 1956, pp. 37–39.

Seasholes, Bradbury, and F. Cleaveland. "Negro Political Participation in Two Piedmont Crescent Cities." In *Urban Growth Dynamics in a Regional Cluster of Cities*, edited by Francis S. Chapin and Shirley F. Weiss, pp. 260–308. New York: John Wiley and Sons, 1962.

Shugg, Roger Wallace. "Negro Voting in the Ante-Bellum South." *Journal of Negro History*, 21 (October, 1936): 357–364.

Sigel, Roberta. "Race and Religion as Factors in the Kennedy Victory in Detroit, 1960." *Journal of Negro Education*, 31 (Fall, 1962): 436–447.

Sindler, Allan P. *Negro Protest and Local Politics in Durham, N.C.* New York: McGraw-Hill Book Company, 1965.

Smith, Stanley, and Lewis Jones. *Tuskegee, Alabama, Voting Rights and Economic Pressure.* New York: Anti-Defamation League, 1958.

Smith, Wilfred H. "The Disfranchisement of the Negro." *Alexander's Magazine*, 1 (May 15, 1905): 17–19.

Spicer, George W. "The Federal Judiciary and Political Change in the South." *Journal of Politics*, 26 (February, 1964): 154–176.

Steinberg, Charles. "The Southern Negro's Right to Vote." *American Federationist*, 69 (July, 1962): 1–6.

Stony, George C. "Suffrage in the South, Part I, The Poll Tax." *Survey Graphic*, 29 (January, 1940): 5–9.

Strong, Donald. *Negroes, Ballots, and Judges.* University, Ala.: University of Alabama Press, 1968.

Strong, Donald. "The Rise of Negro Voting in Texas." In *Race Prejudice and Discrimination*, edited by Arnold Rose. New York: Alfred A. Knopf, 1951.

Stroud, Virgil. "The Negro Voter in the South." *Quarterly Review of Higher Education among Negroes*, 29 (January, 1961): 9–39.

Stroud, Virgil. "Voter Registration in North Carolina." *Journal of Negro Education*, 30 (Spring, 1961): 153–155.

Taper, Bernard. "A Break with Tradition." *New Yorker*, 41, June 24, 1965, p. 68.

Taper, Bernard. *Gomillion versus Lightfoot: The Tuskegee Gerrymander Case.* New York: McGraw-Hill Book Company, 1962.

Toppin, Edgar A. "Negro Emancipation in Historic Retrospect: Ohio: The Negro Suffrage Issue in Postbellum Ohio Politics." *Journal of Human Relations*, 11 (Winter, 1963): 252–286.

Walker, Zack. "Negro Voting in Atlanta, 1953–1961." *Phylon*, 24 (Winter, 1963): 378–387.

Wall, Marvin. "Black Votes." *South Today*, August, 1961, pp. 6–7.

Walton, Hanes, Jr. "Blacks and Conservative Political Movements." *Quarterly Review of Higher Education among Negroes*, 37 (October, 1969).

Walton, Hanes, Jr., and J. E. Taylor. "Blacks, the Prohibitionists, and Disfranchisement." *Quarterly Review of Higher Education among Negroes*, 37 (April, 1969): 66–69.

Wardlow, Ralph W. *Negro Suffrage in Georgia, 1867–1930.* Athens, Ga.: Phelps-Stoke, 1932.

Watters, Pat, and Reese Cleghorn. *Climbing Jacob's Ladder: The Arrival of Negroes in Southern Politics.* New York: Harcourt, Brace and World, 1967.

Weeks, O. Douglas. "The White Primary, 1944–48." *American Political Science Review*, June, 1948, pp. 500–510.

Weeks, Stephen B. "History of Negro Suffrage in the South." *Political Science Quarterly*, 9 (December, 1894): 671–703.

Wells, Janet. "43 Blacks Win Elections in Three Southern States." *VEP News*, May, 1969, pp. 1–10.

"Where Does Negro Voting Strength Lie?" *Congressional Quarterly Weekly Report*, May 4, 1956, pp. 491–496.

White, Walter. "Will the Negro Elect the Next President?" *Colliers*, 120, November 22, 1947, pp. 26, 70–71.

White, Walter. "Win Our Vote or Lose." *Look* 16, October 7, 1952, pp. 18–22.

Wilkins, Roy. "An Interview with Louisiana's Kingfish." *Crisis*, 42 (February, 1935): 41–55.

Wilson, James Q. "How the Northern Negro Uses His Vote." *The Reporter*, 22, March 31, 1960, pp. 11–12.

WRIGHT, T. MORRIS. "The First Colored Voter of Kentucky." *The Colored American Magazine*, 3 (February, 1901): 292–293.
ZINN, HOWARD. "Registration in Alabama." *New Republic*, 149, October 26, 1963, pp. 11–12.

Blacks and the Republican Party

COX, LAWANDA, and JOHN H. COX. "Negro Suffrage and Republican Politics: The Problem of Motivation in Reconstruction Historiography." *Journal of Southern History*, 33 (August, 1967): 303–330.
DE SANTIS, VINCENT P. "Negro Dissatisfaction with Republican Policy in the South, 1882–1884." *Journal of Negro History*, 36 (April, 1951): 148–159.
DE SANTIS, VINCENT P. "The Republican Party and the Southern Negro, 1877–1897." *Journal of Negro History*, 45 (April, 1960): 71–87.
DU BOIS, W. E. B. "The Republican and the Black Voter." *The Nation*, 111 (June 5, 1920): 757–759.
GELB, JOYCE. "Black Republicans in New York: A Minority Group in a Minority." Paper presented at the 54th annual meeting of the Association for the Study of Negro Life and History, Birmingham, October 16, 1969.
HIRSHSON, STANLEY P. *Farewell to the Bloody Shirt: Northern Republicans and the Southern Negro, 1877–1883*. Bloomington, Ind.: Indiana University Press, 1962.
KATZNELSON, IRA. "The Politics of Race in New York City, 1900–1930: A Taste of Honey." Paper presented at the 54th annual meeting of the Association for the Study of Negro Life and History, Birmingham, October 10, 1969.
KRUG, MARK M. "The Republican Party and the Emancipation Proclamation." *Journal of Negro History*, 48 (April, 1963): 98–114.
LOGAN, RAYFORD W. *The Betrayal of the Negro*, chaps. 1–6. New York: Collier Books, 1965.
QUARLES, BENJAMIN. *Lincoln and the Negro*. New York: Oxford University Press, 1962.
RIDDLEBERGER, PATRICK W. "The Break in the Radical Ranks: Liberals vs. Stalwarts in the Election of 1872." *Journal of Negro History*, 44 (April, 1959): 136–157.
RUSS, WILLIAM, JR. "The Negro and White Disfranchisement during Radical Reconstruction." *Journal of Negro History*, 19 (April, 1934): 171–192.
SHERMAN, RICHARD B. "Republicans and Negroes: The Lessons of Normalcy." *Phylon*, 27 (first quarter, 1966): 63–79.
WALTON, HANES, JR. "The Politics of the Black and Tan Republicans." Paper presented at the 54th annual meeting of the Association for the Study of Negro Life and History, Birmingham, October 10, 1969.

Blacks and the Democratic Party

ABRAMS, RAY H. "The Copperhead Newspapers and the Negro." *Journal of Negro History*, 20 (April, 1935): 131–152.
ALLSWING, JOHN. "The Chicago Negro Voter and the Democratic Consensus: A Case Study, 1918–1936." In *The Negro in Depression and War: Prelude to Revolution*, edited by Bernard Sternsher, pp. 234–252. Chicago: Quadrangle Books, 1969.
BENDINER, ROBERT. "The Negro Vote and the Democrats." *The Reporter*, 14, May 31, 1956, pp. 8–12.
BREWER, JAMES H. "Robert Lee Van, Democrat or Republican: An Exponent of Loose Leaf Politics." *Negro History Bulletin*, 21 (February, 1958): 100–103.
FISHEL, LESLIE. "The Negro in the New Deal Era." In *The Negro in Depression and War: Prelude to Revolution*, edited by Bernard Sternsher, pp. 7–28. Chicago: Quadrangle Books, 1969.
LUBELL, SAMUEL. "The Negro and the Democratic Coalition." *Commentary*, 38 (August, 1964): 18–27.
LUBELL, SAMUEL. *White and Black: Test of a Nation*. New York: Harper and Row, 1963.
MEIER, AUGUST. "The Negro and the Democratic Party, 1875–1915." *Phylon*, 17 (second quarter, 1956): 173–191.
WOOD, FORREST G. *Black Scare: The Racist Response to Emancipation and Reconstruction*. Berkeley: University of California Press, 1968.

Black and Third Parties

ABRAMOWITZ, JACK. "The Negro in the Populist Movement." *Journal of Negro History,* 38 (July, 1953): 257–289.

ADDAMS, JANE. "The Progressive Party and the Negro." *Crisis,* 5 (November, 1912): 30–31.

ANALAVAGE, ROBERT. "A Victory in Defeat in Lowndes." *National Guardian,* November 19, 1966.

ANALAVAGE, ROBERT. "Lowndes Party Girds for Future." *The Southern Patriot,* December, 1966.

ANDREWS, E. F. "Socialism and the Negro." *International Socialist Review,* March, 1905, pp. 524–526.

BARNES, ELIZABETH. "Independent Politics: The Significance of the Black Panther Party." *Young Socialist,* October 13, 1966.

CARMICHAEL, STOKELY, and JOHN HULETT. *The Black Panther Party.* New York: Merit Publishers, 1966.

The Case for a Black Party. New York: Socialist Workers Party, 1968.

CROSSWAITH, FRANK A. "The Negro Program of the Socialists." *Crisis,* 38 (September, 1931): 279–280.

DEBS, EUGENE V. "The Negro in the Class Struggle." *International Socialist Review,* 4 (November, 1903): 257–260.

FONER, ERIC. "Politics and Prejudices: The Free Soil Party and the Negro, 1849–1852." *Journal of Negro History,* 50 (October, 1965): 239–258.

FORD, JAMES. *The Negro and the Democratic Front.* New York: International Publishers, 1937.

"Freedom Party Enters Race." *New York Times,* June 1, 1966, p. 34.

GRANTHAM, DEWEY W., JR. "The Progressive Movement and the Negro." In *The Negro in the South since 1865,* edited by Charles Wynes, pp. 62–82. New York: Harper Calophon Books, 1965.

GUTMAN, HERBERT. "Peter H. Clark: Pioneer Negro Socialist, 1877." *Journal of Negro Education,* 34 (Fall, 1965): 413–418.

GUYOT, LAWRENCE, and MIKE THELWELL. "The Politics of Necessity and Survival in Mississippi." *Freedomways,* 6 (Spring, 1966): 120–132.

GUYOT, L., and M. THELWELL. "Toward Independent Political Power." *Freedomways,* 6 (Summer, 1966): 246–254.

HAYNES, JAMES. "Why the Negro Should Be a Progressive." *Crisis,* 5 (November, 1912): 42–43.

HERBERS, JOHN. "Mississippi Freedom Democrats to Run Own Slate for Congress." *New York Times Supplement,* September 23, 1965, p. 1.

JAMES, DANIEL. "Cannon the Progressive." *New Republic,* 119, October 18, 1948, pp. 14–15.

JONES, DAVID R. "Negro Party Pasts Strength to Test." *New York Times,* October 4, 1964, p. 70.

KIFNER, JOHN. "Freedom Party Endorses Candidates." *New York Times,* July 22, 1968, p. 27.

KOPKIND, ANDREW. "The Future of 'Black Power.'" *New Republic,* 156, January 7, 1967, pp. 16–18.

KOPKIND, ANDREW. "The Lair of the Black Panther." *New Republic,* 155, August 13, 1966, pp. 10–13.

LEO, JOHN. "Black Panthers to Oppose Powell." *New York Times,* July 28, 1968, p. 41.

MCLEMORE, LESLIE B. "The Freedom Democratic Party and the Changing Political States of the Negro in Mississippi." Master's thesis, Atlanta University, 1965.

MINNIS, JACK. "The Mississippi Freedom Democratic Party." *Freedomways,* 5 (Spring, 1965): 264–278.

"The Negro Party." *Crisis,* 12 (October, 1916): 268–269.

"Negro Party Files in Michigan." *New York Times,* May 3, 1964, p. 70.

NOLAN, WILLIAM A. *Communism versus the Negro.* Chicago: Henry Regnery Company, 1951.

RANSON, REVERDY C. "Socialism and the Negro." *Alexander's Magazine,* 1, May 15, 1905, pp. 15–16.

RECORD, WILSON. "The Development of the Communist Position on the Negro Question in the United States." *Phylon,* 19 (third quarter, 1958): 306–326.

RECORD, WILSON. *The Negro and the Communist Party*. Chapel Hill, N.C.: University of North Carolina Press, 1951.

RECORD, WILSON. *Race and Radicalism: The NAACP and the Communist Party in Conflict*. Ithaca, N.Y.: Cornell University Press, 1964.

ROBINSON, W., JR. "Democratic Frontiers." *Journal of Human Relations*, Spring, 1954, pp. 63–70.

ROGERS, WILLIAM W. "The Negro Alliance in Alabama." *Journal of Negro History*, 45 (January, 1960): 38–44.

TAYLOR, JOSEPH H. "Populism and Disfranchisement in Alabama." *Journal of Negro History*, 34 (October, 1949): 410–424.

THOMAS, NORMAN. "The Future of the Black Vote." *Crisis*, 38 (February, 1931): 45.

THOMAS, NORMAN. "Socialism's Appeal to Negroes." *Crisis*, 43 (October, 1936): 294–295.

VIDRINE, ERASTE. "Negro Locals." *International Socialists Review*, 5 (January, 1905): 389–392.

WALTON, HANES, JR. *Black Political Parties: A Historical and Political Analysis*. New York: Free Press, 1972.

WALTON, HANES, JR. "Blacks and the 1968 Third Parties." *Negro Educational Review*, 21 (April, 1970): 19–23.

WALTON, HANES, JR. "The Negro in the Progressive Party Movements." *Quarterly Review of Higher Education among Negroes*, 36 (January, 1968).

WALTON, HANES, JR. "The Negro in the Prohibition Party: A Case Study of the Tennessee Prohibition Party" (tentative title). *Papers and Proceedings of the 53rd Annual Meeting of the Association for Study of Negro Life and History*, vol. 1.

WILLIAMS, SAMUEL W. "The People's Progressive Party of Georgia." *Phylon*, 10 (third quarter, 1949): 226–230.

WOODWARD, C. VANN. "Tom Watson and the Negro in Agrarian Politics." *Journal of Southern History*, 4 (1938): 14–33.

WRIGHT, R. R. "A Negro Party." *Christian Records*, October, 1916.

Black Pressure Groups

BELL, INGE. *Core and the Strategy of Non-violence*. New York: Random House, 1968.

BUNCHE, RALPH J. "A Critical Analysis of the Tactics and Programs of Minority Groups." *Journal of Negro Education*, 4 (July, 1935): 308–320.

BUNCHE, RALPH J. "The Program of Organizations Devoted to the Improvement of the Status of the American Negro." *Journal of Negro Education*, 8 (July, 1939): 539–550.

BURNS, W. HAYWORD. *The Voices of Negro Protest in America*. New York: Oxford University Press, 1963.

CLARKE, JACQUELYNE JOHNSON. "Standard Operational Procedures in Tragic Situations." *Phylon*, 22 (fourth quarter, 1961): 318–328.

CLARK, JACQUELYNE. *These Rights They Seek: A Comparison of Goals and Techniques of Local Civil Rights Organizations*. Washington, D.C.: Public Affairs Press, 1962.

CLARK, KENNETH B. "The Civil Rights Movement: Momentums and Organization." *Daedalus*, 96 (Winter, 1966): 239–267.

COX, OLIVER C. "The Programs of Negro Civil Rights Organizations." *Journal of Negro Education*, 20 (Summer, 1951).

GARFINKEL, GERBERT. *When Negroes March: The March on Washington Movement in the Organizational Politics for F.E.P.C.* Glencoe, Ill.: Free Press, 1959.

HUGHES, LANGSTON. *Fight for Freedom: The Story for the Advancement of Colored People*, vol. 1, *1909–1920*. Baltimore: Johns Hopkins Press, 1967.

JACK, ROBERT L. *History of the National Association for the Advancement of Colored People*. Boston: Meador Publishing Company, 1943.

JONES, EUGENE K. "The National Urban League." *Opportunity*, 3 (January, 1925): 12–15.

KELLOGG, CHARLES F. *NAACP: A History of the National Association for the Advancement of Colored People*, vol. 1, *1909–1920*. Baltimore: Johns Hopkins Press, 1967.

LEWIS, ROSCOE E. "The Role of Pressure Groups in Maintaining Morale among Negroes." *Journal of Negro Education*, 12 (Summer, 1943): 464–473.

MEIER, AUGUST. "Negro Protest Movements and Organizations." *Journal of Negro Education,* 32 (Fall, 1963): 437–450.

MEIER, AUGUST. "On the Role of Martin Luther King." *New Politics,* 4 (Winter, 1965): 52–59.

RICH, MARVIN. "The Congress of Racial Equality and Its Strategy." In *Pressure Groups in American Politics,* edited by Harry R. Mahood, pp. 197–204. New York: Charles Scribner's Sons, 1967.

RUDWICK, ELLIOTT M. "The Niagara Movement." *Journal of Negro History,* 42 (July, 1957): 177–200.

SAINT JAMES, WARREN D. *The National Association for the Advancement of Colored People: A Case Study in Pressure Groups.* New York: Exposition Press, 1958.

STRICKLAND, ARVACH E. *History of the Chicago Urban League.* Urbana, Ill.: University of Illinois Press, 1966.

THOMPSON, DANIEL C. "Civil Rights Leadership: An Opinion Study." *Journal of Negro Education,* 32 (Fall, 1963): 426–436.

THORNBROUGH, EMMA LOU. "The National Afro-American League, 1887–1908." *Journal of Southern History,* 27 (November, 1961): 494–512.

VOSE, CLEMENT E. "Litigation as a Form of Pressure Group Activity." *The Annals,* 319 (September, 1958): 20–31.

WALTON, HANES, JR. "The Political Leadership of Martin Luther King, Jr." *Quarterly Review of Higher Education among Negroes,* 36 (July, 1968): 163–171.

WALTON, HANES, JR. "The Politics of Negro Educational Associations." *Negro Educational Review,* 20 (January, 1969): 34–41.

WARE, GILBERT. "Lobbying as a Means of Protest: The NAACP as an Agent of Equality." *Journal of Negro Education,* 33 (Spring, 1964): 103–110.

WATSON, RICHARD L., JR. "The Defeat of Judge Parker: A Case Study in Pressure Groups and Politics." *Mississippi Valley Historical Review,* 50 (September, 1963): 213–234.

ZANGRANDO, ROBERT L. "The NAACP and a Federal Anti-lynching Bill, 1934–1940." *Journal of Negro History,* 50 (April, 1965): 106–117.

ZINN, HOWARD. *SNCC: The New Abolitionists.* Boston: Beacon Press, 1964.

Blacks and the Federal Government

ALEXANDER, RAYMOND PACE. "The Upgrading of the Negro's Status by Supreme Court Decisions." *Journal of Negro History,* 30 (April, 1945): 117–149.

ALILUNAS, LEO. "Legal Restrictions on the Negro in Politics." *Journal of Negro History,* 25 (April, 1940): 153–202.

BAGE, ELVENA S. "President Garfield's Forgotten Pronouncement." *Negro History Bulletin,* June, 1951, pp. 195–197.

BENNETT, LERONE. *Black Power, U.S.A.* Chicago: Johnson Publishing Company, 1968.

BERGER, MONROE. *Equality by Statute.* New York: Anchor Books, 1968.

BETHUNE, MARY MCLEOD. "My Secret Talks with FDR." *Ebony,* April, 1949, pp. 42–51.

BLAUSTERN, ALBERT, and ROBERT ZANGRANDO. *Civil Rights and the American Negro.* New York: Washington Square Press, 1968.

BLUMENTHAL, HENRY. "Woodrow Wilson and the Race Question." *Journal of Negro History,* 48 (January, 1963): 1–21.

BREWER, T. MASON. *Negro Legislators of Texas.* Dallas: Mathis Publishing Company, 1935.

BROWN, CHARLES. "Reconstruction Legislators in Alabama." *Negro History Bulletin,* March, 1963, pp. 198–200.

CATTERALL, HELEN, ed. *Judicial Cases Concerning American Slavery and the Negro.* Washington, D.C., 1926.

CHICK, C. A. "Some Recent United States Supreme Court Decisions Affecting the Rights of Negro Workers." *Journal of Negro Education,* 16 (Spring, 1947): 172–179.

CLAUDE, RICHARD. "Constitutional Voting Rights and Early U.S. Supreme Court Decisions." *Journal of Negro History,* 51 (April, 1966): 114–124.

COULTER, E. MERTON. *Negro Legislators in Georgia during the Reconstruction Period.* Athens, Ga.: Georgia Historical Quarterly, 1968.

DAVIS, JOHN A., and CORNELIUS L. GOLIGHTLY. "Negro Employment in the Federal Government." *Phylon,* 6 (fourth quarter, 1945): 337–346.

DIXON, R. G. "Civil Rights in Transportation and the I.C.C." *George Washington Law Review,* October, 1962, pp. 198–241.

FAGGET, H. L. "The Negroes Who Do Not Want to End Segregation." *Quarterly Review of Higher Education among Negroes,* 23 (July, 1955): 120–121.

FLEMING, HAROLD C. "The Federal Executive and Civil Rights, 1961–1965." In *The Negro American,* edited by Talcott Parsons and Kenneth B. Clark, pp. 371–400. Boston: Houghton Mifflin Company, 1966.

FRIEDMAN, LEON, ed. *Southern Justice.* Cleveland: Meridian Books, 1967.

GILL, R. L. "The Negro in the Supreme Court." *Quarterly Review of Higher Education among Negroes,* 33 (October, 1965): 205–212.

GILL, R. L. "The Negro Standing before the Supreme Court, 1865." *Quarterly Review of Higher Education among Negroes,* 33 (July, 1965): 161–173.

GILL, R. L. "The Role of Five Negro Lawyers in the Civil Rights Struggle." *Quarterly Review of Higher Education among Negroes,* 30 (April, 1962): 31–58.

GILL, R. L. "The School Segregation Cases and State Reactions." *Quarterly Review of Higher Education among Negroes,* 24 (October, 1956): 163–169.

GILL, R. L. "The Shaping of Race Relation by the Federal Judiciary in Court Decisions." *Negro Educational Review,* 11 (January, 1960): 15–23.

GILL, R. L. "Smith vs. Allwright and Reactions in Some of the Southern States." *Quarterly Review of Higher Education among Negroes,* 35 (July, 1967): 154–169.

GILL, R. L. "The Supreme Court, 1963." *Quarterly Review of Higher Education among Negroes,* 34 (October, 1964): 159–176.

GILL, ROBERT L. "Civil Right Legislation, 1865–1965: The Beacon of Ordered Liberty." *Quarterly Review of Higher Education among Negroes,* 33 (April, 1965): 79–93.

GILL, ROBERT L. "Defender of Civil Liberties." *Quarterly Review of Higher Education among Negroes,* 17 (January, 1949): 1–9.

GILL, ROBERT L. "The Negro in the Supreme Court, 1954–1964." *Quarterly Review of Higher Education among Negroes,* 33 (January, 1965): 1–19.

GILL, ROBERT L. "The Negro in the Supreme Court, 1961." *Negro Educational Review,* 13 (April, 1962): 60–75.

GILL, ROBERT L. "The Negro in the Supreme Court, 1962." *Negro Educational Review,* 14 (July–October, 1963): 101–125.

GOLDEN, HARRY. *Mr. Kennedy and the Negroes.* Cleveland: World Publishing Company, 1964.

GOODMAN, JAMES. "FDR New Deal: A Political Disaster for Blacks." *The Black Politician,* 1 (October, 1969): 33–36.

HAMILTON, JAMES. *Negro Suffrage and Congressional Representation.* New York: Winthop Press, 1910.

HERBSTER, BEN M. "FCC Ban Eyed in Mississippi." *New York Times,* December 31, 1964, p. 18.

HOPE, JOHN, II, and EDWARD E. SHELTON. "The Negro in the Federal Government." *Journal of Negro Education,* 32 (Fall, 1963): 367–374.

KAISER, ERNEST. "The Federal Government and the Negro, 1865–1955." *Science and Society,* 20 (Winter, 1956): 27–58.

KALVEN, HARRY, JR. *The Negro and the First Amendment.* Columbus: Ohio State University Press, 1965.

KONVITZ, MILTON R. "A Nation within a Nation: The Negro and the Supreme Court." *The American Scholar,* 11 (Winter, 1941–1942): 67–78.

LLOYD, RAYMOND GRAM. "The States Right Myth and Southern Oppositions to Federal Anti-Lynching Legislation." *Negro Educational Review,* 1 (April, 1950): 78–88.

LYNCH, JOHN R. Letter to the editor. *Journal of Negro History,* 12 (October, 1927): 667–669.

LYTLE, CLIFFORD M. "The History of the Civil Rights Bill of 1964." *Journal of Negro History,* 51 (October, 1966): 275–296.

McKINNEY, THEOPHILES E., JR. "United States Transportation Segregation." *Quarterly Review of Higher Education among Negroes,* 22 (July, 1954): 101–148.

MARSHALL, THURGOOD. "An Evaluation of Recent Efforts to Achieve Racial Integrations through Resort to the Courts." *Journal of Negro Education,* 21 (Summer, 1952): 316–326.

MASSOQUORI, HAN J. "Gus Hawkins—Fifth Negro Congressman." *Ebony*, February, 1963.
MILLER, LOREN. *The Petitioners: The Story of the Supreme Court of the United States and the Negro*. New York: Pantheon Books, 1966.
MORRISON, ALLAN. "The Secret Papers of FDR." *Negro Digest*, January, 1951, pp. 3–13.
MOTLEY, CONSTANCE BAKER. "The Legal Status of the Negro in the United States." In *The American Negro Reference Book*, edited by John P. Davis, pp. 484–521. Englewood Cliffs, N.J.: Prentice-Hall, 1966.
MURPHY, L. E. "The Civil Rights Law of 1875." *Journal of Negro History*, 12 (April, 1927): 110–127.
NELSON, BERNARD. "The Negro before the Supreme Court." *Phylon*, 8 (first quarter, 1947): 34–38.
NELSON, BERNARD H. *The Fourteenth Amendment and the Negro since 1920.* Washington, D.C.: Catholic University Press, 1946.
"New Faces in Congress." *Ebony*, 14 (February, 1969): 56–65.
PENTECOSTE, JOSEPH. "The New Black Television—A White Strategy: A Commentary." *Inner City Issues*, October, 1969, pp. 4–11.
PETERSON, GLADYS. "The Present Status of the Negro Separate School as Defined by Court Decisions." *Journal of Negro Education*, 4 (Winter, 1935): 351–374.
PRESTON, E. DELORUS. "The Negro and the Bill of Rights." *Quarterly Review of Higher Education among Negroes*, 10 (April, 1942): 86–88.
SCHEINER, SETH M. "President Theodore Roosevelt and the Negro, 1901–1908." *Journal of Negro History*, 47 (July, 1962): 169–182.
SHERMAN, RICHARD B. "The Harding Administration and the Negro: An Opportunity Lost." *Journal of Negro History*, 49 (July, 1964): 151–168.
SMITH, SAMUEL D. *The Negro in Congress, 1870–1901.* New York: Kennikat Press, 1966.
TAYLOR, ALRUTHEUS A. "Negro Congressmen a Generation After." *Journal of Negro History*, 7 (April, 1922): 127–171.
TAYLOR, JOSEPH H. "The Fourteenth Amendment, the Negro, and the Spirit of the Times." *Journal of Negro History*, 45 (January, 1960): 21–37.
TEN BROEK, JACOBUS. *Equal under Law*. New York: Collier Books, 1965.
TINSLEY, JAMES A. "Roosevelt, Foraker, Brownsville Affairs." *Journal of Negro History*, 41 (January, 1956): 43–65.
TRENT, W. J., JR. "Federal Sanctions Directed against Racial Discrimination." *Phylon*, 3 (second quarter, 1942): 171–182.
TURNER, ALBERT L. "The Negro and the Supreme Court." *Quarterly Review of Higher Education among Negroes*, 4 (April, 1936): 75–78.
TUSSMAN, JOSEPH, ed. *The Supreme Court on Racial Discrimination*. New York: Oxford University Press, 1967.
VOSE, CLEMENT E. *Caucasians Only: The Supreme Court, the NAACP, and the Restrictive Covenant Cases*. Berkeley: University of California Press, 1959.
WILLIAMSON, HUGH. "The Role of the Courts in the Status of the Negro." *Journal of Negro History*, 40 (January, 1955): 61–72.
WILSON, JAMES. "The Flamboyant Mr. Powell." *Commentary*, 41 (January, 1966): 31–35.
WOLGEMUTH, KATHLEEN L. "Woodrow Wilson and Federal Segregation." *Journal of Negro History*, 44 (April, 1959): 158–173.
WORK, MONROE N. "Some Negro Members of Reconstruction Conventions and Legislatures of Congress." *Journal of Negro History*, 5 (January, 1920): 63–125.

Black Public Officials and Public Policy

"The Black Mayors." *Ebony*, 25 (February, 1970): 76–84.
BOLDEN, RICHARD. "The Role of the Negro Legislature in Georgia." M.A. thesis, Atlanta University, 1969.
BOND, JULIAN. *Black Candidates: Southern Campaign Experiences*. Atlanta: Southern Regional Council, 1969.
CLAYTON, EDWARD T. *The Negro Politician: His Success and Failures*. Chicago: Johnson Publishing Company, 1964.
DAVIS, BENJAMIN T. *Communist Councilman from Harlem*. New York: International Publishers, 1969.

HADDEN, JEFFREY, LOUIS MASOTTI, and VICTOR THIESSEN. "The Making of the
  Negro Mayors, 1967." *Trans-Action,* 5 (January–February, 1968): 21–30.
MILLER, JUDY ANN. "The Representative Is a Lady." *The Black Politician,* Fall,
  1969, pp. 17–18.
MORRIS, JOHN B., ed. *Black Elected Officials in the Southern States.* Atlanta:
  Southern Regional Council, 1969.
National Roster of Black Elected Officials. Washington, D.C.: Metropolitan Ap-
  plied Research Center, 1970.
NAUGHTON, JAMES. "Mayor Stokes: The First Hundred Days." *New York Times
  Magazine,* February 25, 1968, pp. 26–27, 48–62.
NAUGHTON, JAMES, and BERKELEY RICE. "In Cleveland and Boston: The Issue Is
  Race." *New York Times Magazine,* November, 1967, pp. 30–32, 97–130.
"Practical Politician: Julian Bond." *The Black Politician,* 1 (Fall, 1969): 28–30.
ROSE, HAROLD. "The All Negro Town: Its Evolution and Future." *Geographical
  Review,* 65 (July, 1965): 362–381.
WAUGH, JOHN C. "Tom Bradley's Non-partisan, Bi-partisan Coalition Campaign."
  The Black Politician, 1 (Fall, 1969): 9–11.
WEINBERG, KENNETH G. *Black Victory: Carl Stokes and the Winning of Cleveland.*
  Chicago: Quadrangle Books, 1968.

Blacks and the Metropolis

ABRAMS, CHARLES. "The Housing Problem and the Negro." *Daedalus,* 115 (Winter,
  1966): 64–76.
ALLEN, ROSALYN. "The Impact of County and City Government Consolidation in
  Jacksonville Area on Black Political Power." Paper presented to state govern-
  ment class, Savannah State College, December 6, 1966.
BOSKIN, JOSEPH, ed. *Urban Racial Violence in the Twentieth Century.* Beverly Hills:
  Glencoe Press, 1969.
BROWN, CLAUDE. *Manchild in the Promised Land.* New York: Signet, 1965.
CLARK, KENNETH. *Dark Ghetto.* New York: Harper and Row, 1967.
DRAKE, ST. CLAIR, and HORACE CAYTON. *Black Metropolis.* New York: Harcourt,
  Brace, 1965.
ELLIS, WILLIAM. *White Ethics and Black Power.* Chicago: Aldine Publishing Com-
  pany, 1969.
HATCHER, RICHARD G. "The Black Role in Urban Politics." *Current History,* 57
  (November, 1969): 287–289.
KEIL, CHARLES. *Urban Blues.* Chicago: University of Chicago Press, 1969.
MCCORD, WILLIAM, et al. *Life Styles in the Black Ghetto.* New York: W. W. Norton
  and Company, 1969.
MCKAY, CLAUDE. *Harlem: Negro Metropolis.* New York: E. P. Dutton and Com-
  pany, 1940.
MOODY, PETER R., JR. "The Effects of the Adoption of Metropolitan Government
  in Nashville and Davidson County, Tennessee, on Negro Political Influence." Senior
  honor thesis, Vanderbilt University, 1965.
OPPENHEIMER, MARTIN. *The Urban Guerrilla.* Chicago: Quadrangle Books, 1969.
OSOFSKY, GILBERT. *Harlem: The Making of a Ghetto, 1890–1930.* New York:
  Harper and Row, 1966.
PIVEN, FRANCIS, and RICHARD A. CLOWARD. "Black Control of Cities." In *Political
  Power and the Urban Crisis,* edited by Albert Shank, pp. 315–328. Boston: Hol-
  brook Press, 1969.
PIVEN, FRANCIS, and RICHARD A. CLOWARD. "Dissensus Politics." In *Political Power
  and the Urban Crisis,* edited by Albert Shank, pp. 243–252. Boston: Holbrook
  Press, 1969.
Report of the National Advisory Commission on Civil Disorders. New York:
  Bantam Books, 1968.
WARREN, ROLAND W., ed. *Politics and the Ghetto.* New York: Atherton Press, 1969.
WEAVER, ROBERT C. *Dilemmas of Urban America.* New York: Atheneum, 1965.

General Works
on
Blacks and the American Political Process

ANDREWS, NORMAN P. "The Negro in Politics." *Journal of Negro History,* 5 (October, 1920): 420–436.

ANGLIN, ROBERT. "A Sociological Analysis of the NAACP." Ph.D. dissertation, Indiana University, 1950.

BACOTE, C. A. "The Negro in Atlanta Politics." *Phylon*, 16 (fourth quarter, 1955): 333–350.

BAILEY, HARRY, JR., ed. *Negro Politics in America*. Columbus: Charles E. Merrill Publishing Company, 1968.

BARNES, JAMES F. "Negro Voting in Mississippi." Master's thesis, University of Mississippi, 1955.

BLACK, ROBERT. "Southern Government and the Negro: Race as a Campaign Issue since 1954." Ph.D. dissertation, Harvard University, 1968.

BOWMAN, R. LEWIS. "Negro Politics in Four Southern Counties." Ph.D. dissertation, University of North Carolina, 1963.

BUNCHE, RALPH J. "The Negro in the Political Life of the United States." *Journal of Negro Education*, 10 (July, 1941): 567–584.

BUNCHE, RALPH J. "The Role of the University in the Political Orientation of Negro Youth." *Journal of Negro Education*, 9 (October, 1940): 571–579.

BUNCHE, RALPH J. "The Thompson-Negro Alliance." *Opportunity*, 7 (March, 1929): 78–80.

BUNI, ANDREW. *The Negro in Virginia Politics, 1902–1965*. Charlottesville, Va.: University Press of Virginia, 1967.

CALCOTT, MARGARET L. *The Negro in Maryland Politics, 1870–1912*. Baltimore: Johns Hopkins Press, 1969.

CARMICHAEL, STOKELY S., and CHARLES V. HAMILTON. *Black Power: The Politics of Liberation in America*. New York: Random House, 1968.

COLLINS, E. "Political Behavior of the Negroes in Cincinnati and Louisville." Ph.D. dissertation, University of Kentucky, 1950.

COOK, SAMUEL D. "Political Movements and Organization." *Journal of Politics*, 26 (February, 1964): 130–153.

COOK, SAMUEL D. "The Tragic Myth of Black Power." *New South*, Summer, 1966, pp. 58–64.

DORSEY, EMMETT E. "The American Negro and His Government, 1961." *Crisis*, 68 (October, 1961): 467–478.

EDMONDS, HELEN. *The Negro and Fusion Politics in North Carolina, 1894–1901*. Chapel Hill, N.C.: University of North Carolina Press, 1951.

FARRIS, CHARLES D. "Effects of Negro Voting upon the Politics of a Southern City: An Intensive Study, 1946–48." Ph.D. dissertation, University of Chicago, 1953.

FERGUSON, HAROLD B., JR. "Race as a Factor in Presidential Campaigns from 1904 to 1928 in North Carolina." Master's thesis, North Carolina College, 1949.

FLEMING, G. JAMES. "The Negro in American Politics: The Past." In *American Negro Reference Book*, edited by J. David, pp. 414–430. Englewood Cliffs, N.J.: Prentice-Hall, 1966.

FREDRICKS, DAVID. "The Role of the Negro Minister in New Orleans Politics." Ph.D. dissertation, Tulane University, 1967.

GELB, JOYCE. "The Role of Negro Politicians in the Democratic, Republican, and Liberal Parties of New York City." Ph.D. dissertation, New York University, 1969.

GOSNELL, HAROLD. *Negro Politicians: The Rise of Negro Politics in Chicago*. Chicago: University of Chicago Press, 1935.

HAMILTON, CHARLES V. *Minority Politics in Black Belt Alabama*. New York: McGraw-Hill Book Company, 1962.

HILL, D. G. "The Negro as a Political and Social Issue in the Oregon Country." *Journal of Negro History*, 33 (April, 1948): 130–145.

HURT, HENRY. "Negro Politics." *The Reporter*, 35, August 11, 1966, pp. 23–27.

JOHNSON, JAMES WELDON. "A Negro Looks at Politics." *The American Mercury*, 18 (September, 1929): 88–94.

McLEMORE, FRANCES W. "The Role of the Negroes in Chicago in the Senatorial Election, 1930." Master's thesis, University of Chicago, 1931.

MARTIN, ROBERT E. "The Relative Political Status of the Negro in the United States." *Journal of Negro Education*, 22 (Summer, 1953): 363–379.

MARVACK, DWAINE. "The Political Socialization of the American Negro." *The Annals*, 360 (September, 1965).

MERRITT, DIXON. "Politics and the Southern Negro." *The Outlook*, 149 (August 8, 1928): 581.

MILLER, J. ERROLL. "The Negro in Present Day Politics with Special Reference to Philadelphia." *Journal of Negro History*, 33 (July, 1948): 303–343.

MILLER, J. ERROLL. "Major Political Issues Which Directly Concern Negroes." *Quarterly Review of Higher Education among Negroes*, 16 (October, 1948): 140–150.

MILLER, KELLY. "Government and the Negro." *Annals of the American Academy of Political and Social Science*, 140 (November, 1928): 98–104.

MILLER, T. E. "The Negro in National Politics in 1968." In *In Black America: Year of Awakening, 1968*, edited by Patricia W. Romero, pp. 3–40. Washington, D.C.: United Publishing Corporation, 1969.

MILLER, T. E. "The Negro in Pennsylvania Politics with Special Reference to Philadelphia since 1932." Ph.D. thesis, University of Pennsylvania, 1945.

MOON, HENRY LEE. "The Negro in Politics." *New Republic*, 119, October 18, 1948, pp. 9–10.

MORRISON, ALLAN. "Negro Political Progress in New England." *Ebony*, 18, October, 1963, pp. 25–28.

MORSELL, JOHN. "The Political Behavior of Negroes in New York City." Ph.D. dissertation, Columbia University, 1950.

MORTON, R. L. *The Negro in Virginia Politics*. Charlottesville, Va.: University Press of Virginia, 1919.

NOWLIN, WILLIAM F. *The Negro in American National Politics*. Boston: Stratford. 1931; New York: Russell and Russell, 1970.

PRICE, HUGH D. "The Negro and Florida Politics, 1944–1954." *Journal of Politics*, 17 (May, 1955): 198–220.

PRICE, HUGH D. *The Negro and Southern Politics*. New York: New York University Press, 1957.

RAUH, JOSEPH L., JR. "Political Participation." *Civil Rights Digest*, Summer, 1968, pp. 9–11.

ROBERT, CLEO. "Some Correlates of Registration and Voting among Negroes in the 1953 Municipal Election of Atlanta." Master's thesis, Atlanta University, 1954.

ROBINSON, GEORGE R. "The Negro in Politics in Chicago." *Journal of Negro History*, 17 (April, 1932): 183–215.

RUSTIN, BAYARD. "Black Power and Coalition Politics." *Commentary*, 48 (September, 1969): 35–40.

RUSTIN, BAYARD. "From Protest to Politics." *Commentary*, 39 (February, 1965): 25–31.

SEASHOLES, BRADBURY. "Political Socialization of Negroes: Image Development of Self and Politic." In *Negro Self-Concept: Implications for School and Citizenship*, edited by William C. Kvaraceus et al. New York: McGraw-Hill Book Company, 1965.

SILVERMAN, SONDRA, ed. *The Black Revolt and Democratic Politics*. Boston: D. C. Heath and Company, 1970.

SINDLER, ALLAN P. "Protest against the Political Status of the Negro." *The Annals*, January, 1965, pp. 48–54.

STONE, CHUCK. *Black Political Power in America*. Indianapolis: Bobbs-Merrill Company, 1968.

SWEAT, EDWARD F. "State and Local Politics in 1968." In *In Black America: Year of Awakening, 1968*, edited by Patricia W. Romero, pp. 133–146. Washington, D.C.: United Publishing Corporation, 1969.

TATUM, ELBERT L. *The Changed Political Thought of the Negro, 1915–1940*. New York: Exposition Press, 1941.

TATUM, ELBERT L. "The Changed Political Thought of the Negroes in the United States, 1915–1940." *Journal of Negro Education*, 16 (Fall, 1947): 522–533.

United States Commission on Civil Rights. *Political Participation*. Washington, D.C.: U.S. Government Printing Office, 1968.

WALTON, HANES, JR. *The Political Philosophy of Martin Luther King, Jr.* Westport, Conn.: Greenwood Publishing Corporation, 1971.

WATTERS, PAT. "The Negroes Enter Southern Politics." *Dissent*, 13 (July–August, 1966): 361–368.

WILSON, JAMES. "The Changing Political Postures of the Negro." In *Assuring Freedom to the Free*, edited by Arnold Rose, pp. 163–184. Detroit: Wayne State University Press, 1964.

WILSON, JAMES Q. "The Negro in American Politics: The Present." In *American*

Negro Reference Book, edited by J. David, pp. 431–457. New York: Prentice-Hall, 1965.

WILSON, JAMES Q. *Negro Politics: The Search for Leadership.* New York: Free Press, 1960.

WILSON, JAMES Q. "Two Negro Politicians: An Interpretation." *Midwest Journal of Political Science,* 4 (November, 1960): 360–369.

WOLFE, DEBORAH PARTRIDGE. "Negroes in American Politics." *Negro Educational Review,* 14 (April, 1963): 64–71.

Index

240

Subjects